Table of Contents

HORSE BRAIN, HUMAN BRAIN

The Neuroscience of Horsemanship

Janet L. Jones, Ph.D.

T
TRAFALGAR SQUARE
North Pomfret, Vermont

First published in 2020 by
Trafalgar Square Books
North Pomfret, Vermont 05053

Parts of this book have been previously published in some form in *EQUUS* magazine.

Disclaimer of Liability

Library of Congress Cataloging-in-Publication Data
Names: Jones, Janet L. (Neuroscientist), author.
Title: Horse brain, human brain : the neuroscience of horsemanship / Janet L. Jones.
Description: North Pomfret, Vermont : Trafalgar Square Books, 2020. | Includes bibliographical references and index. | Summary: "Horsemanship of every kind depends on mutual interaction between equine and human brains. When we understand the function of both, we can learn to communicate with horses on their terms instead of ours. And, by meeting horses halfway, we not only save valuable training time and improve performance, we achieve other goals, too. We develop much deeper bonds with our horses; we handle them with insight and kindness instead of force or command; we comprehend their misbehavior in ways that allow solutions; and we reduce the human mistakes we often make while working with them. In this illuminating book, brain scientist and horsewoman Janet Jones describes human and equine brains working together. Using plain language, she explores the differences and similarities between equine and human ways of negotiating the world. Mental abilities-like seeing, learning, fearing, trusting, and focusing-are discussed from both human and horse perspectives. Throughout, true stories of horses and handlers attempting to understand each other-sometimes successfully, sometimes not-help to illustrate the principles"-- Provided by publisher.
Identifiers: LCCN 2020000724 (print) | LCCN 2020000725 (ebook) | ISBN 9781570769481 (paperback) | ISBN 9781646010271 (epub)
Subjects: LCSH: Horses--Training. | Horses--Physiology. | Human-animal communication. | Horsemanship--Physiological aspects. | Neurosciences.
Classification: LCC SF287 .J63 2020 (print) | LCC SF287 (ebook) | DDC 636.1/0835--dc23
LC record available at https://lccn.loc.gov/2020000724
LC ebook record available at https://lccn.loc.gov/2020000725

Illustrations by Susan Harris and Jean Abernethy
Book design by Tim Holtz
Cover design by RM Didier
Index by Andrea Jones (JonesLiteraryServices.com)
Typefaces: Berkeley Oldstyle, Perpetua, Avenir
Printed in the United States of America
20 19 18 17 16 15 14 13 12

Dedicated to my father

Gerry Jones

who surrounded me from birth with an exceptional variety of

books, brains, and horses

The Brain—is wider than the Sky—
For—put them side by side—
The one the other will contain
With ease—and You—beside—

The Brain is deeper than the sea—
For—hold them—Blue to Blue—
The one the other will absorb—
As Sponges—Buckets—do—

The Brain is just the weight of God—
For—Heft them—Pound for Pound—
And they will differ—if they do—
As Syllable from Sound—

Emily Dickinson, c. 1862

PART ONE

Animals in a Human World

CHAPTER ONE

The Horse-and-Human Team

"Here. I don't even wanna *hold* 'er. Don't wanna *see* 'er! Nutcase still won't get in the trailer. Jus' set her out by the road with a sign 'round 'er neck: 'Free flippin' *horse*.'" My red-faced friend stomped off, leaving me on the dumb end of a sweaty sorrel's lead rope. Apparently, their teamwork over the past several hours had not gone well.

Horses and people have been working together, or trying to, for at least 5500 years. Evidence comes from Kazakhstan, where Stone Age tools show that horses were milked for human food and bridled for riding or driving. Since then, we've joined these creatures of power and beauty on all sorts of tasks: military, agricultural, transportation, law enforcement, therapy, performance sports, ranch work, companionship, exercise, and recreation. Horses have played starring roles in almost every aspect of human life.

Today, horses are an estimated 60 million strong worldwide. The American Horse Council Foundation reports that our four-legged friends pack a financial punch of $122 billion a year and create almost 2 million full–time jobs in the United States alone. About 27 million Americans ride. That's a lot of cross-species pairs trying to work with each other.

Horse Brain, Human Brain explains and applies principles of brain function that improve horsemanship across the entire spectrum of horse-and-human teams. And what a spectrum it is! Disciplines include driving, jumping, reining, vaulting, foxhunting, cutting, rodeo, barrels, endurance, racing, pulling, ranch work, dressage, roping, trail, and much more—the equine family is über-versatile. We cubbyhole types of riding: Western,

English, dressage, Australian, hunt seat, jumping seat, saddle seat, jockey seat, bad seat, and so on. Okay, I'm kind of kidding with that last one, but not much!

Worldwide, about 833 different breeds of horses exist today. Many of them are specialized for their disciplines. For example, we'd be surprised to see a Clydesdale in a saddle-seat equitation class or a Selle Français roping. *Equus caballus* is a species of tremendous range.

Of the few factors common to such dizzying variety, the most critical is the brain. It controls every behavior, from an eye blink to an aerial capriole. Every horse and every human has one, and it determines the success or failure of our partnerships. So if you want a better team, get to know your horse's brain—and your own.

Trial and Error

Through most of our past, people have used trial and error plus apprenticeship to train horses and riders. We set a simple goal for a horse, try several means of achieving it, and use the one that works. Trainers then teach other handlers the selected technique.

This method has been popular for centuries, but doesn't work all that well. For one thing, trial and error means making a lot of mistakes. With each effort, we run the risk of teaching the horse something we didn't really want him to know. Then we have to "un-teach," which is often difficult and sometimes dangerous. The horse becomes confused—or worse, annoyed—with his career as an experimental guinea pig.

For another, the old method is generic. "One size fits all" doesn't work well with animals. Each horse—like each human—is unique, with a different background, and various experiences, strengths, and weaknesses. Even the brain of a cloned horse differs from the original because his daily experiences are not the same. So, the training technique that achieves a goal for one team might be useless or detrimental with the next.

Add to this the fact that quite a few training techniques are not as teachable as we might like. Raise your hand if your trainer has ever said, "Move your leg like this," in a manner that your leg couldn't approach if it was made of silly putty. Without superb apprenticeship, it takes a lot of time to hunt, peck, and cuss your way to a well-mannered horse and a skilled rider.

And too often, our chosen technique flies in the face of brain function. For example, we can urge a mounted horse straight toward a frightening object, as most riders do, but this method works *against* his brain rather than with it. Riding against the brain occurs more frequently than you might guess. As you learn more about equine and human brains, you'll see the conflict often.

The root of our trouble with trial and error followed by apprenticeship is that it fails to say why or how a particular technique works. Here's where brain science can lighten our load. By learning the why and how of horse and human brains, we can improve a team's skills far beyond the norm. We ask why a horse does something then ask how that behavior can be changed at the level of his brain. When we know the principles common to equine noggins, we have greater ability to predict which techniques will work.

Brain-based horsemanship also helps us design creative new techniques that work best for specific teams. Using the basics of brain function, we can train horses and riders to perform in harmony with the inner workings of their natural minds—while still taking their individual differences into account. It's akin to the old saw that if you give people fish, you feed them for a day, but if you teach them to fish, you feed them for a lifetime. Both parties end up happier and more successful.

Human and Equine Brains

Horse sports are just beginning to include brain science for riders. A few psychologists work with equestrians to build the mental discipline needed to perform and compete. Sports psychology teaches riders to focus even under the circus top of a horse show, to steady our nerves against stage fright, to practice challenging tasks and overcome daily weaknesses with self-discipline, and to accept the criticism that daily training entails. Such lessons benefit horses indirectly because good riders transmit focus, calm, discipline, and confidence to their mounts.

Still, these goals represent only one grain of sand in the arena of brain-based horsemanship. They fail to address the ways that the human brain directs the body while working with a horse—the precise physical timing, tiny balance shifts, and wondrous range of sensitivities that are necessary. They ignore many of the emotional aspects of training a horse—the almost pathological measure of calmness that horses sometimes need from us, combined with the ability to deliver varying degrees of authority. They disregard the communicative aspect of horse-and-human collaboration—knowing when to use which voice or posture, how to transmit zen, and why we must comprehend body language between species.

Our sport offers a tiny grain of brain science for riders at this point, but almost no knowledge of brain function in horses. There's a dollop of anatomy here and a smidgen of physiology there—but the material tends to be speculative, inapplicable, or irrelevant. Too often, it's also inaccurate. Why? There are several reasons:

- Many facts about the brain are new and much of the science is still in flux. Forty years ago, we didn't have brain imaging machines that could look inside the head or parallel processing computers powerful enough to simulate thought. Now we do, but we're still in the process of developing this new knowledge and extending it across scattered domains.
- Horses are hard to test. You can keep a hundred lab rats in a room and experiment with them pretty easily, and you can call in 100 people to volunteer as research subjects—but 100 test horses will run you ragged. They need more space, time, staff, food, water, cash, equipment, and specialized knowledge than other animals do. Not to mention all the liability insurance.
- Most people, horsey or not, don't realize how much training our animals need. The task seems simple on the surface, so people wonder why they should cram a bunch of factoids about equine biology into their busy minds. Just hop on and ride! Too many riding students have swallowed the illusion that one lesson a week breeds true skill. Three-day colt starting contests suggest to newbies that training is completed

in a weekend. Novice owners still pay for 30-day wonders—horses who are expected to meet complex training goals in a month—without realizing these are the province of fraudulent operators.

In fact, freshly started horses don't even know how to walk a straight line. They can't balance the weight of a rider and haven't realized they need to turn a corner when they reach one. They have no idea what the rider's most basic cues mean. These youngsters are still learning the basics of "stop," "go," and "don't you dare buck me off." The human world is a bewildering jumble of chaos to the green horse. Years of work are needed to train him for reliable human interaction and solid performance.

- There's precious little cross-talk between brain scientists and horse trainers. We live in different worlds and don't lean on the barn fence together to chat about our work. The person who links brain science to horsemanship needs to wear a lab coat and breeches at the same time, some crusty old cowboy boots too; somebody who can explain neurology without using the word "neurology." A straight-talking, ink-stained, horse nerd.

Brain Interaction

Beyond learning how horse and human brains operate in isolation, we must reflect on how they interact. Mutual interaction is the key to teamwork. It's the rare partnership in life that lets two brains work together, especially two brains from different species, but that's exactly what brain-based horsemanship offers (fig. 1.1). A flutter of nerve cells fires in your brain as you ask a horse to move forward. The horse takes a step, while his brain sends neural signals back to you. You pick them up, and so on. Two brains dancing together like this is as natural a form of communication as two species can enjoy. How does the process work? Why does it sometimes fail? How can you maximize it for greater success?

One thing to do is reject the notion that horses must always bow to human ways of thinking. Of course, you set clear boundaries and firm expectations, but training is much more effective—and more

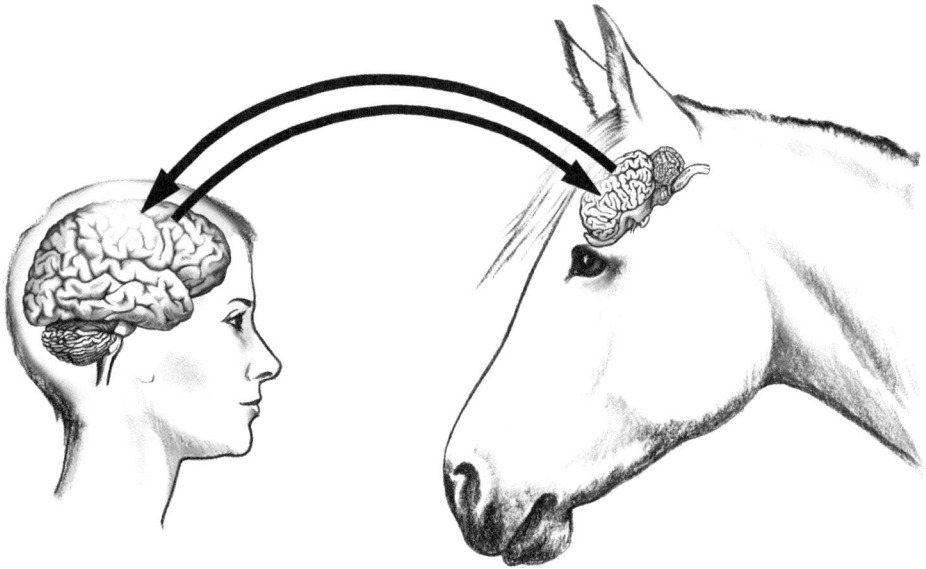

1.1 Mutual interaction within the horse-and-human team depends on communication between two species' brains.

rewarding—when you listen to what your horse is trying to convey. Hollywood sells that romantic myth of horse whispering, but the best trainers don't whisper—they *watch*, *listen*, *learn*, and *think*. The horses do the whispering. The human's job is to rivet attention to their faintest hints. Let's try to connect with animals at their level, instead of demanding that they constantly adjust to us.

To develop mutual interaction of this sort, ask yourself what's going on inside the horse's head. Suppose you want your horse to lead quietly. Most educated handlers start with the question, "How can I teach him that?" But you need to take a step farther back, asking, "How does he learn?" You want him to stop shying at unexpected sights, "How does he see? Why is he afraid?" You'd like to develop a closer attachment with him, "How does he bond? What does security mean to him?"

All well and good, you might say, but tick…tock…. Asking these questions and learning the answers takes time. It's faster to just make a horse follow orders. (Well, sometimes.) But forcing is not teaching, and it doesn't last. Instead, why not pique the horse's interest, appeal to his natural curiosity, encourage him to *want* to meet our needs? And, in turn, let's meet his!

Working with a horse's brain—instead of against it—smoothes every mutual interaction, from a pasture greeting to open flight over an eight-foot puissance wall. Too often, horse-and-human partnerships are a one-way street on which we command and they respond. To a surprising degree, many horses accept unilateral pronouncements. But training improves by leaps and bounds—becoming safer, gentler, faster, more effective, and immeasurably more interesting—when communication within the partnership flows in both directions. We then begin to experience the world through the brain of another species. It's an amazing feeling, and it illuminates everything we can know about true horsemanship.

Cross-Species Communication

Asked which species of animal is best at mutual communication with humans, most people would guess dogs. After all, dogs are the most common pet and have evolved an innate alertness to human signals. But I believe the potential for cross-species communication is much greater between horses and riders. Why? Because in addition to the voice, gesture, and body language we use with dogs, our bodies are in frequent contact with our horses. Each party transmits and receives information through skin, muscles, tendons, weight distribution, and balance. This contact triggers that dance between equine and human neurons that I mentioned a moment ago.

Despite their size, horses are unbelievably sensitive. Imagine asking a horse to slow his pace while working under saddle. One of the cues a good rider offers is to squeeze her shoulder blades together, opening the upper chest. This change causes a neural network to fire in the horse's brain. The trained horse instantly responds by slowing slightly. That response is conveyed through the rider's body directly to her brain, which sends the next message to the horse. And so on, with neurons firing from equine brain to human brain and back. It's the equivalent of a direct neural link with no translation needed—like mainlining nitroglycerine straight to the heart instead of letting a pill melt under your tongue.

Horse Brain, Human Brain explores our own and our horses' minds to achieve several goals:

- We can deepen bonds by adapting our forms of communication to theirs. Connect with a horse, and suddenly he trusts you to take him to fearful places and ask him to perform difficult feats.
- With knowledge of his brain, we can train an animal with insight and kindness instead of force or demand. If the animal knows we understand his fears and will accommodate them while teaching, we are on the road to success.
- We can comprehend a horse's misbehavior in ways that prompt creative new solutions. Why is this sorrel mare refusing to load? Let's look at how her brain works and what she's telling us with her form of communication.
- By analyzing the differences between species' brains, we can reduce our own mistakes. Any animal trainer will tell you that the hardest part of the job is training the human.

Obstacles to the Goal

We could yammer all day about the need for brain science in handling horses. Most people would agree it's a reasonable idea. But in practice, there are obstacles. Let's push them aside right now:

"Brain science? Are you kidding? I barely escaped college." Brains might be the most fascinating frontier in the universe, but they are not the easiest. In this book, I will talk "brains" in the most direct way—without a wheelbarrow full of high falutin' Latin syllables. You don't have to grasp every nuance of neural operation in order to apply some useful knowledge to your riding.

"Pfft. I'd rather ride than read." For sure, riding is a lot of fun. But it's even more fun when you ride well enough to establish a true relationship with your horse. Understanding how he thinks will help you do that. Plus, it's not only about the riding. Your horse wants to get to know you. With his help, you can prove that brains rule.

"Just show me the 'obey' button." Ah, if only I knew where it was! The behavior you want is probably too complicated for one or two buttons—getting a racehorse to stand still, for example, takes scores of buttons. Now, it is true that you could take your horse to a trainer for a year or two of tutoring, and that trainer might create some buttons and teach you how to push them. But then you're not really interacting with the animal. If you just want an "obey" button, buy a golf cart. It eats less.

"Anything with the word 'science' is boring and obscure." Scientists are just regular people. We're curious about the hows and whys of life, and we break our work down into basic steps to manage it from one day to the next. You probably do the same in your job. It's actually kind of fun to learn how your brain works: "Why did I think that? Uh-oh, why did I *say* that?" It also feels good to see the interest in your horse's eye when you try something brainy with him and he gets it.

"I'm the human, the horse does what I say." One very natural aspect of the human brain is that it is centered on itself. It has to be in order to survive. Human egocentrism has been part of horse training ever since the Greek philosopher Xenophon wrote about riding back in 350 BC. But getting a 1,200-pound fear-based prey animal to do your bidding isn't like training a puppy. You can't just press his hips down and say, "Sit!" in an ever-louder voice. Learn about your horse's brain, and you will be much more likely to succeed.

"Riding is easy. Let's not make a big deal out of it." Most anybody can huff and puff onto a mounting block, stretch their legs into the air like long pretzels, and slither up onto a school horse's back just long enough to get dizzy from the height. Real riding, however, is not easy. It takes strength, coordination, effort, knowledge, skill, and a boatload of practice. In return, all that work brings joy and mastery to our lives. It makes for comfortable healthy horses, too.

That Horse Nerd

My interest in horses and brains began in Scottsdale, Arizona, where horses were a way of life and a means of childhood transportation. Scottsdale was a four-square-mile cow town of 10,000 people back then, surrounded by large horse and cattle ranches. Most of my childhood was spent reading in a palo verde tree or sweating on the back of a horse. We kids rode ponies on dirt tracks to each other's houses and hopped bushes in the desert for fun. At some point, my father took me to a horse show where he explained why the riders were bouncing up and down. "It's called posting," he said, and I was instantly obsessed. Riding was now my mission.

For years, I lived at a 60-horse barn, riding under the supervision of two trainers. Most of our mounts were young or difficult because that's what training stables get—a diverse influx of babies who don't know the human world yet and bad actors no one else wants to handle. I schooled seven or eight of them a day and taught beginning riders.

The brains came into it early one morning on a three-year-old Quarter Horse colt. Dee Sea topped out at 16.3 when he grew up, with the mighty engine of a Doc Bar butt to match. We were playing with live cattle for the first time, to see whether he'd have any talent for cutting in the future. Turns out he did.

I thought we were just soaking up the milieu. But shortly into our adventure, Dee Sea pinned his ears at a young steer, dropped low, and whirled 180 degrees in a millisecond—every bit as fast as an established cutting horse would turn. I stayed on but accidentally caught his side with the half-inch spur I shouldn't have been wearing. He bucked high and hard, blasting me head-first into a railroad tie standing vertically as a fence post. This was back in the Dark Ages—harnessed helmets and plastic fencing hadn't been invented.

I regained consciousness that afternoon, having worked several other horses in the meantime—speaking, walking, tacking up, and riding in a manner everyone called normal. (What "normal" says about my early personality is best left unexplored.) I suffered bouts of amnesia for a couple of years, "coming to" at various times and places with no recollection of how I got there or what I had been doing. And I asked myself how my brain could keep me functioning during complete lapses of awareness that lasted anywhere from two hours to two days.

To answer that question, I began reading about brains between rides, eventually earning a Ph.D. in cognitive science. Don't worry, "cognitive science" is just a fancy phrase for figuring out what happens inside normal noggins on a regular day. I then taught college students how human brains perceive, learn, remember, communicate, and think. There's nothing quite like teaching the innards of a neuron to bleary-eyed 18-year-olds at eight in the morning. I had to explain brains in ways that would at least keep these kids awake.

My life ran on two tracks for many years, but horses and brains finally converged in 2014, long after meeting that railroad tie. Leaving my position as a tenured professor, I renewed my equine occupation, running a successful horse training business of my own. Deciphering brain function within the horse-and-human team was now my goal.

The Trail Ahead

Horse Brain, Human Brain is written in five parts. Part One introduces the book and considers the challenges of forming teams between predators and prey, with attention to the pressures of evolution that created our brains.

Part Two focuses on taking the world in—perceiving sights, sounds, smells, tastes, touch, and awareness of body positions. Human egocentrism raises its head right away, with riders often assuming that horses perceive the world just like we do. This incorrect assumption confuses horses and frustrates handlers.

Part Three looks at how horses learn, imitate, solve problems, and remember. Why do equine brains learn best with positive reinforcement, despite the fact that trainers usually rely on its opposite? Why is timing so critical as natural chemicals flow through brain tissue, and why are edible rewards both a blessing and a curse? Why is punishment the worst method of teaching? Once the basics of associative learning are in place, I'll introduce the power of indirect training. Part Three ends by exploring the dangers that crop up when goal-driven human brains try to command stimulus-driven equine brains.

Part Four homes in on equine attention, emotion, and forethought. We have to capture horses' attention and regulate their emotions before we can teach them anything. Fear, anxiety, and trust are addressed, in addition to the ways horses express their emotions and interpret ours. We'll also tackle questions of strategy here. Are equine brains capable of planning in advance? If so, are they culpable for their actions?

Finally, Part Five takes on the topic of *true horsemanship*. Of course, knowledge and skill are part of horsemanship, but I'm also talking about an ethical philosophy of care. True horsemen—both male and female—put the horse's needs first and offer a generous spirit even when the animal misbehaves. *Horse Brain, Human Brain* teaches people to understand the equine noodle not only so that we can ride better, train more effectively, and protect our animals' welfare. It also applies brain science to horsemanship so that we can understand each animal at a deep level that encourages mutual bonds of trust and responsibility between the two species.

All in All

Throughout this book, you'll find barn-side applications of brain science. I want you to ride with your brain in real life, not just ponder a handsome theory from your reading chair. Every chapter includes true stories about real horses I've worked with, stories that illustrate my successes and failures in trying to understand equine minds. Along the way, I'll explain how brain cells work when they fire their tiny electric sparks and shoot homemade chemicals around. Source notes appear at the end of this book and are referenced by page number. Illustrations are offered throughout, with drawings of the horse brain enlarged for visual ease. A glossary and index are included, too. That way, you can find information quickly if your horse makes you run from the arena to look something up!

Horse Brain, Human Brain is written for everyone who interacts with horses. Our group includes raw beginners and seasoned experts, practitioners of any equestrian discipline, and members of all equine professions. An understanding of the horse's brain is pertinent to all of us.

Unfortunately, this breadth gives me the opportunity to offend everyone by either talking down to the expert or talking up to the novice. Please forgive me for points that are pitched to alternate skill levels.

Leonardo da Vinci is credited with the quote, "Simplicity is the ultimate sophistication." I hope Leo's right because no book can convey the full complexity of the human or equine brain. To do so would require many volumes crammed with high-dollar vocabulary. That would dishonor the intent of this project. Explanations here are accurate but simplified, so that we can concentrate on our main character: the horse.

The Horse

Where in this wide world can
man find nobility without pride,
friendship without envy or beauty
without vanity? Here, where
grace is laced with muscle, and
strength by gentleness confined.

Ronald Duncan, Poet
© Ronald Duncan Estate and reprinted with permission.

With brain-based horsemanship, we have access to the immense privilege of collaborating with an individual of another species, of shaping his brain and allowing him to shape ours. But to succeed, we have to work *with* the principles of human and equine brains instead of against them.

CHAPTER TWO
Evolving a Brain

Why do we need to know how brains are engineered? I mean, there they are, fully formed, and ready to go. Why not just "shut up and dance," as the song says? The reason is that the way brains evolved eons ago tells us a lot about how they work today.

Equine brains are engineered to sense and interpret the equine world. Where's the best grass? Which way is the water? Is it safe to lie down here? What's that noise? Is my alpha mare concerned? But they are not designed to take in and interpret the *human* world, and that's what we ask of them most often.

Not only do we expect them to understand the human world, we also expect them to understand *us*! Now, I don't know about you, but even with a human brain I sometimes fail miserably to understand people. Truth be told, I'm not always that great at understanding myself. How can we expect horses to succeed at the task?

Brains—horse, human, or otherwise—are engineered through time in many ways. Some methods of brain design are more easily modified than others. In shaping equine behavior, we need to know which aspects of the brain can be changed and which must be accepted.

- Brains evolve first by natural selection, in which a mental ability helps individuals to survive and reproduce. For example, early horses who noticed peripheral movement quickly tended to stay alive. The physical structure of today's brains is determined by environmental pressures that occurred millions of years ago. We can work around it somewhat, but we cannot eliminate or change it.

- Brains adjust through domestication, which is driven by artificial selection. Here, humans choose stallions and mares with certain traits to yield offspring who carry the same trait. Breeders can select for temperament and trainability, but often choose beauty, speed, or strength instead.
- Brains mature during development from birth to adulthood. The human brain develops for 25 years before it is fully mature, longer than most of us realize. In horses, the length of brain maturation to adulthood is unknown. Physical maturity in general takes five to seven years, depending on breed. Experiences during development alter the brain significantly, so the early training we provide to a horse is critical.
- Brains change physically throughout adulthood in response to daily learning. Every time you or your horse experience something important, new connections are formed among brain cells. With use, these connections form a persistent record in the brain. In addition, new neurons are born throughout adulthood.

Natural Selection

Bone and tooth fossils show that the earliest ancestors of today's horse lived in North America 56 million years ago. The size of small dogs, they had wide-set eyes down near their noses and padded feet with several toes. Warm temperatures of the era had produced subtropical forest across most of the continent, and the lower leaves of those trees kept pre-horses fed and sheltered. Life was good.

But fast-forward 21 million years, when an Ice Age caused temperatures to drop. Polar ice caps formed, glaciers moved in, forests died, and prairies emerged—covered with hard ground, tough grass, open space, and predators. Pre-horses whose bodies could not withstand these new conditions died off. But those few individuals who happened to have warmer fur, bigger bodies, stronger feet, faster legs, and harder teeth survived. They reproduced, their offspring reproduced, and so on—altering the species' bodies and brains over eons of time.

If you have a chance, try a speedy getaway across rough ground on soft padded feet and a bunch of cold toes. Not very fast, is it? So, through natural selection, the horse's outside toes began to disappear. Today, the splint bones in our horses' legs, the chestnuts above their knees, and the ergots on their fetlocks are vestiges of those ancient outside toes. Meanwhile, the central toes hardened and enlarged into hooves that could travel a long way on rigid surfaces.

Natural selection also streamlined the horse for speed, with longer-legged horses better able to survive and reproduce in the new conditions. The bones in equine legs became longer. The "knee" (or carpus) on a horse today is actually the equivalent of a human wrist. Everything below that carpus is the equivalent of a human hand with very long fingers. The horse's ankle or fetlock corresponds to the large knuckles of your hand, where the fingers begin to protrude. With all this lengthening of equine bone came longer tendons. Today's equine legs are lightning fast for running away, but length makes them fragile too. Long legs also lifted the horse's head above the level of tall plains grasses—the better to notice predators lying in wait.

Brains Run the Show

With all of these evolutionary changes in the horse's body, the brain's sensory organs had to adapt. Peripheral motion vision and precise hearing tuned up so that important sights or sounds—the rustle of a predator's movement through grass, for instance—would be noticed instantly. Smell became critical for safety from predators and navigation to water. Motor coordination and fast-twitch muscles became vital for escape. These increases in sensitivity were built partly into the eyes, ears, nose, and muscles. But they are even more apparent in the brain tissue where sensory signals arrive for interpretation and in the hard wiring that carries action commands to various destinations in the brain.

The internal operation of brain cells adapted too. Fatty tissue was produced to surround the long tail (or *axon*) of each *neuron*, so it could transmit information faster. (Neurons are a type of brain cell that transmit

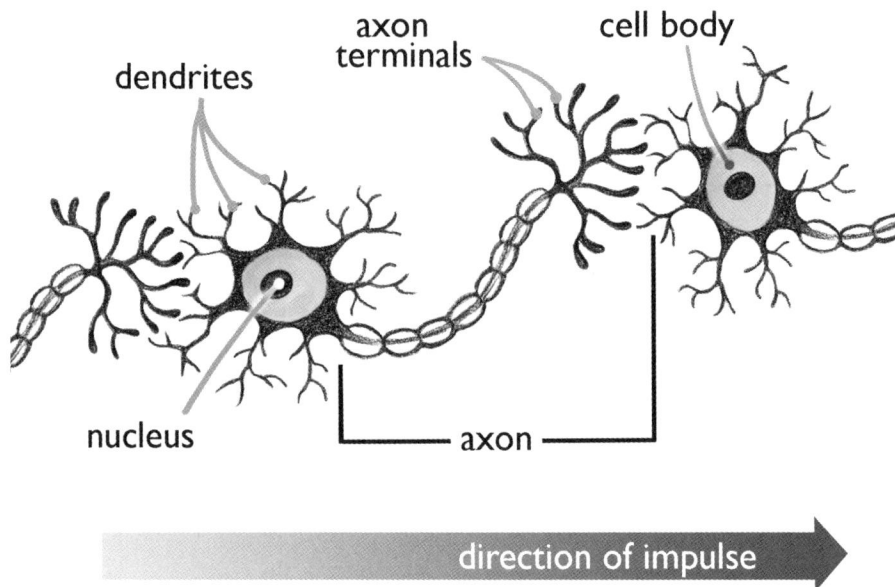

2.1 Neurons transmit electrical impulses through equine and human brains. The dendrites of one neuron send electricity through its axon. Axon terminals then transmit that information to the dendrites of the next cell.

functional information.) In today's horse, some axons are 10 feet long, stretching from the brain and looping around through the body. The fastest can transmit messages up to 394 feet per second. That's nearly 250 miles an hour! *Glial* ("GLEE-ull") *cells*—the brain's janitors—multiplied to keep neurons healthy. The neural ability to form connections became faster and more efficient (fig. 2.1). So did the brain's ability to kill off unused connections that would only interfere with the learning process.

The brain adapted to collect glucose from food more efficiently, because brains hog glucose for fuel. The human brain represents 2% of your total body weight but uses 20% of your body's glucose. Equine brains are downright gluttonous—they comprise only two-tenths of a percent of the horse's total body weight but use 25% of the glucose. Too much glucose can harm our bodies—both equine and human—but too little harms our brains. That's why we get confused when our blood sugar is too low.

Hard-Wiring for Safety

When dangerous sensory signals were detected on the prairie, a horse couldn't twiddle his hooves deciding what to do. He had to run first and be alive to ask questions later. To manage that requirement, the equine brain evolved to connect perception directly to action. A nerve signal comes from the eye to the visual processing area of the brain, for example, and the equine brain instantly sends that signal to the motor control area with the command to RUN (fig. 2.2 A). These processing areas are in the surface, or *cortex*, of the brain. It all happens unconsciously.

2.2 A The horse's brain detects sights at the visual cortex, then sends the new information to the motor cortex for immediate action.

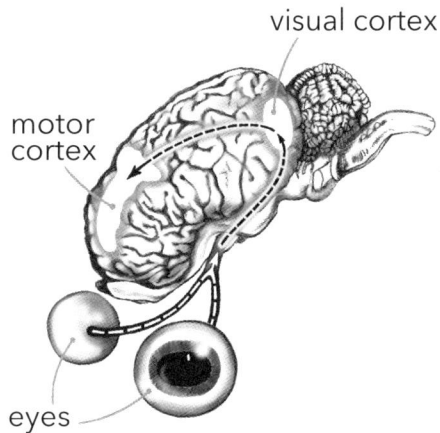

2.2 B The human brain also detects sights at the visual cortex. But it sends that information to the prefrontal cortex for analysis and evaluation before the motor cortex springs into action.

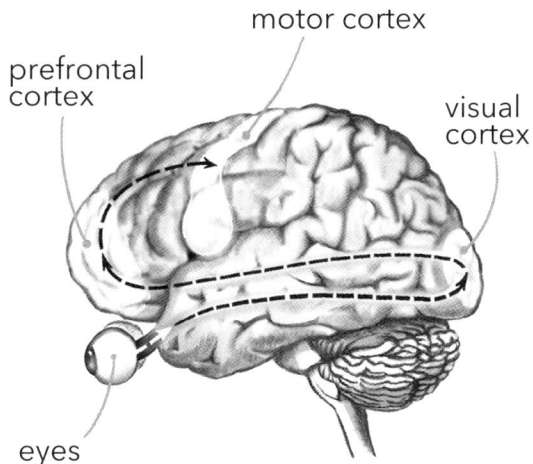

If human perception and action are mediated by thought, you might wonder how we so rapidly avoid pain. Automatic reflex actions are responsible for that—and the brain does not control them. Next time you touch a hot stove burner (please *do not* try this at home!), notice how your arm instantaneously pulls away. This action occurs at the level of the spinal cord, before the pain signal has time to reach the brain. No thought is involved. Horses experience reflex actions when they shake flies off their skin, shiver in the cold, cough, swallow, suckle, or blink.

The wiring between perception and action in the human brain is quite different. A nerve signal comes from our eyes to the visual cortex at the back of our brain, and is usually diverted to a slow path that meanders over to the prefrontal cortex just behind our forehead. There, an unconscious analysis is undertaken: "What have I seen? Have I seen that before? What does it mean? What should I do? Which option is best? Why? Did I have lunch yet? Oh… whoops, let's pay attention… Hmm, option 17c has worked in the past. Let's try that one again." Finally, action kicks in—long after a lion would have punctured an equine throat and gobbled half a leg (fig. 2.2 B).

Innate Instincts

The process of natural selection over millions of years forms the hard wiring of a brain—its major pathways and structures. Evolution always lags behind the present day. So the human brain still functions according to its ability to hunt meat and gather berries, keep its body warm and dry, find mates in the savannah, and try to prevent the children from being eaten by lions. It doesn't matter that today we drive to the grocery store instead of spearing a wildebeest for dinner, meet potential mates online, and try to prevent the children from being shot in their schools.

Some pathways make stops here and there along the route to their brain destinations—and often, these stops occur at places where the path ended a few million years ago. When scientists see an abandoned way station like that, we have evidence that the brain used to work differently than it does now. For instance, in 2018 researchers found links in the human brain between areas for navigation and smell. People no longer need to smell their way to water, but at one time that ability was so critical for survival that our brain structures changed physically to account for it.

Most psychologists agree that the initial stages of romantic attraction are hard-wired. You don't turn the process on, and you can't just flip a switch to turn it off. The feelings are involuntary. But that doesn't mean we have no recourse. We can work around attraction by learning to notice and identify it, pausing to think carefully about its implications, listening to Mr. or Ms. Perfect's point of view, and removing ourselves from awkward situations. The feelings are still there, but we don't have to act on them.

Shying is a good example of hard-wired behavior in horses. Equine brains evolved to whirl and bolt when potential danger occurs. Horses are captive to the naturally selected aspects of their brains, just as we are to ours. In addition, horses have far less ability to manage their hard-wired behavior than humans do. They're super-smart but do not have the prefrontal cortex to control their instincts fully. We cannot expect a horse to smell a bear a few feet away and simply walk on.

This, by the way, is not a hypothetical example. Aspen, a furry dun pony belonging to a friend, tended to shy out in the back forty. One area near a thicket of willows was especially difficult for her to negotiate. She was convinced of danger there, tightening her muscles, doing the quick-step as if on *Dancing with the Stars*, and opening her eyes wider every time she approached. In frustration, her owner hired a trainer to get Aspen past this foolishness.

The trainer hopped on one fall day and rode Aspen to the thicket, where she pulled her usual shenanigans. He insisted she move closer to the bushes and, trembling, she eventually agreed. Just about then, a black bear bounded out of his cover, moving on all fours straight toward Aspen—who took off hell bent for election. Everyone learned some lessons: Sometimes it really is best to listen to the horse. And don't poke the bear!

So do we have to allow every horse to spin out from under us whenever a leaf wiggles? Of course not. We can teach the horse to get to know a frightening area over time, to shy with smaller movements, to slow down and investigate after shying, to trust our leadership. We can teach ourselves to distinguish between equine nerves and true fear. We can overcome our frustration—after all, the horse is behaving in a perfectly natural way. Horses shy just like car passengers slam their useless brake feet into the floorboards and gasp for air when expecting a crash. It's the brain's involuntary method of staying alive.

Social Dynamics

Because of their distant past, horses are strongly social animals with herd instincts. They respond to their buddies at all times. We humans fail to notice much of this subtle interaction, and it weakens when we are around. But left on their own, horses rely on group perception, learn by imitation, seek leadership from dominant guides, and soothe themselves through social contact.

As the horse evolved to survive predators on open grasslands, his brain became more dependent on activity within the group. Imagine 10 horses grazing in a field that is familiar to them. By nature, they will adopt slightly different positions with their bodies aimed this way and that for greater surveillance. Although their heads are usually down, each horse pays attention to the others. If the most sensitive horse glances up to check a noise, the others cock an eye or ear toward him. If one horse startles, the group looks in that direction immediately. To stay safe, they need each other.

When removed from the group, horses transfer their need for leadership from a dominant equine to a human. So, in the absence of a higher-ranking horse, your mount is going to look to you for help. He doesn't need a friend or a follower—he needs you to be his leader.

Social behavior among horses is partly learned but largely innate. Brain scientists in 2018 found that mammalian brains are hard wired to regulate the rank hierarchies, group status, social vocalization, and peer observation that horses use all the time. To train well, we need to understand these evolutionary motives.

Evolution's Behavioral Tendencies

Because of their need to escape predators, horses are innately afraid of being restricted or confined. Tying, for example, needs to be taught in a gradual gentle way to overcome the horse's natural fear. Blocking the horse's side view in narrow passageways causes trouble —and, unknowingly, people do it all the time. At least 35 million years of evolution tells an equine brain that the dark, restricted, metal box of a trailer spells D-E-A-T-H. A horse who balks at these practices is not being ornery. He's being a horse.

We all know that horses are attuned to unexpected sights and sounds. But many people don't realize that the least obvious of these are the most likely to startle the horse: short rapid movements and low-volume sounds. Predators did not announce their presence in advance—they tried to hide. If you've ever seen a non-horse person try to "hide" from a horse so as not to bother him, you know what I mean. Once while I was giving a lesson, a visitor tried to hide her Labrador Retriever under the bleachers in an indoor arena. Every horse in the ring flipped out. Once the dog was in plain view, they settled. Hiding from a horse is impossible, and the very act of attempting to remain unseen and unheard unnerves the horse much more than a serene open approach.

Some of the most critical brain differences between horses and humans are wrought by the distinctions between predators and their prey. Horses (along with rabbits, deer, cattle, and many other species) are prey animals—food for predators. Their brains evolved to notice tiny movements instantly, hightail it out of there with no analysis, and live in groups for safety. Prey animals are easily identified by sideward-facing eyes that survey a wide horizontal range for potential danger.

Hard-Wired Fears

Natural selection causes horses to fear:

- restriction
- confinement
- darkness or narrow passages
- sudden movements
- unusual sounds
- predators
- isolation from the group

Predators have forward-facing eyes. Their brains evolved for visual focus, depth perception, stalking, and killing. These include lions, wolves, cats, dogs, and um (how can I say this gently?)…humans. You and I are predators, and every horse knows it with one glance at our close-set eyes. The fact that horses allow us to work with them at all—let alone straddle their backs—is a testament to their generosity, curiosity, and domestication. But we do well to remember that the horse's brain is still hard-wired by evolution to fear us.

Fear of isolation is another by-product of equine evolution that we can't change. Safety lies in the group. Even super-chill horses tend to be more nervous when they are alone. Equine misbehavior caused by fear can often be relieved by introducing another horse. Give the worried animal the comfort of a buddy—a horse who walks quietly into a trailer, a horse who relaxes on trail rides, a horse who has seen scary objects but survived to tell the tale.

Domestication

Today's species of horse, *equus caballus,* includes all breeds and represents the domesticated version of its forest and grassland ancestors. Technically, domestication refers to artificial selection, which has occurred for at least 6,000 years. Key breeding characteristics for the purpose of taming a wild animal are calmness, ability to learn, submission to captivity, and willingness to allow human contact. By selecting mares and stallions with these traits, people have produced horses who are much easier to train than their undomesticated counterparts would be.

Many people assume that "wild" horses today are undomesticated. That's not accurate. Some are feral individuals who have lived without much human contact but are descended from domesticated ancestors. They live in bands on their own, but are not truly "wild." Until recently, the Przewalski horse of Mongolia was thought to be the only remaining undomesticated horse. But DNA evidence now shows that even this breed descends from domesticated ancestors.

Many allegedly "wild" horses are abandoned. During the 2008 recession in the United States, for example, some impoverished horse owners turned their animals loose in undeveloped areas to fend for themselves. A few lucky survivors formed groups that are sometimes referred to as "wild" even though they grew up in stalls and enjoyed years of training.

After several thousand generations of domestication, we now have horses whose bodies and brains are mostly naturally selected, but whose behavioral traits of calmness and acquiescence are largely artificially selected. Variation among breeds is also a feature of artificial selection. The American Thoroughbred, for example, is bred to be light, long, lean, and agile—perfect for speed. Belgian Warmbloods are bred to be bulky, thick-muscled, wide, and slow—great for power. Along with these physical traits come differences in temperament, with the flighty nervous racehorse contrasting the stolid reliable Belgian. Within each breed there are individual differences, of course.

Today's Brain

Throughout evolution, brains have become bigger. Yet brain function in both horses and humans is determined far more by neural connection than absolute size. According to the Internet, the horse's brain is the size of a walnut. Or a human fist. Three baseballs. Next thing ya know, they'll be likening it to a peanut or a watermelon. Sounds like some facts are in order.

Pop a human brain out of its skull and you have a 3-pound lump of squishy tofu that's 75% water. The average horse's brain has the same consistency but weighs 1 pound 5 ounces, not quite half the weight of its human counterpart. A basketball weighs the same, as does the brain of a six-month-old human baby. In terms of size, the adult human brain is about 4 inches high, 6 inches wide, and 7 inches long. The tissue of both the human and horse brain is especially dense in some areas, often corresponding to "structures" that are identified in diagrams.

The horse's brain is about the volume of a grapefruit. In shape, the grapefruit is elongated and partly squashed. It's lumpy and bumpy but measures about 4 inches high, 4 inches side to side, and 6 inches front to back. It rests on a 45-degree angle pointing downward rather than sitting level as a human brain does.

Most important for function, the horse's brain contains slightly over 1 billion neurons, far fewer than the human brain's 86 billion. Depending on its type, each neuron can accept up to 10,000 connections. These connections are the magic behind equine perception, learning, emotion, and athleticism.

Brain Change through Maturation and Learning

One of the linchpins to any form of animal training—or human learning, for that matter—is to identify what can be changed and what cannot be changed. We've seen that evolution drives certain equine behaviors that are innate and physiological. By respecting them, we reduce the horse's fear and can then alter more malleable aspects of his brain.

Brain connections are built by daily experience. Few people realize just how physical a process learning is. When a foal takes that first step toward you, a new physical connection within a group of brain cells is formed. It's weak, it will disappear if it's not repeated, and it's prone to mistakes. But every time the fledgling connection is used, it becomes stronger. The foal's second step forward strengthens it, tomorrow's positive approach reinforces it, and so on. Eventually you have built a brand new network of connected neurons inside your foal's brain that forms an initial bond.

That one physical connection is the basis for everything the foal will do in the human world. You will build on it, little by little, until this baby trots at your shoulder, halts on a slack lead when your feet stop moving, follows verbal commands, accepts a saddle and rider, learns to jump, wins a world championship, retires with you to the trails, and eventually enters the old-age pasture.

Neural connections form throughout all of life, so you can continue to shape your horse's brain—and your own—until the day one of you leaves this earth behind. Pause for a moment to think about the immensity of that power. And the responsibility that comes with it. You are shaping your horse's physical brain, and he is shaping yours. That is an extraordinary—almost supernatural—ability. Cherish it.

PART TWO

Taking the World In

CHAPTER THREE

How Horses See

See that sliver of light on the sand, shining through a gap in the roof of the indoor arena? Every time she goes past, Hawkeye arches her neck and skirts the boundary as if it's a rattlesnake. The sliver changes in size and shape with the sun's movement, and the horse seems to see each tiny difference as a brand new snake. When a concurrent sound erupts—oh say, the sound of a grain of sand shifting—she leaps sideways.

These are normal behaviors caused by the way a horse's visual system is hard-wired into his brain. We can teach the horse to overcome some of them, but we can't force such behaviors away. Nor can we make a horse see the way we do. How we respond to our mounts depends largely on human vision, and it biases our expectations of what horses see.

When we ponder equine vision, we know it must differ from our own; but when we're busy handling a horse, that fact is easy to forget. Equine vision is fuzzy—contrary to our assumptions, horses cannot make out details or see strong edges. They have trouble focusing on objects, especially those that are near to them. We can't see the periphery of the world, but it's the equivalent of front and center for horses—they get a complete double-side view that we never see. They're also tuned to identify tiny flicks of motion that the human eye misses. And objects can fall into many equine blind spots, becoming invisible until they suddenly pop up like trick-or-treaters saying, "Boo!"

Eye and Brain

We construct sight using information from our eyes combined with knowledge in our brains. Things can go wrong at either end—the eye or the brain. People whose eyes become blind still see images and dreams. Those whose visual cortex is damaged, but whose eyes are intact, often see lights and shadows but can't make sense of them. In rare cases, people who are completely brain-blind can navigate around invisible objects or reach accurately to grasp coffee cups they cannot see. This ability, called *blindsight*, isn't limited to humans—cortically blind animals can do it, too.

Rarely, a snippet of visual cortex is impaired so specifically that its owner—having otherwise normal sight—suddenly cannot see color, shape, or perhaps movement. Imagine trying to cross a busy street with your intact eyes open when your brain can't perceive motion. Cars travelling 50 miles an hour become a series of still images stopped along the road. A moment later, they're stopped in different locations.

Neuroscientist Gerald Edelman said it best: "Every act of perception is, to some degree, an act of creation." The trouble for a horse-and-human team is that equine brains create perceptions in ways that are very different from ours. Visual information travels from the eye to the brain in both species, of course. But the human brain sends back six times more neural information in the opposite direction, from the brain to the eye. This wiring boosts perceptual interpretation: lots of knowledge is melded with the human eye's pictures of the outside world. So, who's more objective in seeing reality, you or your horse? Hate to break the news, but it's probably your horse. Equine brains should be less prone to illusions than human brains are.

Visual Acuity

Horses often give the impression of superb eyesight. Walking in an open field, a bird flicks a wing and they'll raise their heads, point their ears, quiver their nostrils, and widen their eyes with what seems to be intense focus on the bird's location. Some trainers refer to this as the look of an eagle, and it is indeed an impressive display of intelligence and sensitivity. However, the reason for it depends less on good vision than bad vision. Horses try to improve blurry views by raising their heads and enlarging their eyes. Their ears perk up to listen because they can't see stationary details well. Their nostrils expand to optimize an excellent sense of smell.

Equine eyes are eight times larger than human eyes, larger than those of any other land mammal. But a horse's *acuity* is considerably worse than ours. Acuity refers to the ability to make tiny discriminations in detail while focusing on something in the center of the visual field. Reading is a great example for humans—right now, your eyes are picking up tiny differences in the black marks on a page. You can see the difference between an "e" and a "c," for example. The distinction is meaningful—witness the confusion if you misread that you have "cars" on both sides of your head.

By convention, normal human acuity is 20/20. What a person with normal vision can see from a distance of 20 feet is the same as what *you* see from a distance of 20 feet—if you have normal vision. But normal equine acuity ranges from 20/30 to 20/60.

Let's consider the visually gifted (20/30) horse first. Details you can see from 30 feet away, a sharp-eyed horse can only see from 20 feet away. In other words, he has to be 50% closer to see the same details—he has half your acuity. What if your sweetie-pie is near the low end of normal equine acuity at 20/60? Details you make out from 60 feet away, he cannot see until approaching within 20 feet. That's a 200% impairment compared to human vision!

Even the 50% deficiency is enough for any rider to consider. Imagine what a horse sees when the two of you approach a jump (figs. 3.1 A & B). For you, it's clear, sharp, and bright. You'd be mighty nervous if it looked fuzzy and faded. But equestrians are often startled to see photographs constructed to show what a jump looks like to a horse. Even in sunshine, the horse's view of a jump is blurry, hazy, dim, flat, vague—all the adjectives you'd rather not deliberate as you're galloping 30 feet per second to a big oxer that could break your neck.

Beyond the normal range from 20/30 to 20/60, horses differ in individual acuity just as people do. Twenty-three percent of horses are nearsighted (they do not see details clearly until they get much closer than equine normal to an object). Forty-three percent of horses are far-sighted (able to see more clearly only as they get farther away). It stands to reason

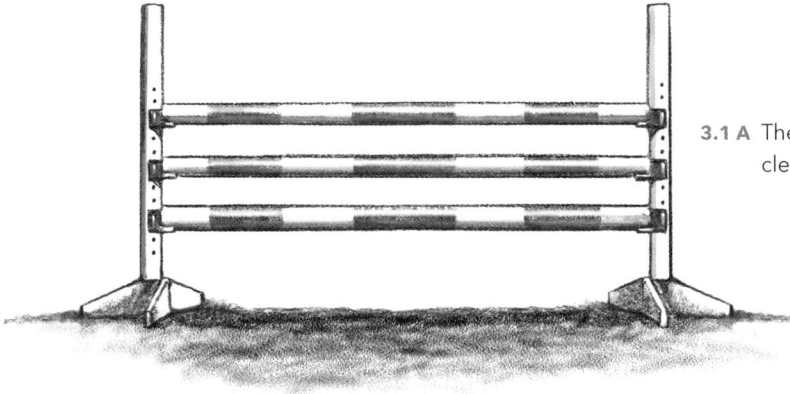

3.1 A The rider sees a jump clearly on approach.

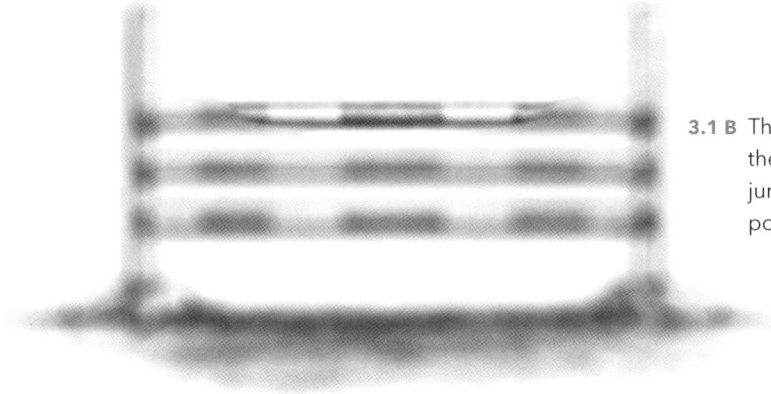

3.1 B The horse's brain sees the same oncoming jump with less acuity and poorer focus.

that slightly far-sighted horses excel in disciplines like jumping because the ability to drill down on fine points from a distance fuels their athleticism.

Acuity for objects close to us worsens with age because the natural lens inside human and equine eyes hardens over time. If you're over 50, you know what I'm talking about. The best acuity in horses occurs around age seven. Prior to that it's not fully developed, and afterward it begins to decay. Breed makes a difference, too. Horses with long convex faces, like Standardbreds and Thoroughbreds, have better acuity than horses with short concave faces, like Arabians.

Focus

The human eye is superb at focusing on one detail of a scene. Muscles holding the flexible lens of the eye pull it into a more convex shape to focus on objects close up. You can feel these muscles working if you hold a finger up in front of your eyes. Focus on the finger then look past it (without moving your eyes) to a distant object. Go back and forth, getting the feel of the ciliary muscles that flex your lens. This ability—called *accommodation*—allows us to inspect objects while working on them with our hands. Humans excel at visual accommodation.

Horses do not. Their ciliary muscles are too weak to pull the lens into a more convex shape for greater focus (fig. 3.2). So when you hold something near your horse's face—a bridle or clippers—he can smell it but will have great trouble focusing his eyes on it. To show your horse something new, hold it near his nose for a good sniff or on his shoulder where he can feel it with his excellent sense of touch. If it must be seen, hold it out in the air several feet away, and wait a bit. What little focus horses can achieve happens slowly. That's why sudden movements near their bodies can surprise them.

3.2 Like the human eye, the equine eye contains a pupil, iris, ciliary muscle, and lens. However, it is a bit more compressed, or flatter, in shape than the human eyeball.

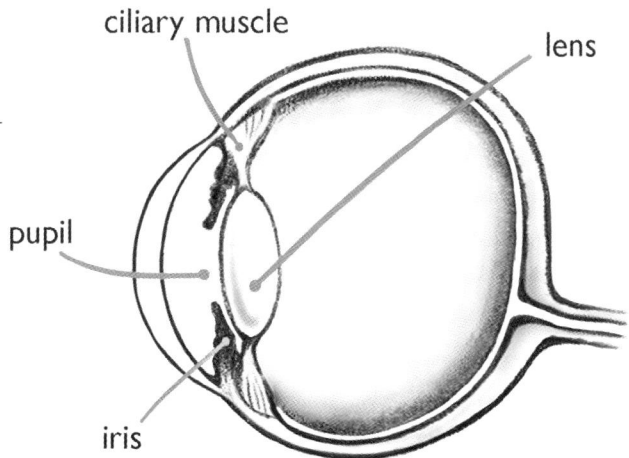

Range of Vision

Ask a child to describe a horse's eyes. One of the first things the child will mention is that they are very large and set on the sides of the head, unlike small human eyes that point forward. This simple observation generates profound differences in the ways humans and horses see. Eye position affects visual range, peripheral motion detection, and depth perception. Equine eyes can even move independently to scan one side of the world more intently than the other.

Human sight is accurate enough to decode tiny marks on a page, but only for a very small slice of the view. While reading, a few words in your central vision are truly clear; the rest are blurred. Stretch your arm out to the side, holding something like a pencil vertically in your hand. Look straight ahead. You won't see the pencil in this position. You can't even see your arm. Now move your arm slowly in a wide outstretched semi-circle toward the front, keeping your eyes focused on a distant point in front of you. No cheating! The pencil remains invisible until it reaches almost a 45-degree angle. Human vision is limited to roughly 45 degrees on either side of our noses, for a total of about 90 degrees (figs. 3.3 A & B).

By contrast, if we held a pencil straight out from the side of a horse's head, it would be almost in the center of his vision. With eyes on the sides of his head, he catches a 340-degree view, almost four times greater than the range we see. Imagine what would happen if we humans had four times more vision to process every second of the day. We'd be edgy, too!

The horse's visual range stretches from the outside of the nose all the way around to an imaginary line extending back from the hip. The last few degrees of angle near the hind legs and hips permit only very poor vision. When leading or riding your horse, the vehicle that you cannot see approaching from behind your shoulder is within his line of sight, but it's not too clear. It's coming toward him, often at a rate faster than he is moving. Green horses see this as a chase, and every fiber of their being says that the way to survive a chase is to run. Now!

3.3 A Human range of view is about 90 degrees, so the rider in this drawing only sees someone moving hay near a wheelbarrow.

3.3 B Equine range of view is about 340 degrees, so the horse sees everything except the bird behind him.

Working with the Side View

One of the most common mistakes made with nervous horses is to thwart their side view. Humans can't see it, so we forget it's there. We lead horses through narrow passages forgetting that the walls completely block their primary lines of sight—then we wonder why the horse is skittish.

Because it's best for our forward-facing eyes, humans assume that the frontal view is also best for the horse. Some equestrian websites even advise this position. Let's return to Hawkeye, a lovely appendix hunter shown by an excellent equitation student who was new to me. We were working in the indoor arena when Hawkeye skirted the sliver of light that I told you about. At first, I just watched.

The rider was annoyed. In keeping with standard technique, she pushed Hawkeye straight toward the sliver of light on the sand that already scared the bejeebers out of her. She tried to make Hawkeye stand still and stare at the sliver head on, eyes bugged out like tennis balls. The horse danced back and forth, trying to turn to the side, and each time the rider cued her back to center. These demands—which good riders carry out every day—provide a perfect example of riding against the equine brain.

How so? Well, let's think it through.

- From the front, human eyes can see an object clearly, but a horse's wide-set eyes cannot. All Hawkeye knows is that her rider is upset, forcing her forward to a place she considers a threat.
- Without radically moving their heads, horses can't see much below the level of their eyes, and they see nothing under their noses. So, as Hawkeye reluctantly approaches the light-snake, it vanishes from her line of sight. This makes it all the more frightening.
- Standing still concentrates a horse's fear rather than alleviating it. Frightened horses need to move; that's what their brains are telling them to do.
- Each time Hawkeye cocks her head and pivots to the side for a better view, her rider pulls on one rein and presses with the opposite leg, pushing her back to the frontal stance where equine vision is worst.

We might scoff at a big horse who is afraid of a sliver of sunlight or an evil paper cup—but fear is in the eye of the beholder. When was the last time you felt good about a big hairy tarantula running through your hair?

Hawkeye refused to obey the frontal commands, and by now the rider was very frustrated. At such moments, it's tempting to dismount and drive to the nearest ice cream store for solace. But that only teaches a horse that shying buys her a nice safe stall for some couch time. Because the horse was afraid but not terrified of the light-snake, I asked the rider to remain mounted and distract the horse with a task that moved her away from the threat. Yes, this sounds like "letting her get away with it," but work with me for a minute here.

The best technique is to ride to any distance the horse considers safe, with the object in view (fig. 3.4). Trot back and forth in a series of loops that place the object most frequently at the horse's side. Focus on pace, relaxation, and inward bend; ignore whatever's scary—don't even glance at it. When the horse settles at that distance, gradually enlarge the loops,

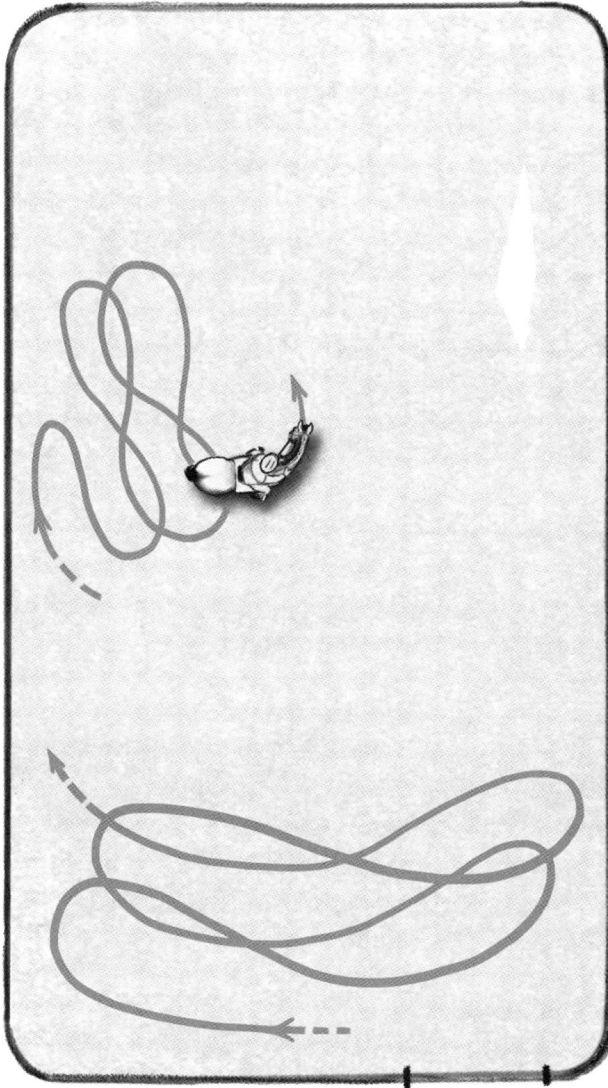

3.4 When the horse is frightened of something, like a sliver of light on arena sand, avoid a frontal approach. Instead, work gradually back and forth from the sides with a distracting task until the horse settles. This method accommodates equine vision instead of expecting the horse to adopt human frontal vision.

maintaining the distance that keeps him tranquil. Ride a foot or so closer to the object each time you go by. When the horse passes it calmly, even from a distance, stroke his neck and speak kindly but keep moving. We want the horse to believe that the task is to form loops with an inward bend— period. If he skirts the fright-sight at some point, decrease the loop to make the task easier. Move closer when *the horse* is ready, not when *you* are ready.

A simple lesson like this might take 1 minute or 100, two days or two months. Don't push or punish fear. If the horse needs a 50-foot berth to negotiate an object calmly, give it to him. The priority is mental composure, not physical distance. Tomorrow you can set the goal for composure at 45 feet. If you're rushed ("I've got an appointment!") or you're annoyed ("You've seen that thing a million times!"), start the lesson another day. Forcing horses is a good way to destroy their trust in you, frighten them all the more, and wake up with Nurse Ratched beside your bed.

Within 10 minutes of this exercise, Hawkeye was walking, trotting, and cantering past the light sliver without looking at or bending away from it. She was relaxed and calm, with no struggle between horse and rider. But it's not always that easy.

My Horse Is Still Scared

Suppose you try this exercise, but your little knucklehead is still freaking out. Here you revert to groundwork. Ride to a spot he considers relatively safe. Dismount and immediately put him to work. If necessary, longe him to get his mind off the problem. Test his progress by gradually moving the longeing circle so that the fright-sight is closer to the horse's side.

Now slow to a walk, remove the longe line, and try leading the horse in the same loops you used before, at the closest distance he considers safe. Give him a chance to discover that the patch does not bite. If necessary, use some vicarious learning: Let him watch a familiar human friend walk to the object, stand next to it, and speak calmly. Stroke his neck and encourage him to approach from the side. A step or two more than the horse wants equals success. Offer praise and stop for today.

If the horse is so deep into his fraidy-hole that this technique fails, have your friend bring a known, preferably dominant horse to the object the next day. (Verify ahead of time that this horse is unafraid.) Speak slowly and stroke your horse's neck while he watches his buddy survive the terror. If this also fails, move out of sight of the object and put your horse to work on a completely unrelated task. Tomorrow, start building his trust using objects that he considers less frightening. Eventually, he will be calm enough to return to the original fright-sight and try again.

When your horse is finally relaxed enough to advance face-first, let him stretch down and forward for a good sniff. He'll probably startle a couple of times—that's okay, you'd jump too if you had to sniff a tarantula in your blind spot. Touch the hazard so your hand makes a soft noise against it; this will allow the horse to learn more through his ears. Gently roll or push the object around as the horse becomes accustomed. It's important to wait for this frontal approach until the horse is completely relaxed while approaching from the side and standing next to the object.

Groundwork

Most trainers use groundwork when starting young horses under saddle. Groundwork refers to any form of training in which the horse is not being ridden. We use it to teach leading, longeing, ground manners, and respect for human space. But we often forget that it's useful in adult years as well, to teach a horse to back, spin, jump, or move laterally, for example. And it's an excellent technique to revert to when problems arise.

The key is to realize that it's a lot harder for horses to relax and learn while we're sitting on them. So, step off and give them a better chance. Don't worry, you'll get back on again before the lesson is over. Remain quiet and calm, moving the horse with your eyes, hands, body position, voice, lead, reins, and/or a whip used only as an extension of your arm to touch the horse's hindquarters. Groundwork does not require chasing a frightened horse in tight circles with flapping plastic bags tied to a stick. This is more properly called "frightwork," in my opinion, and it usually causes more harm than good. Good groundwork takes skill and practice. Take the time to learn it well, and it will help your team.

Peripheral Motion

The back of an eye—horse or human—contains 55 different types of cells specialized for vision. But relax, we only need to discuss two: rods and cones. Stop reading for a minute and look at a scene. Anything: your living room, a view out the window, your hand, whatever. Every pixel of light or dark that you see in that scene is transmitted through your rods and cones. Each cell corresponds to a tiny part of the visual scene, and if that part of the scene is bright, its rod or cone sends a signal to your brain. If another minute piece of the scene is dark, the rod or cone corresponding to it stays mum. Every part of the visual scene is coded by 210 million rods and cones in the human eye, until your brain contains a neural pattern of light and dark that represents the entire view. Every time you move your eyes, your rods and cones transmit a new set of signals. Pretty cool, huh?

Rods are especially good at picking up off-center motion in poor light. They do not transmit detail. Equine eyes are loaded with rods, and rods are connected to cells that send information about motion on a fast track to the brain. This combination gives horses an extraordinary ability to notice tiny rapid movements. If we had a horse's rods, we'd shy all the time at the countless zips of motion flying through our view. Riders often complain that their horses are "shying at nothing"—in fact, they are shying at very real sights that we have too few rods to sense. What's truly remarkable is that horses don't shy more and that they allow us to modify the behavior at all.

So, rods and cones transmit a scene's pattern of light and dark to the brain. The human brain then takes half a second to process each glance at the world and determine what it has seen—shape, color, size, distance, meaning, importance, and so on. Half a second of processing is out of the question for a horse in the wild: He needs to notice the faintest wave of the grasses and step on the gas. If the movement turns out to be a bicycle instead of a lion, that's okay. Little is lost by running from a bicycle.

By nature, the horse relies on peripheral motion vision for safety. It dictates his need to startle or bolt—and otherwise "misbehave"—while ridden. Help him out by sharpening your own peripheral senses. Try to become more aware of objects behind and to the sides of your eye, putting your ears, nose, and knowledge to work. Begin to notice with your body where your horse is looking—it's an intuitive skill that develops with attention and practice. If horses are all jacked up in an area where they're normally calm, investigate. Chances are good that they notice something you do not and are trying to tell you about it.

Blind Spots

Despite its horizontal band of panoramic vision, equine eyesight includes a number of blind spots. Without changing position, the horse cannot see above his neck or back, beneath his belly or neck, or directly behind him. The sharp acuity needed to inspect or identify objects is best in a horizontal streak at the horse's eye level, due to the distribution of rods and cones in the eye. So nearby dogs or children on the ground, or balloons and birds above eye level, are hard for the horse to spot until they move.

The area to the outer sides of the horse's back legs is only barely seen. Surprised from behind, even the sweetest horse can kick in any direction, causing severe harm or death. That's why we approach a horse's hindquarters from the shoulder, moving back while speaking, standing close, and touching his side. Lesson number one to new riders is never to walk up behind a horse.

Another blind spot exists in front of the horse's face, from eye level to the ground below his nose and out to about six feet. A hand suddenly raised in this area appears to come from nowhere. Horses cannot see the grass they eat, the bit they accept, the fingers that stroke their muzzles, or the ill-supervised child who stretches up to kiss their soft noses. Instead, they use their long mouth whiskers to sense this area. A horse whose whiskers are shaved is at a sensory disadvantage.

Finally, there's a blind spot inside the equine eye that projects onto the visual scene when horses move. All those cells at the back of the eye transmit their signals along the optic nerve to the brain. To carry them, the optic nerve has to connect to each eye, and where it connects, rods and cones cannot exist. This location is called the *optic disk* (fig. 3.5). It occludes sensory receptors just like a manhole cover hides the drain below a street.

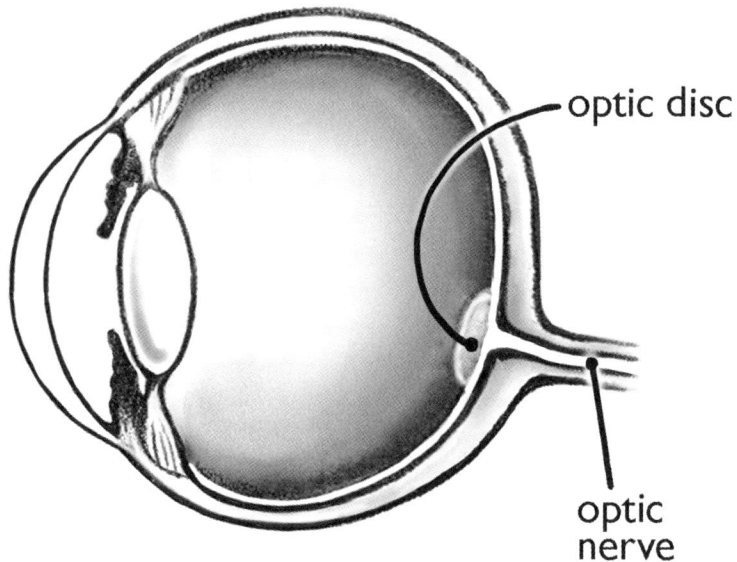

optic disc

optic nerve

3.5 The optic nerve creates an internal blind spot where it exits the human and equine eye. Cells at the optic disk cannot sense visual information from that part of a scene.

When the head and eyes remain still, the visual area of the world that corresponds to the optic disk becomes invisible. This is true for people and horses—although the equine optic disk and its corresponding blind spot are larger than ours. In daily life, we move our heads and eyes around to solve this problem. Human brains also fill in the blind spot by imagining objects that must be there even though our eyes can't see them.

If you find the blind spot in your eye, it will be easier to understand the blind spot in your horse's eye. Take a look at figure 3.6. Hold the book up so that the cross is in front of your left eye. Close your right eye and stare at the cross with your left eye. Without moving your left eye, begin to notice the outer periphery of your vision so that the black circle is visible. Now move the book in and out slowly—closer and farther from you. When the book is 4 to 12 inches from your left eye, the circle will disappear. That's *your* blind spot! When you find it, make tiny movements with the book so the circle falls into and out of the blind spot. It will vanish then reappear.

3.6 Find your blind spot. (Please see text for instructions.)

You can play games with your blind spot. Don't tell anybody, but in boring academic meetings, I used to focus my eye just to the side of where a trying colleague was seated. Then with imperceptible movements, it was possible to move the person's face into and out of my blind spot for some private entertainment. You can learn to do the same. Stand far enough back at a horse show, and you can even make a naughty pony disappear.

More importantly for our purposes, your horse has a roaming blind spot large enough that an object can disappear at the right distance. This object could be a bird, dog, or small child, for example. If we step silently out of a horse's blind spot, or even if we remain stationary but the horse moves, we might startle him. Sudden discoveries make horses nervous—no prey animal wants predators popping in and out of sight, or demanding frontal views and preventing escape, all while the brain says, "Run!"

CHAPTER FOUR

Training with Vision

W e've seen that equine acuity and focus are poor, but peripheral range and motion detection are excellent. Let's round out our understanding with a few added aspects of equine eyesight: night vision, depth perception, visual capture, and color vision.

By nature, equestrians ride on the basis of human assumptions, imagining—if we ponder it at all—that the horse visualizes depth and color the same way we do. We also assume that other equine senses are subordinate to vision, as ours are. Because of misinformation concerning night vision and our own inexperience with it, we presume that horses see details in the dark with superhero sensitivity. The reality is quite different. Doubling down on these discrepancies between human and equine sight explains many common problems within the horse-and-human team.

Night Vision

Horses can see in the dark, right? So they have no trouble jumping at dusk or loading onto the trailer before dawn? Well, not so much! Take a look at your horse's pupil sometime. See how much longer and larger it is than a human pupil? Large horizontal pupils take in more light across a wider range of visual angle. Having entered the eye, this luminosity filters toward the back of the eye, shining onto that patch of rods and cones that changes particles of light into neural impulses. Those impulses are then routed to areas of the brain that interpret their meaning.

Horses also have iridescent collagen fibers in an upper area of the eyeball called the *tapetum* ("TAP-uh-tum"). These fibers reflect light from the ground into the eyeball, allowing the horse to gather small amounts of illumination while moving in darkness. Human eyes have a similar mechanism, the choroid coat, but it is not as large or strong as the tapetum and cannot reflect light to an equivalent degree. In both species, the collagen fibers become visible when reflected in a camera flash or headlight. Ours appear to be red, but in horses, the eye-shine varies among green, yellow, or blue depending on a horse's coat color and age.

With large pupils and a reflective tapetum, horses have a reasonable degree of night vision—enough to wander from hay bin to water trough in the dark and notice movements in the shrubs. It's more acute than human night vision, which is about as effective as underwater breathing, but still not sharp enough to identify details, hop a cross-rail, or load into a trailer comfortably. The fact that a horse will try to complete these tasks in the dark is evidence of a willingness to obey, not proof of good nocturnal eyesight.

Dark Adaptation

The real rub with night vision comes when we realize that horses can make out shapes in dark conditions only after a long period of pupillary adaptation. This makes sense because equine vision developed when horses stood outside as dusk settled very slowly on the earth. But today, we expect them to enter dark barns and indoor arenas from bright sunlight.

Show riders often expect horses to move from sunlight into an indoor arena during performance. Top facilities use intense lights for illumination, but lesser locations tend to skimp. And at home, most winter riders work horses indoors, where footing is good but lighting is not. How do these changes affect equine performance?

Although all disciplines are affected, let's consider jumping because it is so dependent on acute equine eyesight. Jumping horses have to judge the height and width of fences very quickly, often scanning distances on a short approach, adjusting stride length for takeoff, carrying riders who transmit countless cues, and coordinating their bodies to clear obstacles by only an inch or two. These are meticulous feats that would cause many human athletes to stumble.

Riders all over the world warm up hunters and jumpers in bright sun prior to competition. After a typical warm up, Twinkletoes' pupils are constricted to the maximum degree to admit as little light as possible. The chemicals that transduce light into neural impulses are at their ebb. This combination of pupillary contraction and chemical paucity allows the horse to jump in bright sun without being blinded by the glare. High elevation, central latitudes, low humidity, pale arena sand, and white fences demand even greater adaptation.

Twinkletoes is jumping well in the warm-up when the gate steward calls him to the indoor show arena. His rider removes her sunglasses at the in-gate, instantly improving her indoor vision. Too bad Twink can't shove his face into some military night goggles. Through the gate they go, galloping into the murk to leap over 8 or 12, sometimes 15, jumps that the horse can barely see. And oh, by the way, like all of us, Twink's rider expects top-quality performance. But he hasn't come close to the 45 minutes he needs to accommodate to indoor lighting. Typically, he's had one minute, if that.

The scenario described here is common. We allow it because we are not aware of the visual hardship for the horse. Most of us reprove mounts who balk at the in-gate, weave between fences, skirt the flower box, or refuse to jump. We assume that if we can see the course, they can, too. But imagine moving from a sunny parking lot into a darkened movie theater, then dashing around under a heavy backpack—hurdling seats, slipping on buttered popcorn, and dodging angry patrons. The fact that horses try to perform under such circumstances is a testament to their generosity.

Time to Dark Adapt

Eyes adapt to light by *contracting* their pupils, and they adapt to darkness by *expanding* their pupils. Human eyes require about 25 minutes to adjust from bright sunlight to complete darkness. But equine eyes need 45 minutes, almost twice as long. So, upon entering a dim building from daylight, your horse will struggle with darkness long after your eyes have adapted. After adaptation, his eyes are 25,000 times more sensitive than they were at the beginning. Now he can see. Unfortunately, his 45-minute training session is about done by then.

Like humans, horses differ in individual visual abilities. One horse might require a little less than 45 minutes to adapt to dim light; another will require even more. Age plays a role, too. Older horses with healthy eyes take in less light than younger horses do. This age difference occurs in humans as well—in fact, the average person's eyes take in 66% less light at age 60 than at age 20. No wonder the world can seem a little glum as we get older.

How can we help our horse's eyes adapt before performing? No suggestion is ideal, but some will help. Allow your horse to walk in the shade before entering an indoor arena. Stand at the gate for a few minutes while the preceding team competes. When possible, schedule a jumping performance right after a flat class, giving your horse 15 minutes of adaptation time prior to starting over fences. Remember that a jumping round, no matter how easy it looks, is a complicated and unnatural coup for a horse. He can't just phone it in.

The best solution is to require show organizers and facilities managers to brighten indoor arenas with strong artificial lighting. Exhibitors, trainers, boarders, and owners have the power to make such requests as a group, especially when safety is at stake. Veterinary schools and organizations can help the cause by publicizing the need for strong indoor lighting. Professional associations like the United States Equestrian Federation (USEF) and Fédération Equestre Internationale (FEI) should revoke horse show ratings when a venue's lighting is not up to snuff.

As a show participant, suggest that officials cordon off a small strip of the indoor as a wait-and-walk area for horses about to perform. Ask that they open doors to illuminate the area inside. Be sure they have turned on all the lights—this sounds so elementary, but many show riders and trainers have experienced events at which the managers powered up only half of the indoor arena's lights. When all else fails, scratch—and tell the event organizers why. Your horse's long-term welfare and your own are more important than three minutes spent hopping around in Aladdin's cave.

Horses need to see their surroundings, whether leaping 7-foot walls or just chillin' in the barn. Those who can't see well compensate by using other senses to a greater degree. This can yield new kerfuffles, as when the horse begins to listen to a dark indoor arena so closely that he spooks at the sound of two air molecules colliding.

Depth Perception

Eyes admit physical views, but it takes a brain to compute visual distance. When staring straight ahead, humans take in two views of a given sight— one from each eye. To see this for yourself, hold your finger in front of your nose at arm's length. Close one eye and line your finger up with something vertical in the distance—a door frame or a fence post, whatever. Now open that eye and close the other. Your finger will appear to jump back and forth as you alternate eyes. Those are the two views that your right and left eyes send to your brain. The brain calculates the difference between them, and as if by magic, you become aware of depth. Using this automatic computation, you can look at a field of horses and note that the cute roan is farther from you than the pretty paint.

Human depth perception is extremely precise because our eyes are so close together. They are also yoked, moving in concert with each other for precise tracking. With this design, the average person can distinguish ⅛ of an inch in depth from a distance of 16½ feet. In other words, if you were standing one long stride away from the takeoff to a double-rail vertical, your brain could tell you whether one of the rails was set ⅛-inch behind the other one. That's depth perception on steroids!

By contrast, the smallest amount of depth a horse can detect when standing the same distance away from something is 9 inches. Human stereoacuity is 72 times sharper than that (fig. 4.1).

Horses' ability to see depth is limited because their eyes are set so far apart. From most angles, horses cannot get a left-eye and right-eye view of the same object in one glance. We hominids can see an outstretched finger with both eyes simultaneously. But even in a rearing position, Twinkle-toes would have to be a contortionist to get his hoof in front of both eyes at the same time. As prey animals, horses are built for peripheral motion detection at the expense of depth perception. As predators, we're built in reverse.

4.1 With two eyes from a stride away, the equine brain can sense a minimum of only 9 inches in depth from front to back. In contrast, the human brain can sense 1/8 inch in depth from front to back. We perceive differences in depth that the horse cannot see.

For horses in disciplines like dressage, reining, or pleasure, depth perception is not so critical. But consider cutting, barrel racing, or jumping. A horse needs to know how far away relevant objects are and how fast those distances are changing as he moves. A horse can improve depth perception by raising his head, dropping his withers, or lifting his nose, but this often complicates his task. In cutting, for instance, horses need to keep their eyes down on the cow and their heads low to make quick turns. In jumping, they need impulsion from their hindquarters to power off the ground and abdominal tuck to lift their legs. The physics of such movements require horses to maintain a round back for core strength, which often precludes the position of a high head.

The distinction between hunters and jumpers is also important here. Top jumpers are judged by the clearance and speed of their rounds over high, wide fences—fences that are often approached off sharp turns from short distances. Such horses are often selected as jumpers because their necks are set high on the withers, with head position proportionately higher. Those without that conformation are encouraged to approach jumps with their heads raised. If you watch a jumper approaching a fence, you'll see his head lift in the last stride or two. This natural form provides both eyes with a brief view of the jump, so that the equine brain can determine its height and width. But the view is indeed brief—fractions of a second—and it's late.

Occasionally, we hear that jumpers are aided in depth perception by wagging their heads back and forth on approach, to allow each eye a view of the jump. This suggestion does not hold up in terms of brain science. To compute distance, the brain requires a *simultaneous* view of the object with both eyes. Wiggling the head back and forth only interferes with centering the horse. It probably also prevents him from concentrating on other cues from the rider that are much more important.

Depth perception is easier for hunters. These horses are judged on the quiet beauty of their jumping form and are taught to maintain a long frame with hindquarters engaged, necks arched long, heads low, and faces nearer the vertical to form a strong topline. This position can be preserved over fences because hunters are given a long approach with which to see relatively low jumps without raising their heads. Good hunter riders encourage horses to look at a fence while rounding a distant corner. This supplies the horse with a better side view, a longer front view, and more time for the two eyes to send images of the jump to the brain. It's still a good idea, of course, to allow any jumping horse some freedom in moving his head to improve his view.

In terms of width, only about half the area visible to two human eyes at the same time is visible to a horse's two eyes at the same time (fig. 4.2). Stand

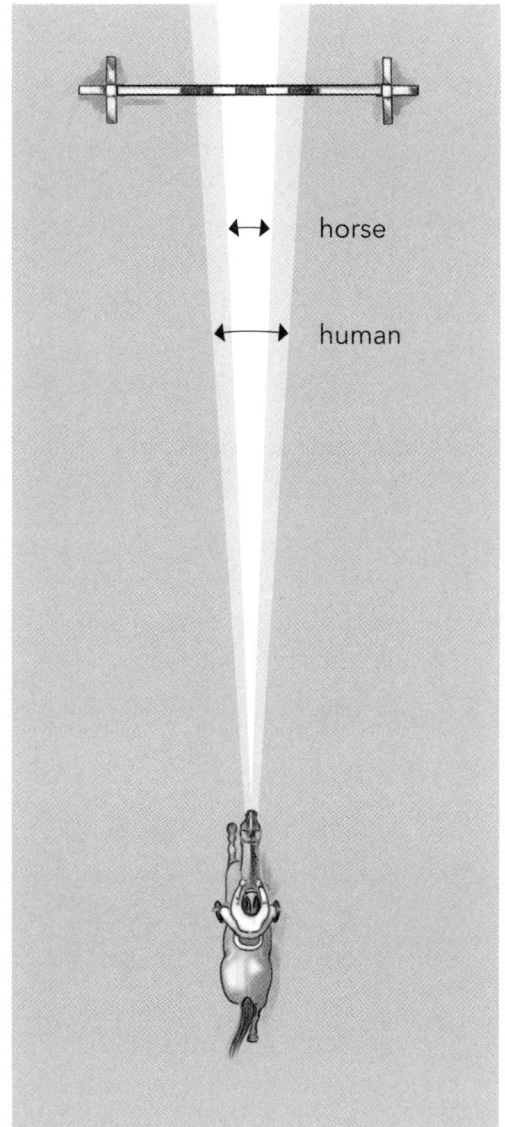

4.2 With two eyes focused straight ahead, the horse sees only half the width of the human view.

about 30 feet back from an arena fence. Roughly 5 feet of that fence is clear and sharp to both of your eyes as you hold them still. From the same position, only half of that—about 2½ feet—is clear to both the horse's eyes. And it is only that small portion visible to both eyes for which a brain can calculate depth by stereoacuity.

When you're aiming a horse toward a fence, center him on the narrow middle portion that *he* can see with both eyes. Many early jumping errors occur when a rider does not steer the horse to the center of a jump. These problems are frequently blamed on the horse—he ran out, he refused, he chipped, he jumped in bad form. Well, that's not because he's a bad horse; it's because the rider didn't let him see the fence!

Visual Capture

Vision is our strongest human sense—it hogs more neural real estate than any other sensory system, filling almost one-third of the human brain. With such clout, it can override other senses, a neural ability known as *visual capture*.

Visual capture is responsible for the fact that ventriloquists can fool us. We believe that speech is emanating from a dummy's mouth, even when the human speaker is standing right there. The visual movement of the fake mouth captures our attention and links it to the spoken words. Magicians use visual capture to hide actions of their hands in plain sight. Moviegoers gesture toward an actor's mouth on the screen when asked where the sound is coming from—even when theater speakers are placed at the back or sides of the house.

Because we rely so heavily on sight, we suppose our horses do, too. Yet we've seen that many aspects of equine vision are worse than ours. The horse compensates for his visual weaknesses with good hearing and a fantastic sense of smell. We help him by encouraging reliance on these stronger senses. The next time your horse skitters away from a safe spot, think about what he might hear or smell that is imperceptible to you. In his world, it's not all about vision.

Color Vision

Harley was a six-year-old red dun Quarter Horse who knew how to be led and longed. Nothing else. An adult horse who knows so little is not the safest animal. (Let me make a plea to backyard horse owners everywhere: Hire a trainer when the horse is young and small!) I was holding this over-grown baby in an indoor arena one day when snow slid off the roof. Many horses shy from this, but most don't try to jump in my lap. Harley jumped a foot high and a couple feet forward off all four hooves and landed on the arch of my left foot.

The ensuing injury interfered with my ability to use a stirrup, so a friend suggested mountain bike shoes with rigid soles that would support my foot. Off I hobbled to the cycling store, where the only inexpensive pair pulsed on the shelf in blazing yellow with a chartreuse afterglow. To accommodate the padding around my wrapped foot, they were also two sizes too big. They were probably visible from the surface of the moon. But riding is more important to me than style—a good thing, because I looked absurd wearing these shoes coupled with some old sunburned half-chaps.

On Day One of the new fashion, every horse at the ranch stared in surprise at my feet. They knew me well; some I'd ridden daily for years. They'd seen me wear a variety of neon shirts in an effort to liven up the atmosphere. But this was clearly a strong visual sight for them. All day, as soon as I mounted, every horse turned to my stirrups and sniffed each shoe carefully. We joked that the horses were embarrassed, but in reality we had proven a feature of equine color vision.

What colors do horses see best? Yep, you guessed it: bright yellow with a chartreuse tint, just like my shoes! Horses also pick up bright turquoise and teal hues well. Hang a few jackets on your arena fence someday. Notice how the horses are much more aware of the bright yellow rain jacket than they are of the equally flappable bright purple or flame red versions. A horse who needs to pick up his feet over fences can be reminded to do so with the simple use of some bright yellow or turquoise rails. A young horse who is just learning to negotiate ground poles will excel with other colors—he needs to see the poles without feeling provoked by them.

Remember the eye's rod and cone cells from chapter 3 (p. 42)? Where rods sense movement in dim light, cones pick up detail and color. Horses have many rods and few cones; humans have the opposite. So, all colors visible to horses—even the bright yellows—are faded in comparison to human perception of color. Most critically, horses do not have any cones that pick up red and green. Because of this a horse (like a dog, squirrel, or pig) cannot distinguish between red and green—as journalist Wendy Williams has noted, a horse looking across a green pasture cannot see a stationary person dressed in bright red. Both pasture and person appear to be grey.

Saving Lives with Color

In 2018, British researchers demonstrated horses' inability to see the bright red-orange poles used to mark the base of steeplechase jumps that they sail over at high speed. Against green grass, white poles were much more visible to the horses. Jockeys could see both colors equally well, so the choice didn't matter to them. The British Racing Association now plans to change the color of steeplechase poles throughout the United Kingdom, increasing safety for thousands of animals and their riders. That's brain science saving lives: in 2018 alone, 201 horses died on British steeplechase racecourses. Invisible ground lines likely played a role in some of those deaths.

Next time you need to mark off an area to keep horses from entering a reseeded portion of their pasture or a weekend construction job, throw away the fuschia survey tape. It's salient to you, but invisible to your horse. Tie bright yellow tape around your temporary fence instead.

Seeing Equine Vision for Yourself

By exploring just a few important features of the brain, we can already see that equine vision differs dramatically from our own. An excellent 2016 video clip pulls a few of these differences together. (It's online—see the Source Notes on p. 270 for the link.) In the video, a horse-and-human team is simply walking through a grassy meadow and forest to a barn. The view seen by each species is shown simultaneously at the top and bottom of the screen, so they're easy to compare. In two minutes, you'll get an idea of the vast changes caused by differences in range of vision, acuity, dark and light adaptation, and color vision.

All of us who work with horses need to think about the senseless difficulties we impose on our horses by assuming they see like we do. Let's try seeing through their eyes for a change.

CHAPTER FIVE
"Did You Hear That?"

Reno, a blood bay off-the-track Thoroughbred, stood in the cross-ties one afternoon while his owner's toddler went inside for a nap. A nursery monitor in the barn allowed the mother to hear the two-year-old in his crib while she worked. The horse was accustomed to baby and monitor, so he paid no attention to the noises of adult speech and the movement of blankets and pillows as the baby was put to bed. But a few minutes later, when the baby began babbling, Reno came to military attention. He lifted his head and peered around the corner, ears nailed to the monitor.

"Ba-ba-ba-ba-ba, na-na-na-na, muh-muh-muh-muh," the baby repeated one syllable after another. Reno pushed his nose forward and jiggled the cross-ties; he seemed to bob his head in time with the repetition. Out of curiosity, I led him to the baby monitor to see what he would do. He approached eagerly, showing no fear, and sniffed every corner of it. He cocked his head from one side to another, listening. He did not want to turn away, even though the baby's babbling continued for perhaps 15 minutes. Reno was spellbound.

Loudness

To explain equine hearing, it helps to distinguish between loudness, pitch, and localization. The easiest to describe is loudness. The volume of a sound is measured in decibels (dB). By convention, 0 dB represents the softest sound that human ears are capable of sensing. It's the tiniest tick in a soundproof room of dead silence—a tick that can be detected only by that rare 18-year-old who's never gone to a rock concert or cranked up her earbuds. Even the most sensitive horse will not hear that sound.

According to the best available data, the softest sound an average horse can hear occurs at 7 dB. That's the volume of a person breathing quietly. In general, then, the same noise seems a little quieter to a horse than to a person. Horses hear us speak to them but at slightly lower volumes than we believe we have used. On one hand, we might be surprised that horses do not perceive hushed noises as well as humans do…after all, spooky horses certainly seem to have bionic hearing out on the trail! On the other hand, we have to give them credit for hearing something as quiet as an easy breath.

Pitch

Within the volumes that people and horses can detect, a second aspect of sound is pitch. Pitch refers to the range of low to high frequencies that corresponds to musical notes from low bass to high soprano. Horses can hear pitches from about 55 to 33,500 Hertz (Hz). That's similar to the 10-octave range (20 to 20,000 Hz) humans can sense. By comparison, Indian elephants hear lower pitches, and wild mice sense tones up in super-squeak territory (fig. 5.1).

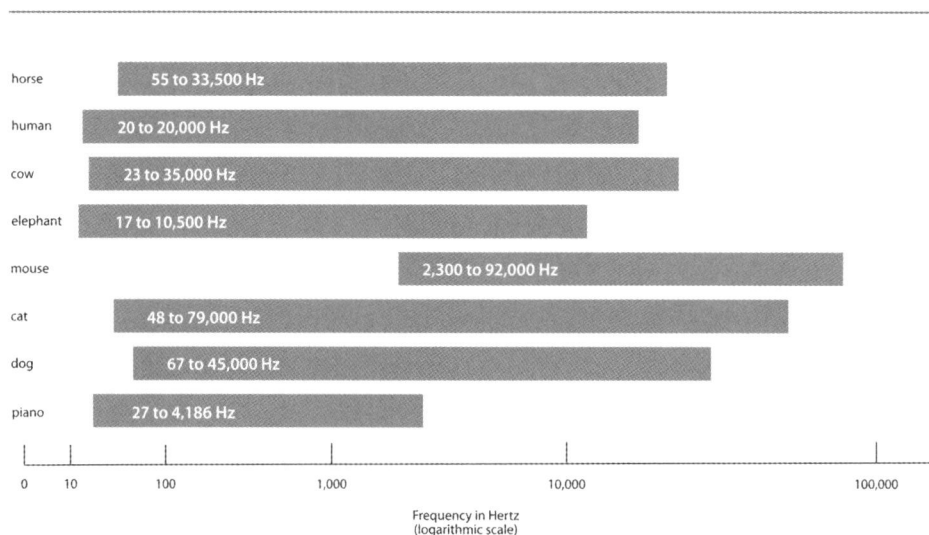

horse	55 to 33,500 Hz
human	20 to 20,000 Hz
cow	23 to 35,000 Hz
elephant	17 to 10,500 Hz
mouse	2,300 to 92,000 Hz
cat	48 to 79,000 Hz
dog	67 to 45,000 Hz
piano	27 to 4,186 Hz

0   10   100   1,000   10,000   100,000

Frequency in Hertz
(logarithmic scale)

5.1 Pitch ranges of various animals in young adulthood, with a piano range included for comparison. Horses hear pitches slightly higher than human range, but fail to notice pitches that we experience as very low.

Equine ears miss about an octave and a half of the lowest bass notes we can hear, those between 20 and 55 Hz. However, horses can pick up many of these low frequency sounds through vibrations in their teeth and jawbones while grazing. Their hooves also transmit low vibrations. Ears aren't everything!

At the high end of the sound spectrum, equine ears surpass ours by half an octave (from 20,000 to 33,500 Hz). Horses can hear the ultrasonic squeal of a bat or dolphin, the silent dog whistle, and the noise that insect and rodent repelling machines produce—all inaudible to humans. Although researchers have found no difference in hearing sensitivity between male and female horses, males do pay more attention to sound. This heightened reaction probably occurs because it is the male horse's job to warn mares and youngsters of danger.

Hearing Over Time

Equine hearing declines with age just as human hearing does. By the time a horse is 20 years old, he's usually experiencing mild to moderate hearing loss. Humans decline much faster in proportion to our life span, with higher frequencies generally inaudible by age 30. A controversial anti-loitering system called the "Mosquito" is used in many countries to disperse young people from public areas that are prone to vandalism. The frequency of the noise it makes (17,400 Hz) is too high for older adults to perceive, but young people won't hang around in such an annoying environment. Nor will horses!

You know how your mount sometimes stops dead and goes taut to listen to something that you keep telling him "isn't there?" I'm only the messenger, but uh…if it's high frequency, it probably *is* there. Our ears just can't hear it. An older rider on a younger horse is at a particular disadvantage in terms of being unable to hear high frequencies as well as the horse does. Often the horse freezes in place to reduce ambient noise—a squeaking saddle, hooves striking the ground, the soft jangle of a bit. Grazing horses stop chewing when they hear a quiet noise—that's because the grinding of their jaws interferes with their ears' ability to transmit sound signals to the brain.

Aside from their physical range of hearing, horses have evolved to pay much greater attention to small noises than humans do. Although the two of you are often capable of hearing the same sounds, you might heed the voice inside your head—your plans and thoughts and worries—more than the crackling of a dry twig.

Interpreting Sounds

All sensory organs—eyes, ears, noses, tongues, skin—pick up patterns in the external world, transform them into neural impulses, and send them to the brain for interpretation. Tiny differences in loudness and pitch are critical to comprehending human speech, tonal emotion, music, environmental noises, and animal vocalizations. A horse or human who can't discriminate sounds well is going to have some trouble communicating.

So, once a horse's ears pick up a sound wave and send it to that squashed grapefruit called his brain, what happens there? All sorts of things. We often study those processes by considering what happens when the brain isn't doing its job. Humans with good ears but damage to the auditory cortex often experience auditory *agnosia* ("ag-NO-zhuh"). The sounds come in, but they don't make sense. Patients report that sounds—often voices—are too loud, unpleasant, blurred, crackling, echoing, sometimes painful. They're not sure whether a sound is real, but they usually don't realize that anything is wrong with their brains. Instead, these patients complain that the noises themselves are to blame for the misperception.

Intact human and equine brains order sounds, allowing some tones to fade into the background and others to come forward. They become accustomed to typical sounds and use atypical ones as warning signals. They associate learned sounds with sights, smells, touches, knowledge, or experiences. What horse, for example, does not link the sound of the feed truck or bucket with the time of day?

Thanks to their brains, horses are whiz kids at interpreting the whinnies, nickers, snorts, blows, groans, snores, and squeals of daily equine life. A horse can hear one whinny and know who's calling, what mood he's in, and what he wants. Horses whose owners arrive by car to feed them will nicker a greeting when that car arrives, yet ignore other cars. They know who's who. Some ignore all transport rigs except their own, heading to the farthest corner of a pasture when the trailer arrives, as if to say, "No, thanks, I'd rather stay home."

Stories abound: Have you heard about the retired circus horse who knew the command "high" as an instruction to rear? It worked all too well around his retirement barn when folks said, "Hi," to each other. How about the American import who refused to canter on a longe until the English handler faked a strong American accent to pronounce the command, "Canter?" Once the horse understood the word, he picked up the gait.

Horses scope out a wide range of human emotion from tone of voice, and they respond to it well. A horse who knows to hold still while being tacked up, for example, might wiggle while the handler murmurs, "Oh, stop that," or even voices a known command like, "Stand." But the minute a respected handler says the same words in a sharp sudden tone, the horse reverts to good manners. Of course, he has learned the desired behavior in advance—unfortunately, we can't just train a horse from scratch by speaking louder. If only!

Music

Normal human brains interpret certain pitch patterns as music. We take this ability for granted because it feels completely effortless and is common among almost all people. To comprehend music, though, our brains are working up a sweat. They have to analyze:

- Relationships between pitch, time, and volume
- Variations and consistencies in grouping and phrasing

- Patterns of rhythm and tempo
- Expectations based on memory
- Sensory illusions designed by the composer
- Emotion

This is complicated stuff.

I am often reminded of musical rhythm while riding—a horse who's "behind the leg" is much like a singer behind the beat. And like music, the location of the rhythmic pocket changes with riding discipline: We teach Western Pleasure horses to work behind the leg, jumpers to work in front of it, and trail horses to stay on it.

Rarely, specific damage to the brain interferes with music perception. When listening to a song, people with *amusia* ("uh-MYOO-zhuh") hear random disconnected tones. One patient, formerly a music composer and performer, described her post-injury perception as a collection of equal notes in which no one instrument or tone emerges as superior to the rest: "When I listen to an orchestra I hear 20 intense laser voices [each belonging to a separate instrument]. It is extremely difficult to integrate all these different voices into some entity that makes sense."

An even tinier handful of people have congenital amusia, a lifelong disability in which their hearing is fine and their brains are normal in every other way. One described listening to a lilting lullaby like this: "If you were in my kitchen and threw all the pots and pans on the floor, that's what I hear!"

We can infer that horses perceive music. It certainly has an effect on them that is different from the sound of kitchen pans landing on a floor. The equine brain is calmed by lyrical tunes without sudden changes in volume. Horses prefer Mozart to Beethoven, soft rock over techno, and country or folk more than heavy metal. Dissonant music agitates them, so it's best to leave Stravinsky at home. Human brainwaves synchronize when a group of people listen to music together. Chances are that the same synchrony occurs among horses.

Despite the complexity of music perception, the horse's brain makes sense of tonal patterns. How do we know this? Because his emotions change when listening to varied types of music. Even more intriguing, the same correspondences between music and emotion occur in a human as in a horse. A song that relaxes, invigorates, or annoys us is likely to have the same effect on our animals.

Winning with Music

A recent study explored the effects of music on Arabian racehorses. Thirty of them were housed in a barn where harmonious background music was played for five hours every afternoon. Forty of their peers were in a different barn at the same facility where there was no music. Conditions like feed, exercise, companionship, cleanliness, and handling were held constant. Within a month, the Arabians exposed to daily music developed significantly lower heart rates and won their races more often.

The positive effect lasted for three months. After that, the horses became accustomed to the music and its effect waned. But three months is long enough for a good trainer to change a smart aleck who becomes relaxed enough to learn. Once that foundation is set, the horse will remain trainable for the long term.

Where's That Sound?

A third aspect of hearing is sound localization. Close your eyes and listen for a noise. (Have a friend hide a timer and set it to ring quietly in a few minutes, if necessary.) When you hear the noise, you know where it's coming from— behind you, from one side or another, above, below, or from some angle in front of you. Horses seem to be likely candidates for localization genius: They have large cupped ears with a turning radius of 180 degrees front to back and about 90 degrees top to side. Sixteen muscles per ear are devoted to flicking all that cartilage around quickly and accurately. These movements operate independently, so one ear can be pointed toward the front, for example, and the other toward the back. Fur protects equine ears from insect bites, cold, foreign objects, dirt, and rain, so they can function well.

In addition, equine ears are set far apart, which increases the time difference in the arrival of a sound as it approaches the horse's head. This is a key feature for good localization. Physically, a sound is a wave of air molecules that strikes the eardrum. Suppose the wave is coming toward the left side of the head. This sound will arrive in the left ear before it arrives in the right. The greater the distance between ears, the greater the difference in arrival time. This tiny interval tells the brain that the sound is coming from the left. The horse—or human—then knows to turn to the left and look for more information or run toward the right to escape potential harm.

All these advantages should produce excellent sound localization in the horse. Humans, after all, have meager little ears set close to the head. We have three weakling vestigial muscles connected to our ears that are only good for party tricks in those rare funsters who can wiggle their ears. A human's head is narrower than most horses', though the placement of our ears down the sides of the head increases the time difference of sound arrival to the two ears. Still, with all the advantages a horse has, plus the evolutionary pressure to survive by sound localization, we would expect horses to excel.

Yet, research does not bear out this suspicion. Humans can locate the origin of a sound within less than 1 degree of precision; elephants 1 to 2 degrees; cats 5 degrees. Horses? Their precision ranges from 22 to 30 degrees, depending on the type of noise that is studied (figs. 5.2 A & B). That's like a D minus! If a lion is sneaking through the meadow, a horse needs to identify the lion's location with greater precision than a 30-degree angle of "maybes."

Why would horses have such weak ability to hear the origin of a sound? I'll speculate with two guesses. First, when this kind of anomaly occurs in science, we check the research methods. Sometimes the sample sizes are too small—we can't generalize across 60 million horses worldwide on the basis of one or two individuals. Often the method of gathering data is weak or confounded by other variables. Subjects, especially horses, don't always cooperate with the process. Research flaws are part of science—with something

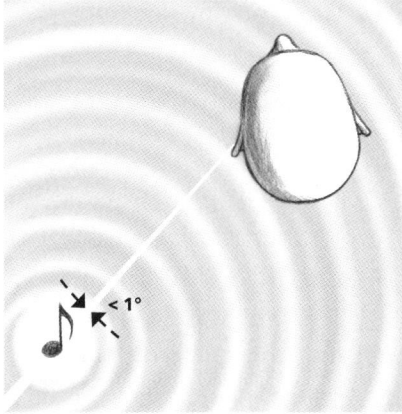

5.2 A The human brain identifies a sound's location with less than one degree of error.

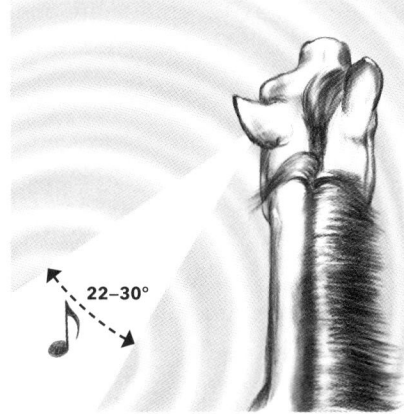

5.2 B The equine brain identifies a sound's location with 22 to 30 degrees of error.

as complicated as a brain, nobody fashions the perfect experimental design every time. We replicate and revise studies to overcome such problems.

But the second guess is this: maybe horses don't need excellent sound localization because they have other ways of protecting themselves. The horse's excellent peripheral vision for along the horizon might render sound localization moot. His outstanding sense of smell is also working to locate a threat. Remember Aspen the Bear Hunter? She didn't need to hear the location of the bear in the bushes—she could smell him from much farther away (see p. 23).

Noise

People design equestrian facilities in all sorts of interesting ways. Which way should the wash racks face? Where should the grooming areas be? How much of the world should horses see from their stalls? Should the barn be tightly closed for warmth or wide open for air? And so on, ad nauseam. Many choices depend on our assumptions about how horses experience the human world.

For several years, I trained at a barn where the owners believed random noises were an aid to schooling. Located next to their indoor arena was the shop where paint sprayers were blown out with high pressure air hoses, snow plows were sledge-hammered, and power saws were blasted through plastic fence posts at unexpected moments. Horses and riders working in the indoor could not see out, so we had no visual warning of these impending explosions. At times it was dangerous, especially for beginning riders with insecure seats or horses who were green or anxious. The layout was "grumpifying," to say the least.

One would imagine that the shop had been located near the indoor by accident. But no. It was a conscious decision, intended to help the horses "get used to unexpected noises." This way, the rationale went, they would be calmer at horse shows. Hmmm. The equine brain doesn't work like that. Although some level of desensitization is necessary with young horses, plunking a tender filly into a flaming bowl of frightening distractions is not the way to go about it.

Environments marked by loud, unexpected, and unfamiliar noises cause horses much distress. Even consistent unpleasant noises bother horses, like wind or idling diesel engines. Wind makes things flap around, and engines mask sounds that might be important to a prey animal. Decades of research prove that constant noise is not good for human ears, minds, or emotions, either. Animals—and humans—cannot relax in such settings, and without the security of relaxation, true learning is impaired. Within days of moving to a quieter barn, my training horses were much easier to handle at home and at shows.

"Say What?"

Horses have powerful pitch perception, but why? Why does a horse need to analyze sound frequencies across a 10-octave range? The rustling grasses of a predator's approach don't vary by that much. The answer lies in the horse's position as a social animal. To survive, he must be able to hear and interpret the vocalizations of herd mates.

Horses communicate with each other all the time. Much of this communication is hidden from humans—not because our four-legged friends are keeping secrets, but because most of us don't notice the subtle ways that animals reach out to each other. And when we do notice a movement or vocalization, we often fail to understand what it means.

Let's reflect on a simple whinny. It averages 1.5 seconds in length and can be heard half a mile away. It's produced in three phases—a high-frequency introduction, a rhythmic collection of medium frequencies in the middle, and a lower-frequency waffle near the end. Many of these frequencies sound simultaneously, like a musical chord, but some waver in and out. Minute variations in these parameters convey meaning to the equine brain.

Compared to neutral, a fearful whinny is higher in fundamental pitch, and the highest frequencies within it are produced at stronger intensities. A greeting whinny is much lower in pitch, and there is greater range and more time in the wavering or vibrato between tones. A separation whinny cuts off early in the ending phase. And so on, through the whinnies that mean, "Good to see you," "Why won't that mare come over here?" "Feed me now," or "Help, the barn's on fire!" Horses might produce 10 million variations of whinny, and each variation will have different physical characteristics from the next.

The brain of a listening horse analyzes all these components instantly and automatically. Cells in the horse's inner ear encode the varied frequencies within each whinny; cells in the auditory cortex calculate the differences and mark the timing. The brain's association areas apply meaning: "Oh, that's Mirror. She's worried about something." We hear the whinny and, if we are observant, we notice the response. But all of the complicated neural work is hidden, so we assume the analysis is easy. Or magical. It's not. There's a lot going on inside your horse's forehead.

In addition to gradations of emotion and meaning, each horse's whinny is also unique—it's a signature. Reno's fearful whinny, for example, differs in its physical composition from Dee Sea's fearful whinny. So, in addition to decoding what a whinny means, a listening horse also knows without sight who produced it. Knowing who's sounding off provides even more information, because horses differ in their sensitivity just like humans do. The fearful whinny of a horse who's generally laid back is a stronger warning than the fearful whinny of a horse who's got the willies most of the time.

Horses also cull information from a whinny even when they do not know the horse who produced it. From sound alone, they can identify an unfamiliar animal's size, sex, and rank in the equine hierarchy. By contrast, humans can usually determine sex from the sound of a voice, but size is harder, and rank is not something we hear. After all, rank is less important to human survival than to equine survival.

Identifying Human Voices

Do horses identify a familiar human by her voice? Absolutely. Imagine two human friends whom your horse knows. Record their voices saying the same words. Now play the recordings while these two silent friends stand within the horse's view. He will match the recorded voice to the person who owns it—looking immediately and for a longer period of time at the one whose recorded voice is played on a speaker. Incidentally, this type of *cross-modal perception*, in which vision and hearing are used in tandem, was once thought to be unique to humans. We now know that dogs and horses use it, too. Chances are that many species tap cross-modal perception. What's remarkable is that we assumed they couldn't.

For the full effect of the equine brain's ability to decode what it hears, remember that we have considered only the whinny. Horses must also take into account the meanings of their neighbors' nickers, squeals, groans, blows, and snorts. Their brains must analyze all the acoustic variations within those vocalizations, sort out which sound belongs to which horse, and figure out what it means in the context of the particular horse who produced it. Throw horses in a new setting where they don't know anybody, and all this becomes a cacophony of confusing noise. And we wonder why they're upset by change!

CHAPTER SIX
Powers of Smell and Taste

A few months into his early training over fences, Shimmer was trotting tiny verticals with assorted flower boxes and varied poles. Many budding hunters are intimidated by fences they can't see through, so it was time to begin working on jumps that were solid but easy. A small brick wall was selected.

Now, for those of you who don't jump, don't worry: A solid brick wall in a hunter arena is not solid and it's not made of brick. It's a standing rectangle with narrow wood supports covered in lightweight plastic that's colored like brick. It falls over easily if anything goes wrong. The wall that this four-year-old powerhouse was jumping was only 2 feet high and 8 inches wide, no larger than his usual fare.

Shimmer trotted toward the little wall, sailed over it, and cantered out, seeming quite pleased with himself. Everyone smiled—he was a fancy Warmblood from Amsterdam, the color of a new penny with the friendly personality of a cruise director, so we all liked to watch him learn. He repeated his new accomplishment several times.

But when trotting the same wall from the opposite direction, Shim stopped. First time ever! Now, unless you like becoming a human catapult, you don't let a green horse get the idea that stopping is an option. Shim's trainer and rider overcame the problem fairly quickly, but it was the topic of the barn aisle after the ride. Why would he stop when approaching from one direction but jump so willingly from the opposite direction?

The process of asking why a horse behaves in a certain way is critical to good training. In refusing the wall, Shim was headed away from the arena gate. Was he gate-bound? No, he worked past the gate all the time without hesitation. Was he tired? No, the stops occurred only 20 minutes into his daily one-hour ride, and he showed no fatigue over other obstacles. Was the wall too big? No, Shim routinely jumped fences the same size, and he showed no hesitation from the opposite side of the same wall. The jump looked identical on both sides. The two approaches to it were similar in length. What else could it be?

Naturally, the answer didn't come to me until after the conversation ended. Shimmer had been jumping around noon, when there was no shade in the arena. But at other times of day, the side of the wall he disliked cast a deep shadow. Four big coonhounds slept in that shade daily, flopped out with their backs against the cool fake brick. Their scent would have been especially strong on that side of the jump. Also, when snoozing there, the black dogs were hidden in dark shade, easy for a horse to miss visually. Shim knew this from his usual morning workouts, when the dogs' side of the wall was shaded.

So, back to the noontime jumping: Neither side of the wall was shaded on the day Shim stopped, and the hounds were nowhere near it. But their scent sure was! In addition, the horse knew the dogs' usual location in the shade and knew that they were often hard to see. If my theory is correct, the dogs' scent would have been most condensed just as Shim's eyes entered the blind spot below and in front of his nose. And that's just how his behavior appeared—he approached at a fluid forward pace with his ears up, then stopped at the last minute—not a dirty stop, but short, sudden, as if surprised.

Could he also have smelled the dogs' residual scent from the "good" side of the wall? Maybe, but that side was upwind of their typical spot. The odor would have been much weaker on the side the dogs avoided and the wall was never shaded on that side, so the horse had no memory of them being there.

The Stepchildren of Perception

Equine smell and taste get little attention from scientists despite the fact that the horse's sense of smell is probably his strongest source of perception. Observation and brain anatomy suggest that it puts equine vision and hearing to shame. But our human brains are biased so strongly toward vision that we have studied it to the exclusion of other senses. And science is complicated enough that we usually develop research designs fully in one area (like vision) and for one species (like humans) before applying them to others.

Another issue that limits progress in studies of smell and taste is that the stimulation is chemical. Vision and hearing are based on mechanical stimuli—particles of light or waves of sound striking the eyes and ears. Scientists have become familiar with these forms of stimulation over three and a half centuries of intense study, ever since Isaac Newton picked up a prism in 1666 and demonstrated that white light contains all colors. But chemical molecules present many mysteries to this day. Not until 2017 were we even able to predict the scent of an odor from its molecular structure.

So, calling all equine scientists: We need the scoop on equine olfaction! It's deeply underestimated and largely ignored. What we know about it so far suggests that the horse noggin analyzes and interprets complex smells all the time, much like the human brain deciphers sights whenever our eyes are open.

Do Horses Rely on Smell?

They sure do. Horses are fascinated by scents. Often we are not aware of this because we hold our horses back from sniffing or teach them that it is unacceptable. Not to mention the fact that we don't even know the scents are there. But halter your horse up someday and give him his head away from the distractions of grass. Conjure up your best Type B personality—saunter slowly, stand around as if you have nothing to do, and mosey past various objects. Once your giant hound dog realizes it's okay to use his nose, he'll sniff himself silly.

Suppose your horse is alone in a field. He sniffs some manure left by another horse he's never met. From that one inhalation, your horse can determine the sex, state of health, and social rank of the mystery horse. He will know how long ago it left the area, and if necessary can drop his nose to the ground, cast for a lost scent, and follow a scent trail for a long distance. If the deposit was left by a mare, your horse will know whether she is in season. All this from a few road apples slouched in the dirt!

Now, imagine your horse is familiar with the mystery animal. In this case, equine research tells us that a sniff of manure provides all of the above information and more. Your horse will know which equine buddy it belongs to, the buddy's state of aggression toward your horse (regardless of social rank), and whether the buddy was nervous, frightened, or calm at the time he left his calling card.

In addition to the knowledge that comes to a horse by sniffing manure or urine, much can be determined just by sniffing the air. From a few inhalations on a day without wind, typical horses can:

- Locate water
- Avoid predators
- Determine how long ago other horses left the area
- Know whether those horses are familiar or unfamiliar
- Identify each familiar horse specifically
- Suss out the emotions of their herd mates
- Recognize a familiar horse or human from long ago
- Distinguish between familiar humans and strangers
- Notice new scents on clothing, blankets, or tack
- Follow scent trails
- Find the way home by smelling the barn or the body odors left on trail

Instead of shaking hands like we do, horses use their noses for social introductions—an important part of joining a new herd. They approach each other's noses and exchange air through their nostrils. If that goes well, they sniff each other's flanks and tails. We can aid this process by allowing potential herd mates to sniff from either side of an open fence at first. Leave the halters off and get out of the way, because "help" from humans often creates trouble. Once two horses have become friendly through a fence, it's much safer to turn them out together.

Using their noses and long muzzle whiskers, horses are experts at sorting various grasses. Some even sort their grain. This is easiest to observe when the horse is not particularly hungry. If you own Warmbloods, that might sound impossible, but many breeds are not bound so tightly to their food. The typical Thoroughbred, for example, is sometimes captivated by other activities: Like running. Or shying. Playing, bucking, testing—did I mention running? Using smell, they'll sort the alfalfa pellets from the Equine Senior®, the Strategy® from the beet pulp, like children who want each type of food separated on the plate. Many horses push tiny capsules of medicine off to the side while eating a bucket of processed feed. Their noses and whiskers help to discern which pellet is grain and which one is medication.

Working that Nose

Can horses smell fear in humans? I won't dispute the possibility, though it would be nice to see some solid empirical evidence. We do know they can smell the stress hormones cortisol and adrenaline, which signal fear.

Stallions can locate a mare in season up to a mile away and will break or jump fences to get to her. Mares and foals recognize each other from smell, so that a nursing mare can reject another mare's foal to reserve milk for her own. Pungent ointments like Vicks® VapoRub™ are sometimes smeared on a mare's nostrils to prevent her from rejecting an orphan foal who needs to nurse. The same technique helps transport companies reduce equine spats that are caused by close quarters during shipping.

Because we humans have such frail powers of smell, we often forget to safeguard our horses by locking feed rooms. Horses can smell grain from a long distance even when it's behind a closed door, the way we smell steaks sizzling on the grill. There is no horse who can't break through a standard door to seize such mouth-watering goodies. For those of you who are new to horses, the feed room door should be barred at all times to prevent horses from eating their way to founder or colic—either of which can be fatal.

A Noseful of Confidence

Horses also use their noses to build confidence. This activity is especially strong in foals, who should be encouraged to sniff everything. But even adult horses feel more secure when their vision and hearing are confirmed by their sense of smell. Knowing that equine vision is poor up close, I routinely hold new items near a horse's nose before using them. It takes two seconds. The horses angle slightly, sniff then turn back to center much more relaxed.

Many horses derive confidence from sniffing their handlers. A horse knows when you last washed your barn coat (ugh, not since last winter?), whether you lent your hat to a friend yesterday or allowed another horse to nuzzle it, when you cleaned your bridle or ate a meal. He'll smell your new toothpaste or deodorant and knows whether you just shook hands with someone new or stroked a dog or cat. Varied fabrics carry different odors (who knew?), so your horse will even notice unusual clothing. My horses' veterinarian once arrived at the barn after showering twice to remove the odor of a fetal calf that had died prior to birth. I couldn't smell a thing, but the equids curled their lips back, licked their muzzles, flapped their tongues, and shook their heads at the scent.

As If One's Not Enough…

Normal horses have an excellent nose for odors and scents. But even more impressive? They have two! In addition to the receptors that pick up odor molecules at the top of the nasal passages and send impulses about them to olfactory bulbs in the brain, horses have a separate system called the *vomeronasal organ*. It's a pair of long tubes that extend 5 to 6 inches vertically inside the nasal cavities.

Let Them Sniff

Why is it helpful to let a horse sniff your body and clothes? So he can verify that you will not cause harm. Remember, horses are prey animals–they need reassurance in predatory environments. It's our job to comfort them so they can learn and perform well. Horses notice residual scents of predators near their barns and display indirect reactions to them. These indirect changes spell greater vigilance–the horses show more sniffing, more visual seeking, more interruptions while eating, and in some cases, a higher heart rate. Meanwhile, we–unable to smell a predator, and unwilling to accept that we, our dogs, and our cats *are* predators–wonder why the horses seem nervous. Respond to vigilance by calming the horse, not by losing patience. He didn't choose the wiring of his brain.

Many people worry that a horse who is encouraged to sniff objects will become a nosy pest. But with good training, that doesn't happen. Horses learn the conditions under which sniffing is acceptable–it's okay at home but not at group trail rides; fine on a halter but not with a bridle; allowed on the ground but not under saddle. Be consistent, and they'll figure it out. Preventing a horse from sniffing his environment is like blindfolding a child who's learning to read.

Until recently, the vomeronasal organ was thought to be specialized for receiving *pheromones* ("FEER-uh-moans"). Pheromones are natural chemicals that affect animal behavior within the same species. Examples include ant trails that trigger following behavior, human androstenol that encourages sexual interest, and mammary pheromones that allow newborns to find their mother's milk. We now know that both olfactory systems can transmit information about pheromones to the brain. The vomeronasal organ originally evolved in underwater animals to detect water-soluble chemicals, which it can still do. It's especially good at detecting predator and prey odors.

You know how horses sometimes extend their necks, raise their heads, and curl their upper lips back? This *flehmen response* occurs when our four-legged friends eat or smell something unusual or especially flavorful. To get more information, they collect odor molecules by inhaling, then raise their noses and curl their lips back to hold those molecules inside the nostrils. The vomeronasal organ can then work at its leisure, transducing odor chemicals and sending neural data to the equine brain for interpretation.

Unfortunately, we don't yet know exactly how the vomeronasal organ interacts with the brain. But while researchers find out, respect your horse's double-barreled sense of smell. The flehmen is not, as legend would have it, a meaningless action or a sign of amusement. It's a hint that your horse's brain wants more information about a particular odor or flavor in the environment—and a clue to his likes and dislikes.

Dog or Horse

The dog's sense of smell is legendary, estimated as being 100,000 times more powerful than the human's. Dogs can sniff out malaria, Parkinson's disease, diabetes, urinary tract infections, and many forms of cancer, aiding in diagnosis of human illness and preventing medical emergencies. They find bombs, drugs, and post-fire arson accelerants with their noses. Well, that's peachy for dogs—but what about horses? Michel-Antoine Leblanc's review of equine smell offers anatomical comparisons among dogs, horses, and humans. Humans lag way behind, of course, with evolution having sacrificed much of our smelling ability in return for improved color vision. But, compared to dogs, horses have almost the same number of functional genes to build cells that distinguish varied odors, about the same amount of sensory space in the olfactory bulbs of their brains, and similar numbers of neural axons carrying smell information to the brain (fig. 6.1).

And it gets better: humans can differentiate about 10,000 different odors, using roughly 6 million receptor cells to pick them up. Sounds impressive, huh? But bloodhounds have 300 million receptors—50 times

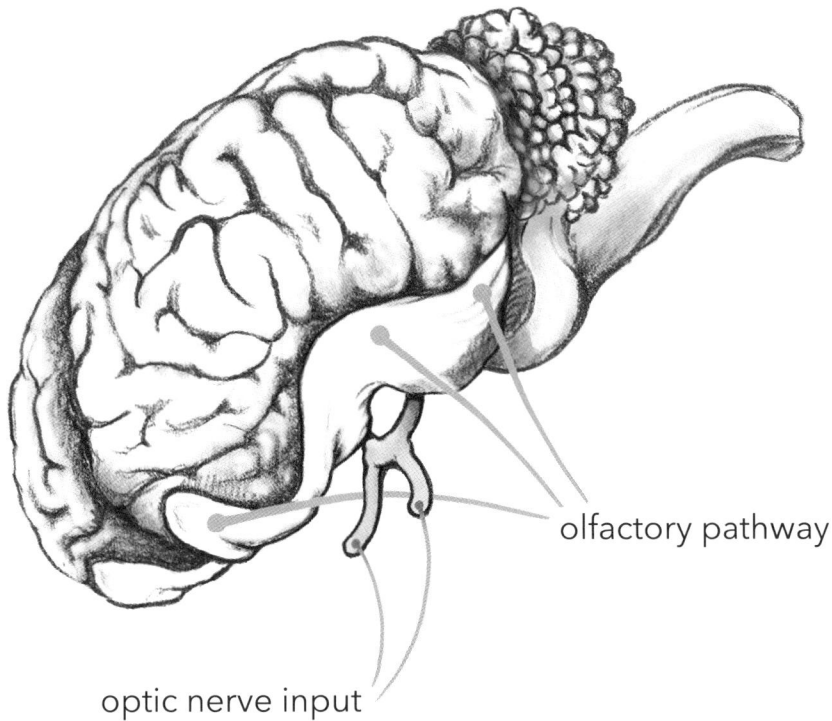

olfactory pathway

optic nerve input

6.1 The horse's olfactory pathways cover almost the full length of his brain. Comparatively, the horse's visual pathway is small. This contrast shows that the horse's brain gathers and receives much greater input via smell than sight.

more than our paltry collection. And here's the real surprise: horses have *more* olfactory receptor cells than many breeds of dogs do! Anatomy isn't everything, but taken together all of this implies that horses might be able to smell with canine sensitivity—a remarkable feat.

I suspect that horses use smell more often and with far more precision than we know. As research develops, we will likely find that it is more important to equine functioning than either vision or hearing. All sorts of equine behaviors and attitudes could be controlled by smell, leading us to brain-based explanations that will alter training methods to better suit the horse. In addition, we egocentric humans are likely to be humbled yet again—many of the equine perceptions we assume are "nothing" are in fact examples of vital sensory information that our big noggins are too weak to discern.

Taste

About 80% of the sense of taste comes from the sense of smell in both horses and humans. Remember that steak being grilled near the feed room a few minutes ago? Mmmm. Our noses can't help but smell the odor molecules wafting up from the meat. When we place a bite on our tongues, our taste buds come into play. Chewing releases more odor molecules, and that scent is carried upward from the throat into the nasal passages for further analysis. The bottom line is that the steak "tastes" great, even though we have smelled most of its flavor.

Horses have taste buds on their tongues just like we do. And the horse's tongue, by the way, is huge! The average equine tongue weighs 2.5 pounds and is almost 16 inches long. The taste buds on it translate molecules into neural impulses that are carried to the brain. Information about sweet, salty, sour, and bitter flavors is gathered and interpreted there. In addition, the tongue contains receptors for the texture and temperature of anything entering the mouth.

The horse's tongue transmits pleasant sensations to the brain when tasting salty or sweet flavors. These flavors are critical for nutrition: human and equine brains run on glucose—sugar—and will steal it from other body parts if it's scarce. Sodium balances the function of brain and motor cells, and salty flavors entice the horse to take it in—that's why every horse needs a salt block near his water. Horses are more tolerant to bitter tastes than humans are, allowing some of them to eat Banamine® without resentment. Cold temperatures reduce bitterness, so with luck you can sometimes sneak a bitter medication past a horse's lips by refrigerating it first. (Although in my experience, "sneaking" anything past a horse is quite the challenge.)

Contrary to assumptions, horses are not particularly good at avoiding toxic plants or bad water by taste, especially when they are very hungry or preferred foods are scarce. This means that we humans are responsible for removing noxious plants and cleaning water sources. When you travel with your horse, encourage him to drink by spiking water with sweetener, peppermint or apple essence, or the water drained away from soaked beet pulp. For short jaunts, bring water with you from home.

Each horse has taste preferences just like people do, determined in the horse's earliest years. A natural pasture contains between 100 and 150 different types of grass—you can see your horse sort through them to select the tastiest morsels. In addition to sweet and salty flavors, horses prefer the types of grass they grew up on, both from direct feeding and from their mother's milk.

The same is true for treats. A brief inventory from my current equine friends shows that the well-named Apple loves apples, but dislikes carrots. She spits out commercial treats that are advertised as "healthy." Cabernet munches carrots with glee. Punkin asks, "What's your angle?" before accepting anything. Cory goes ape for grapes, but rejects bell peppers with eye contact that suggests heartfelt betrayal. Kheluaa accepts or denies a carrot, depending on her assessment of your moral character. Ezra eats anything. If you want to reward your horse with an edible treat—something I don't recommend except when mastering a truly complicated maneuver—find something he really likes.

One of the most critical training aids we use with horses is the bit. We expect horses to accept bits, carry them for long periods, and remain soft to our fingers as the team communicates between hand and mouth. It seems only fair in return that we consider the taste and temperature of a bit. Ice cold metal is not pleasant on the tongue—try it sometime if you dare—so use an electric bit warmer, or warm the bit inside your jacket before offering it to a horse in cold weather. Rubber bits, or bits wrapped in adhesive or leather, contain flavors that are not palatable to all horses. Several types of metal bits hold flavors of their own. If you prefer these, experiment with different types to see which one your horse likes. Of course, the size, style, and action of a bit are important too.

The wrong bit can create all sorts of problems—refusing to bridle, tossing the head, grinding the teeth, opening the mouth while working, pulling on your hands, working behind the bit, flattening the back, evading the bit by inverting the neck, stopping when you want to go, and going when you want to stop. If you experience these problems with your horse, have a professional trainer check your bit and your hands. Most hard mouths are caused not by poor bits, but by hard hands—a topic I'll explore more deeply in the next chapter when we take a look at brain-level perceptual processes.

CHAPTER SEVEN

Pulling the Senses Together

Patch ran the Kentucky Derby without a left eye, starting from a post position where all his competitors were invisible. Gunner cleaned up the World Championship Reining titles from 1996 to 2002, fully deaf. Addy is blind in his right eye, but that didn't stop him from winning the Hickstead Derby—famous for its tricky high-speed course over obstacles that stand 5 feet high. There's no doubt that horses with sensory disabilities can compete with the best, but how do their brains manage these feats? And how do those same brain processes affect horse-and-human teams with no disabilities?

Chickpea is dead to the leg from years of spurs resting against her sides. Strong contact with unforgiving hands has hardened her mouth. She makes no move on her own, waiting for her rider to command her pace and placement from moment to moment. Her sister Mac is just the opposite—she's highly sensitive to every aid and carries her own body without a helicopter parent up top. What is happening inside their brains to cause this disparity, and how can we ride with their brains to address it?

Take Cory for a ride, and he'll show you whether the barn hose was wound to the left or the right last night. Seriously! Horses notice tiny alterations—and most will tell you about them if you're listening. One reason for this is that horses don't group similar items together the way we do. The tractor that grooms the arena might be fine, but the same tractor coming down a barn aisle is a fire-breathing dragon from Dante's seventh circle of hell. Why? And what does this mental process mean for the horse's performance and welfare?

Each of these three situations rest on brain-level processes that fuse perception from all senses, including the horse's superpower of touch:

1. Sensory compensation—the ways the brain overcomes the loss of one sense by beefing up its use of another.
2. Neural fatigue—the ways neurons adapt to stimulation and require dynamic change rather than static constancy to drive their action.
3. Categorical perception—the tendency to perceive varied items as a group so that the brain can treat them as a whole.

Sensory Compensation

Horses with sensory disabilities like blindness or deafness usually perform well, especially if they have learned their disciplines prior to losing the use of an eye or ear. Eye ulcers require an infected eye to be removed after gradual deterioration of sight. That's what happened to Addy and Patch. Because many horses continue their work with partial blindness, we tend to guess it's not a big deal. But cover up your left eye then run as fast as you can on an angle to the left, amidst 20 of the fastest galloping stallions in the world. It's not as easy as it looks!

Deafness is rare in horses, with the exception of those who have bald white faces extending way up the forehead. That lack of pigmentation can cause a congenital form of "splashed-white" deafness because it alters receptor cells in the horse's inner ear. In both horses and humans, these cells transform sounds into neural impulses. Horses born deaf require visual cues during groundwork but use typical body aids under saddle. They startle more easily at unexpected sights and smells, or at sudden touches. We might guess they are calm as can be when the paint sprayer is blown out with an air gun, but in fact, deaf horses pay close attention to nearby animals and will spook from their friends' or handlers' responses to noise. In general, deaf horses do very well—just ask Tough Sunday, who's earned $362,000 so far as a hearing-impaired racehorse in California.

Horses who become blind or deaf during their lives—for example, when an infection damages the organ gradually—have few problems adapting.

Their brains have developed with normal sensory input; in other words, neural networks have already formed by virtue of learning and experience. Once the brain has at least partly developed, it adapts very well even when big chunks are surgically removed. Human babies can lose as much as half a brain—an entire cerebral hemisphere—and still grow up to read, write, speak, love, play, work, and live just like the rest of us do. We'd never know there's nothing but cerebrospinal fluid sloshing around inside half the skull.

In humans and horses, when one sense is deprived of information, the brain pays more attention to input from other senses. So a deaf horse pays more attention to sights, and a blind horse pays more attention to sounds. The same compensation accounts for blind riders like Karen Law, who listens for directional cues while jumping mid-level cross-country and stadium courses, or Kristen Knouse who navigates flat classes by hearing hoofbeats echo off the rail. The sense organs have not changed, but the brain is now zeroing in on stimulation we usually ignore. Neurons in the auditory cortex strengthen in response to blindness, so that poorer vision creates better hearing.

Training Indoors

Views to the outside are diminished in any indoor arena, but some are fully enclosed with no windows, creating an environment in which horses cannot see out at all. Poor lighting adds general dimness, which, as we have seen, the horse cannot overcome for 45 minutes or so (see p. 49). Under these conditions, we would expect hearing, smell, and touch to become sharper—and indeed they do.

Cory is an 18-year-old, off-track Thoroughbred, dark bay with especially delicate legs for his 17.1-hand height. His spookiness piggybacks on the many advantages of his super-sensitivity. He's what I call a "fiber ride"—all of your aids are delivered with precisely timed alterations of only a few muscle fibers. Override this horse, and you're off to the races or face down in the dirt. Lighten up, and you're floating on perfection.

One winter day, Cory and I were warming up alone in an ice-cold indoor arena. It was silent, his ears were speared forward like lasers, and every muscle was taut. You know—the pre-missile demeanor! Suddenly a gunshot went off outside the long wall. Cory whirled and bolted, fortunately at the same time and in the same direction I did, so we stuck together. Determined not to reward the whirl with a halt, I put the horse into a strong trot. When we finished our session, and my heart began to beat again, I went outside to see what had happened.

Two barn friends had set chairs against the metal wall of the arena to enjoy a sunny sky in 3 feet of snow. The "gunshot" that scared Cory and me was the back of a lawn chair placed against that wall. The sound would have been barely noticeable outside. But riding indoors, your horse's brain—and your own—is paying much greater attention to sounds, smells, and touches because vision is limited.

The effects of sensory deprivation are cumulative. When horses cannot see out of an indoor arena, they rely more on hearing. If they are close to age 20, chances are good that their hearing is impaired. The combination of visual limitation and hearing impairment forces the equine brain to attend even more astutely to smell. And so on.

When you work with horses in varied environments, consider which senses contribute most to their understanding. This way, you can anticipate what sort of behavior the horse will offer, and anticipation is a pillar of horse training. We have to know how and why a horse is likely to react before we can prevent that reaction. And preventing it in the first place is much more effective than training it away after it happens.

Seeking Cause

A related aspect of sensory compensation is the brain's desire to find cause. Young mammals develop partly by learning that actions have consequences. Push on a lever and water comes out; whinny and a buddy looks over; fiddle with a loose latch and the gate opens up. Non-actions have consequences, too—miss a flattened ear and the alpha mare bites. With practice, the brain discovers that cause and effect is part of normal life, so it seeks the agent of cause and relies on it to predict upcoming events.

Indoor arenas hide the cause of many unusual noises, reducing predictability. Outside, an approaching storm can be predicted—we feel the wind picking up, see the clouds moving in. But inside, all we know is that the walls suddenly moan in a high wind, the metal roof is deafening in hard rain, the big track doors open from outside with no warning. The arena "ticks" when wood supports expand and contract with invisible temperature change. Snow loads slide off the roof, ice dams drop to the ground outside, spring melt pours through gutters, thunder echoes inside four walls. And have you ever been schooling a hot horse indoors when lightning strikes the roof? I don't recommend it.

Radio stations mask some scary noises in an indoor arena. Novice horses often look for the origin of radio voices, becoming calmer when they identify the source. When horses see someone walk to the radio and adjust its volume, they are less frightened than when an equivalent volume change has no apparent agent. These observations refute the notion common among many scientists that animals like horses do not seek the agents of cause.

But My Horse Isn't Nervous

People often remark that their horses aren't nervous. It's certainly true that there are individual differences: Breed, experience, training, age, and temperament all play a role. But research on trailering and clipping shows that many horses worry about these activities even though their nerves don't show. They experience increases in heart rate, blood pressure, eye temperature, and cortisol levels. The intervals of their heartbeats vary more from one moment to the next. And all of these internal signs of nervousness occur while the horses display calm outward demeanors!

So your horse might be more distressed than you know. Go easy on him during sensory deprivation—build up time in the indoor arena gradually, ask staff to minimize unpredictable outdoor noises, encourage relaxation, and praise calmness. Introduce scary places with a sniffing expedition on halter and lead, making the adventure as pleasant as possible. Add an experienced equine buddy, if necessary.

Consider sensory compensation when you're training outdoors as well. Wind excites the horse's powerful motion-detector cells, creating unusual sights. Some of them are not even visible to you. At the same time, the noise of wind reduces information from hearing, and its sweep carries scents away. With a triple whammy like this, your horse will appreciate some reassurance.

Riding Blind

Riders can use brain-based compensation to advance their skills. Back in the day, we used to train bareback and blindfolded. We'd jump through chutes or on longe lines, learning to feel the horse leave the ground. That way, when riding sighted we wouldn't jump ahead or get left behind. I don't endorse blindfolds—when something goes wrong, you can't rip those babies off fast enough. But riders who are ready for this exercise can gently close their eyes while riding, opening them at any time.

Start on a longe line with a qualified trainer, or at a walk on the long side of a familiar arena. As soon as your eyes are closed, you will begin to feel much more of your horse's movement. Try to sense each foot as he sets it down, feel his shoulders and hips moving back and forth. Identify which leg is doing what. Your horse's back will suddenly feel wider, so locate the central place of greatest balance.

By forcing your brain to pay attention to information it normally ignores, this exercise builds skill, balance, strength, and confidence by the bushel. Of course, you can't go hog-wild with it: Talk with a trainer who has observed your sighted skills first, choose a calm experienced school horse, use a quiet paddock or round pen, and start with a few slow steps. And for goodness' sake, wear a helmet. *Always* wear a helmet when you ride. They're available in English and Western styles for 50 bucks and can save you from a lifetime of mental impairment.

Neural Fatigue

The second brain-level process we'll take on here is *neural fatigue*. Imagine you're a receptor cell (a rod or cone—see p. 42) in the human eye. (It's a stretch, I know, but work with me.) There you are, faced with a beautiful pony. Millions of receptor-cell buddies are standing near you, each responsible for one teensy pixel of the view. Your portion is an infinitesimal gleam of shine on the pony's shoulder. Together all of you send your neural impulses to the visual cortex of the brain. The brain interprets them and says, "Aha! Look at that gorgeous shining pony!"

Great fun. Okay, but here's the thing: You can't send that glimmer of shine to the brain forever. At some point, you're going to get tired standing rooted to the spot saying, "Glimmer of shine, glimmer of shine, gli...." Receptor cells fatigue. Fast. In fact, human visual receptor cells can transmit a signal for only a few seconds. Normally, our eyes make tiny involuntary movements all the time, like automatic tremors, so that each receptor cell gets a different view from one fraction of a second to the next. This prevents them from tiring. When an image is held still artificially, it disappears! This occurs because the cells cannot continue firing their impulses to the brain.

Illusions of Movement

You can experience neural fatigue for yourself by staring at movement. Stand by a rushing river or a waterfall, even a heavy rain, washing downhill, and watch the water move in one direction. Stare at the motion for a couple of minutes then turn your eyes to a stationary sight. You'll notice that the water seems to have stilled while the banks of the river, or the sides of the waterfall, appear to be moving in the opposite direction. What happened? The motion-detector cells in your eyes became fatigued after sending "downward, downward, downward" signals to the brain. When they stopped due to exhaustion, nearby opponent cells sent the brain a flurry of "upward, upward, upward" signals and your brain briefly interpreted that as the motion of a stationary object. It's an illusion of movement that horses can experience, too. They just can't tell us in speech, "Hey, that ground is *moving*!"

I've used the example of vision for neural fatigue because it's easy for us to understand. But all sensory neurons—visual, auditory, olfactory, gustatory, tactile—get tired and stop responding until they have recovered. The brain adapts to static cues; that's why we stop feeling rings on our fingers or hearing fans a few seconds after they're on. Instead, the brain picks up *change*. Change, after all, is most important to survival. If a horse is grazing in a field, he doesn't need to know that a blade of grass is still. He needs to know when it moves.

Many trainers—unaware of neural fatigue—advocate constant aids. Examples crop up in all riding disciplines:

- Dressage trainers often teach riders to hold steady on the outside rein at all times, as a support to the horse.
- Racing trainers encourage jockeys to apply constant pressure with both hands, to help horse and rider balance on the bit as they run.
- Hunter/jumper trainers frequently ask that riders maintain strong lower-leg pressure, to keep the horse forward and the rider secure.
- Many Western Pleasure trainers teach drape reins even at the slowest possible jog, so that the horse receives a steady lack of contact on his mouth.
- Some eventing trainers advocate that the rider should match with her hands the weight of pressure produced by the horse's mouth. For example, if your horse gives you 5 pounds of mouth pressure, you respond with 5 pounds of hand pressure and keep it constant.

All of these are static cues; they are applied, maintained, and unchanged. They defy the reality of neural fatigue, causing us to ride against a horse's brain rather than with it. Very quickly, receptor cells in the horse's mouth or sides tire. They can't continue to send "pressure" signals to the horse's brain. That's why constant aids become meaningless—it's not that the horse is refusing to respond, it's that he has to override his own brain cells to do so. To ride with a horse's brain, apply aids intermittently. Teach the horse to carry his own body at other times. Self-carriage is easy for a horse to learn because it matches the way his brain works.

Self-Carriage

Green babies under saddle must learn to balance the weight of a rider, maintain consistent pace, hold straight lines, bend inward on curves, and attend to a rider's aids. Trainers spend a lot of time in the first few months helping horses with these basics. But once taught, a horse can manage them on his own. Riders don't need to place every foot, round the horse's back every minute, or balance the horse around every corner. There won't be enough attentional capacity for all that when the horse-and-human team begins complex maneuvers.

The basics of teaching the horse to carry his body can be summarized in the phrase *correct-and-release*. Suppose you are teaching a horse to trot at a consistent pace. You pick up the trot, but even with accurate rhythm, weight distribution, and upper-body position on your part, it's too slow. You correct the horse by applying leg pressure. If he speeds up, praise him! If he doesn't, try again. But either way, *release* the pressure after you have made the correction. Horses are not cars—they do not require constant weight on the accelerator to continue moving forward at the same pace. They are thinking, feeling animals who can learn to maintain any pace you teach.

A couple of caveats might help here. A *correction* is not a punishment or a lingering coercion; it is simply a piece of information that tells or reminds the horse what you want. And a *release* is not a drop. We release a correction back to the neutral point, not back to zero. So, for example, we adopt a neutral amount of leg pressure for each horse, depending on his needs, and hold it steady. Increasing that pressure momentarily is a correction; returning the increased pressure to neutral is a release. Altering it to zero would be the equivalent of hopping off the horse for a quick burger.

Often, correct-and-release becomes a series of small touches at this early stage. When the horse trots too fast, we sometimes use correct-and-release in our hands, reminding him to slow down, but always releasing. We don't hang on the reins in an effort to slow the horse, because neural fatigue will make his brain unable to sense that pressure. He'll only learn to pull. By releasing, the horse learns to trot at a set pace until you ask him to change it. He learns that he is responsible for doing that. The horse's job is to respond to new stimulation, not to make you do all the work.

A very common mistake occurs when riders cluck incessantly to a horse in an effort to increase speed. The sound interferes with every other horse-and-human team within earshot, teaching all of them to ignore clucks. Every month or so—to encourage a horse to leave the ground on a sketchy jump approach, or to increase the pivot angle of a reining spin— you might need to cluck. Once. And you want it to mean something! Clucking till the chickens come home ruins the effect entirely.

Spurs or crops are also misused far and wide because of a failure to understand sensory adaptation. Sometimes an uncooperative horse needs spurs. But letting them rest against his sides at all times is a huge error. Just as the receptor cells in the skin of your wrist adapt to your watch, the horse adapts to your spurs and soon loses sensation of them entirely. Riders end up pressing harder and harder, or using stronger spurs—all to no avail. Instead, the horse needs to feel the spur or crop rarely but firmly, as a reminder that is immediately released. The purpose of a spur, crop, or cluck is not to make the horse go faster. It's to teach him to respect your leg.

Categorical Perception

The barn hose adorns the same place every day. When it's moved a few inches, no one notices except the horses. Some of them only cock an ear toward the change; others go goggle-eyed and giraffe-necked as they scoot past with their bellies arched sideways like bows. Annoying, isn't it? They walk past that hose every day. But there's a very good reason that horses notice tiny differences that we miss, and it's called *categorical perception*.

Human brains operate on the basis of categorical perception—the natural tendency to organize sights, sounds, smells, tastes, and touches into meaningful groups. We hear the same word spoken by a hundred different people—male or female, hoarse or smooth, high or low, children or adult, foreign or local. Every version sends a different acoustic form to the ears, but the brain's categorical perception tells us they're all the same word. We taste cheddar, jack, brie, limberger, chevre, and mozzarella, but bind all of them into the category of cheese. We see doors from different angles all the time, yet we group all of them together as doors. In fact, we are so accustomed to the brain's automatic grouping of different instances that we rarely notice it (fig. 7.1 A).

The downside of human categorical perception is stereotyping; our brains are designed to sort rapidly according to external traits. They automatically assume that every Latina is dark-haired, dark-eyed, and olive-skinned; that people who say, "Hey," are from the southern United States; or that all Saddlebreds are nervous. We have to work to avoid these false

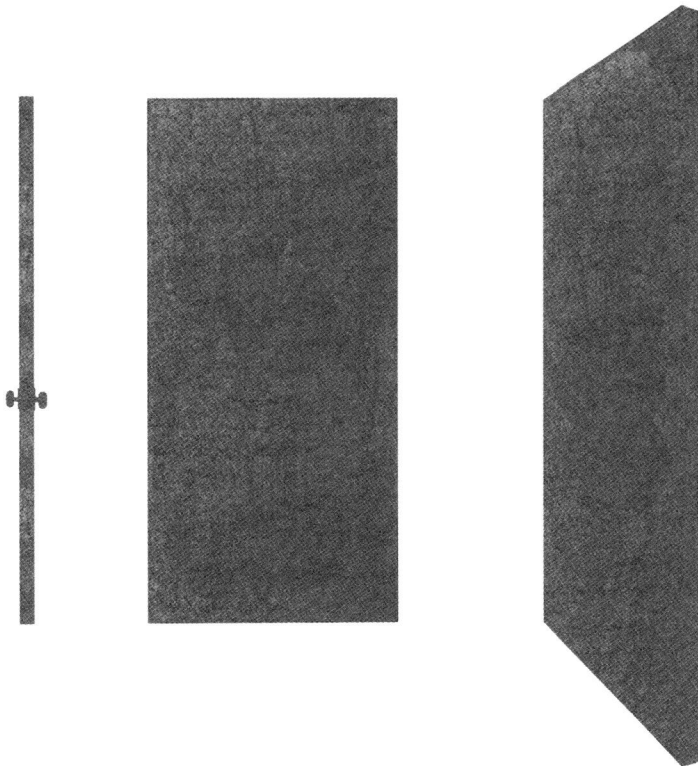

7.1 A The human brain categorizes different physical views into one group automatically, like "doors."

biases because our brains are so good at producing them. The upside of categorical perception is speed—we group separate items instantly without thinking. Most of us are not aware that our brains categorize items automatically, and we cannot imagine what our lives might be like if our brains didn't do that.

With effort, we can stave off the brain's tendency toward categorical perception temporarily. It's hard to do, though. Conjure up the image of a horse you know. Think for a moment of the view your eyes receive. Viewed head-on, Cutie looks nothing like the view you get from her back or side. She's light grey, but when caked in dried mud after a good roll, she looks like a buckskin. If she suddenly lifts a hind leg and scratches her ear, we are not fooled by our eyes' view into thinking she is a dog. Categorical perception is so powerful that it's hard for us *homo sapiens* to even imagine that each view of the same horse could represent an entirely new animal (fig. 7.1 B).

Equine brains don't have much categorical perception. And that's why horses notice minor discrepancies among items within what we would call the same group. To a horse, a different view of a familiar object is the equivalent of a new object. When we see a barn hose, our neural networks are firing simply for "hose." We take a glance, and yup, it's a hose. There's no need for human brains to specify further. But our horses' neural networks are firing "new hose," "faded hose," "muddy hose," "green hose," "black hose," "hose wound in 24-inch loops," "hose wound in 14-inch loops," "stretched-out hose," "hose stored by sloppy human," or "hose stored by OCD human." Because they look different, to a horse they *are* different.

Every perception is separated in the equine brain, so that the same non-categorical effect occurs with sounds, touches, smells, and tastes. We say the horse "has seen that hose a million times." But in fact, he hasn't. He's seen a slightly different view of a hose many different times. We are the ones whose brains assumed those different views all represent the same hose. Their lack of categorical perception is one of the reasons horses don't need to have precise visual acuity or excellent sound localization. Their brains notice tiny differences instead, and that ability allows them to survive.

7.1 B The human brain unconsciously groups items together on the basis of conceptual similarity, using categorical perception. The horse brain tends to process each instance independently.

A horse who is exposed to the same jumbled scene every day will get used to it. But because of categorical perception, our brains assume that the jumble remains constant, when in fact it changes. At one ranch, I used a round pen located next to a storage area for large equipment. Horses who had used that round pen for years still skirted the jumble because the equipment was moved slightly, or added to and deleted from, almost every day. I had to study the scene at length to identify those changes—or use logic to infer that someone had used the hay rake yesterday and probably parked it differently afterward. Horses take one glance and see such variations instantly.

Training and trust help horses learn to ignore their lack of categorical perception just as humans learn to override stereotypes. But we should remember that equine and human brains are working against their respective natures under these conditions. When humans are tired, distressed, or pumped up with adrenaline, our brains revert to stereotyping behavior. And when horses are pressed into uncomfortable situations or lose patience with handlers who do not understand them, their brains will direct them to whirl and bolt from familiar objects. That's just the nature of each beast.

Put these three brain-level processes of perception—*sensory compensation, neural fatigue*, and *categorical perception*—to work for you and your horse. Try to experience the world through his brain. Notice how different it is from yours and caution yourself from assuming your horse perceives the world like you do. Stepping inside a prey animal's brain, even for a brief moment, is a special honor.

CHAPTER EIGHT
Mutual Communication by Feel

T he horse's brain is focused on the present external environment and
does not mull internal plans, intents, and thoughts. His eyes, ears,
nose, and skin catch some information that human senses cannot detect,
but he misses other sensations that the human can detect. With all these
differences, we might despair at the idea of communicating directly, brain
to brain, with a horse.

Yet there is one means of sensory communication that is direct—that
is, not mediated by language, symbol, gesture, or equipment. It's called
proprioception, the sense of body awareness that tells us where our bodies
are in space and where our horses' bodies are while we ride them. With
practice, human proprioception allows us to feel where our horses' legs
are, how they are moving, whether their backs are relaxed or tense, how
their bodies and minds change in response to the slightest human motions.
Equine proprioception, in turn, permits our horses to sense the pressures,
locations, and tensions within their own bodies and ours. At any mounted
moment, a horse with sharp proprioception knows not only where his legs
are, but also where your legs are and what they're doing.

Let's suppose that when you bend one knee a tad and press that calf
against your horse's side, he canters forward. Both of you have just made
use of proprioception. Your brain initiated the amount of calf contraction
that was necessary then released that contraction smoothly just as the
horse's brain picked up your signal. Sensing your leg pressure, he changed
gaits. His brain calibrated the speed of that gait according to the amount

and velocity of pressure against his side. It's like a very complicated close-contact dance, with you and your horse fused in muscular coordination at the level of both brains. Some of your neurons transmit a signal, some of his pick it up, and so on back and forth between the two species.

Author Mark Helprin has noted the connection between horses and dancing. "The horse moved like a dancer, which is not surprising. A horse is a beautiful animal, but he is perhaps most remarkable because he moves as if he always hears music." We humans can learn to join that equine dance as full partners.

Horse sports place steep demands on the human proprioceptive system. All athletes have to control muscle contraction, but we have to contract our muscles while simultaneously keeping them relaxed—almost the perfect oxymoron. We must isolate muscles within a natural group, flexing some while loosening or neutralizing others. Equestrians need precise gradation of muscle tension to cue prey animals in smooth gentle ways. Our brains need to sense not only our own joint angles, muscle lengths, tendon tension, and postural balance, but also our horse's joints, muscles, tendons, and balance. Every athlete's proprioceptive nerves work hard, but the riders are really huffin' and puffin'.

We can improve riding skill by turbocharging the brain's proprioceptive power. As a nice side effect, our horses' proprioception also develops and mutual communication within the team soars. These improvements require some work, but they pay off big time in:

- Creating more precise aids
- Establishing a common balance between horse and rider
- Building the horse's straightness, bend, engagement, and agility
- Reducing the risk of human or equine injury

Most importantly, proprioceptive fitness helps your horse solve the largest obstacle to training: understanding what you want him to do. Too often, we assume horses are refusing to do what we want, when the real problem is that they don't *know* what we want. Good proprioception makes our requests clear.

Life without Proprioception

Proprioception is easy to take for granted because vision usually compensates for its mistakes. But give this a try: Stand on one foot with your eyes open. A little shaky maybe, but possible. Now do the same thing with your eyes closed. Much harder, isn't it? When you close your eyes, your brain has to rely on proprioception alone, without benefit of vision.

Without proprioception or the vision to overcome its loss, people fall into a heap. Really. Consider Ian Waterman, a man who suffered a very rare virus that attacked his proprioceptive nerves. The damage destroyed their ability to send messages from his body to his brain. All other senses, plus his motor function, were intact. But without proprioception, Ian couldn't sit up, stand, speak, drink, or eat. His body flopped like dead weight, and his brain didn't know where his limbs or torso were positioned. Imagine trying to eat if your brain doesn't know where your mouth is. Or mount a horse after losing consciousness of your foot.

Only by virtue of vision and extreme determination did Ian teach himself to sit up, and later, stand. By staring at his feet, he learned to position them for an upright stance. Then, he'd look at his legs and get them in the right spots, and so on for the remainder of his body. Just to stand still, he had to learn the visual position of each joint and muscle. Once all the parts were consciously placed, he could stand while staring at his body. If he looked away, closed his eyes, or lost concentration, Ian collapsed like a string of boiled spaghetti.

Proprioceptive Nerves

A normal human or equine brain receives signals from the body through muscle spindles, Golgi organs, and joint angle receptors. Spindles are located inside the fibers that make our muscles strong. They allow the brain to monitor changes in the length of a muscle as we move, and in the speed of that lengthening process. These buggers are super-sensitive: They can pick up a difference of only .002% of the muscle's total length. After detecting that minuscule change, they send impulses to the brain so that it knows what's going on. The impulses arrive much more quickly than visual information does, so the brain can correct an error in muscle tension in less than half the time that vision would require. Such speed is helpful when you're reacting to a horse!

Spindle Illusions

Muscle spindles are powerful enough to create illusions. When scientists zap the correct spindles with electrodes, the brain thinks that its arm is bending backward at the elbow or that its knee is bending forward. Some illusions are so strong that people report feeling their lower leg fold upward until the foot touches the front of their hip! The brain can't distinguish between a neural signal that comes from a real stimulus and one that comes from a fake stimulus, so it interprets artificial signals in the usual manner. That interpretation causes us to feel as if these limbs are actually in impossible positions when in fact they are lying still.

Located where tendons meet muscles, *Golgi* ("GOAL-jee") tendon organs monitor muscle tension. They tell the brain how much force is being exerted on a muscle by censoring the degree to which it is flexed. When a horse pulls on you with his mouth, Golgi tendon organs in your hands, arms, shoulders, and back signal the amount of force that is exerted against you as well as the amount of force you are returning. If you heed it, this information reminds you to stop the pull by releasing pressure, which in turn relaxes the horse.

Spindles and Golgi organs send instant messages to your brain, while your horse's proprioceptors send similar information to his brain. Suppose you correct your horse after misbehavior with a sharp fast contraction of the calf or a bump with your heel. The horse's proprioception signals his brain that this intense burst is quite different from gradual leg pressure. The brain translates varying signals into different content. The sharp bump scolds, "Hey, whatcha doin', buster?" The gradual rise in pressure encourages, "Okay, now let's canter...."

Angle receptors come into play when our joints straighten or bend. To accommodate the horse's center of gravity, we bend our hips in the air over a jump. This deeper flexion is communicated to the brain through nerves located inside the hip's joint capsule. (The hip, incidentally, contains angle receptors that are more sensitive than those in most other joints, with the ability to detect a change of only .2 degrees. By contrast, toes are working at their outer limits to tell the brain of a 6.1-degree change in angle.) Some angle receptors adapt quickly to joint flexion, signaling only that a change has occurred. Others adapt slowly, telling the brain that this new joint position is being held in place.

Proprioceptive nerves of all types enjoy a special fast lane to the brain. It's a highly insulated portion of the spinal cord that allows signals to travel much more quickly than bodily indicators do for touch, temperature, and pain. Rapid signaling of proprioceptive information is required for efficient feedback to nerves that cause muscles and joints to move. We don't want to be twiddling our thumbs waiting for the brain's instructions while ducking low branches on a runaway horse.

It's Complicated

Proprioception sounds almost simple when we analyze each step independently. But even the most basic equestrian movement—say, one leg's pressure—puts many different nerves to work. A human leg contains 43 major muscles from hip to ankle. To squeeze a horse's barrel, each muscle must sit at the proper location while flexed or relaxed to varying degrees. Thousands of proprioceptive nerves are sending messages to both brains simultaneously when you press your horse's side with one leg. And we're not even counting all the tendons, ligaments, and joints that are involved in such a "simple" act.

Testing Proprioception

Before you can tune proprioception, you have to find inaccuracies in the way your brain perceives body locations. The fact that your brain adapts quickly is both a blessing and a curse: It permits you to align your body by retraining your brain, but it also allows temporary misalignments to become ingrained. Many events can cause temporary misalignment—an injury, the physical compensation that allows it to heal, repetitive misuse, or sloppy form. Over time, your brain grows accustomed to the alteration, accepting it as the new normal.

Proprioceptive training teaches your brain to demand alignment rather than accepting an uneven body position. Why bother? Because your horse picks up every imbalance and alters his body, and then his brain, to accommodate it. Soon you and your horse are listing to the side or stepping short with one leg while both brains say everything's hunky-dory. Every trainer knows the surprise with which clients greet a well-timed video: "I'm leaning that far forward? It sure doesn't feel that way."

General Test

For an easy general test of your proprioception, try the Stork Toe Raise (fig. 8.1). Compare your performance to standard norms and see where you fit in. Don't grind your gears if it's poor—proprioception improves quickly with practice. Stand with your hands on your hips, right foot on the inside of the left calf, knee angled outward.

8.1 The Stork Toe Raise tests your proprioception. (Please see text for instructions.)

Hold a small timer in one hand and start it as you raise onto the ball of your left foot. When you lose that position, stop the timer. Now try the other foot then rate yourself using the table below.

If you hold the position for	your proprioception is
less than 10 seconds	poor
10-24 second	fair
25-39 seconds	average
40-50 seconds	good
more than 50 seconds	excellent

Formal proprioceptive assessment is available through physical therapists and advanced athletic trainers. Most of them aren't familiar with our sport, though, and fail to recognize how delicately we use horse-and-human body awareness to communicate. You can do an informal assessment by asking a friend to view your stance from the front, sides, and rear, jotting down discrepancies in your alignment or the direction, extent, or coordination of your movement (see the following exercises). Close your eyes during assessment to test proprioception without benefit of vision—after all, you can't ride and watch your body at the same time. This process takes a while, so you might want to spread sessions over several days.

Standing Joint Alignment

Put on fitted clothing and have your friend start by checking your joint alignment. Stand comfortably with your feet hip-width apart, eyes closed, and arms at your sides. Don't shoot for Marine Corps boot camp perfection; just stand like you do all the time. Are your shoulders even on an imaginary horizontal line? What about your elbows, wrists, hips, knees, and ankles? From the side, are your ears, hips, knees, and ankles in a vertical line? Is your spine straight, with your weight distributed evenly along the heels and balls of your feet?

Moving Level Alignment

This second part is more fun. Keeping your eyes closed, extend your arms straight out to the sides. Are your hands level? Bring both index fingers together way out in front of you. Do they touch? Is one landing consistently higher than the other? Now bring your arms back out to the sides and touch each index finger to the opposite big toe. Quickly, please! Your proprioception needs to work right now on a horse, not after a bunch of conscious planning. Did your finger connect accurately with each toe?

Touch each elbow to the same side hip joint, moving in a sideways downward arc. Arms out to the side again, and bend one elbow to touch that index finger to the same side ear. Place the sole of each foot on the front of the opposite knee, one after another. Your eyes are still closed, right? Continue these tests as your friend chuckles and looks for discrepancies from various angles.

Distance Assessment

Part three involves standing with your back against a wall. For ideal posture, the back of your head, shoulder blades, sacrum, and heels should all touch the wall. Is there a hollow between the small of your back and the wall? Can your friend fit a hand in it? Play with the amount of abdominal contraction needed to bring your low back into alignment with your shoulders and hips. You'll have much greater strength on your horse with a straight back instead of a hollow one, and the abdominal engagement will center your weight vertically so that your horse isn't carrying a lumpy sack of potatoes.

Now step forward so that your body is about an inch away from the wall. Move your left shoulder back to touch the wall, then your right shoulder. Do the same with each cheek of your seat, each heel, and each elbow. Lift each shoulder an inch toward the same side ear; lift each hip joint an inch toward the shoulder. Then face the wall and bring each shoulder, hip, and knee toward it by an inch. You can experiment with all sorts of movements, while your friend watches for faulty internal measurement.

People often lift one shoulder three inches and the other not at all then report that they've made the same move on each side.

Postural Balance

Balance is mighty important as we riders go whipping around a barrel on huge animals with centers of gravity that differ from ours. Stand arm's length from a wall and hold your arms out to the sides with your eyes closed. When you feel balanced, stand on one foot for 30 seconds then stand on the other. Which foot is most stable? Try it with your arms hanging straight down. If that's too easy, stand on your toes one foot at a time. Touching a solid object, stand on your heels. Ah, that one's tough, isn't it? If you can stop laughing long enough, try standing on one heel to see if you're more stable on one side than the other.

Weight Distribution

Your horse senses the distribution of your body weight while you ride, leaning or becoming tense when it's off. Check weight distribution by placing two weight scales on the floor about a hip distance apart. Calibrate the two scales so that each reads the same weight for a given object. Then close your eyes and stand comfortably with one foot on each scale. If your weight is distributed evenly across both legs, the scales should read the same on each side, even when your knees are bent. Most people stand with more weight on their stronger leg.

Muscle Tension

For the sixth section of proprioceptive assessment, you need to explore the brain's awareness of muscle tension. Find a 10- to 20-pound object you can hold with both hands—hand weights are fine if you have them, or just use some books, a grooming box, whatever's handy. (Leave the 50-pound feed sacks for another time—and if you have bad knees, sit this one out.) The average woman needs about 10 pounds of weight for this test, and the average man needs around 20. Adjust the amount for your personal size and strength.

Now, stand on one foot and center the extra weight over that leg. Gradually bend the knee, bringing your seat down toward the floor, then back up gradually onto your tiptoes. Now try it with the other leg. Are they on par in strength, flexibility, range of motion, and balance? Does one wobble more than the other? Do you lean in a persistent direction when trying to reestablish balance?

Symmetrical Flexibility

Finally, seek differences in flexibility by stretching the same muscles on each side of your body independently. When you stretch, let's say, both legs simultaneously, one leg's flexibility often compensates for the other leg's stiffness. So you want to test the proprioceptors and neurons that control each leg separately. Once you've tested the flexibility of your arms, neck, upper back, mid back, low back, waist, abs, hips, thighs, calves, and Achilles tendons, begin to rotate each major joint independently: the left hip, the right, the left shoulder, then the right, and so on. Ask your friend to identify disparities in the flexibility of each muscle group as compared to its counterpart, and in each joint's range of motion.

That's it! Almost everyone finds some discrepancies—places where your brain says, for example, that your left hip is in a horizontal line with the right when in fact it's an inch higher. Your brain has adapted to an uneven body position and is providing incorrect proprioception. Wherever you find something askew, repeat the movement without trying to correct it. You want to see whether it's a consistent imbalance in your proprioceptive system or just a mistake. I'll explain how to resolve misalignments and imbalances in chapter 9 (see p. 111).

Brain Damage in Proprioception

The assessment I've suggested here explores the function of nerves, muscles, tendons, and joints. But in very rare cases of impaired proprioception, all those are fine. Instead, the brain is to blame. Brain damage can cause people to lean, tip, stoop, fall in an invariable direction, lose awareness of a body part, or become unconscious of one side of their face.

The neurologist Oliver Sacks described an unnamed patient who tried to discard his own leg due to a brain tumor. The young man came in for testing because his left leg felt "lazy." He spent the night in the hospital. When he woke up, he found a dead severed leg in his bed. He threw it out of the bed, but his body followed. Horrified, he realized the dead leg was attached to him. Brains rationalize inexplicable events, conjuring fairy tales about cause—and his brain told him this had to be a joke: The nurses had sneaked a dead leg into his bed while he was asleep, just for fun. Well, he didn't think it was funny.

With further testing, doctors discovered a tumor near the motor cortex in this gentleman's right brain hemisphere. The tumor had begun to bleed overnight, impairing the neurons in that area. Without neural signaling from the leg, the young man's brain assumed it was no longer part of his body. And seeing the leg did not change his mind.

The *motor cortex* is of interest to us because it allows horses and riders to use their bodies in direct cross-species communication. It's a long strip of brain tissue that sends signals to various parts of the body to make them move. In one location along your left-hemisphere motor cortex is a network of neurons responsible for moving your right leg. A similar strip of brain tissue called the *somatosensory cortex* lies next to the motor cortex. ("So-matt-uh-SEN-suh-ree" comes from the Greek word "soma," which means "body.") It receives signals from various parts of the body. So specific neurons in your motor cortex fire when you transmit pressure from your right leg into your horse's side, and specific neurons in his sensory cortex fire when he receives that pressure (figs. 8.2 A & B).

The human sensory and motor cortex areas have been mapped, so we know which spot of brain tissue corresponds to which body part. But the equine sensorimotor cortex has not been mapped for body parts yet. It's hard to strap down an unsedated horse, stick electrodes into his brain, and watch which body part wiggles when we turn on the juice. We do know that the horse's neck and shoulder hold the majority of neural

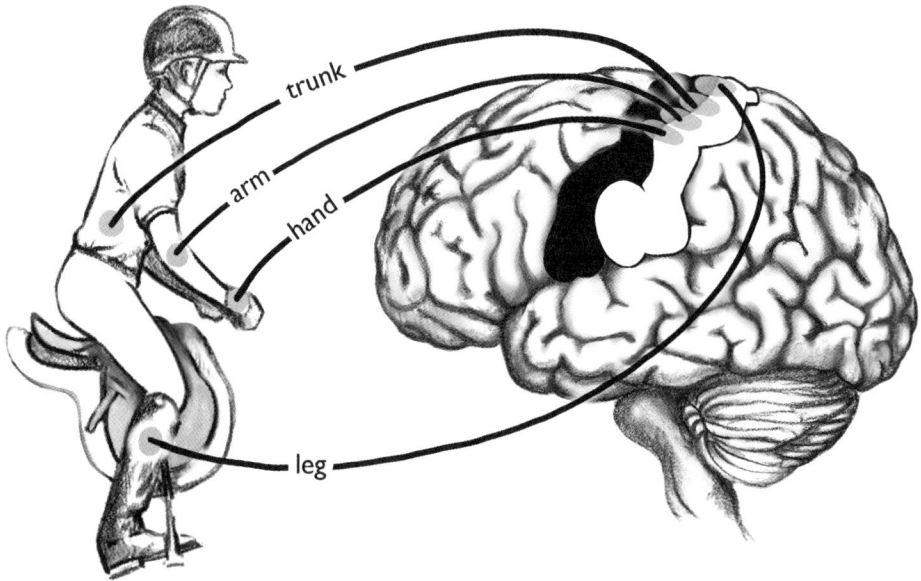

8.2 A Body locations are mapped onto specific neural sites in the human brain. Here, the black area represents the motor cortex, and the white area shows the somatosensory cortex. Pale grey ovals mark human brain sites that have been mapped to various parts of the human body.

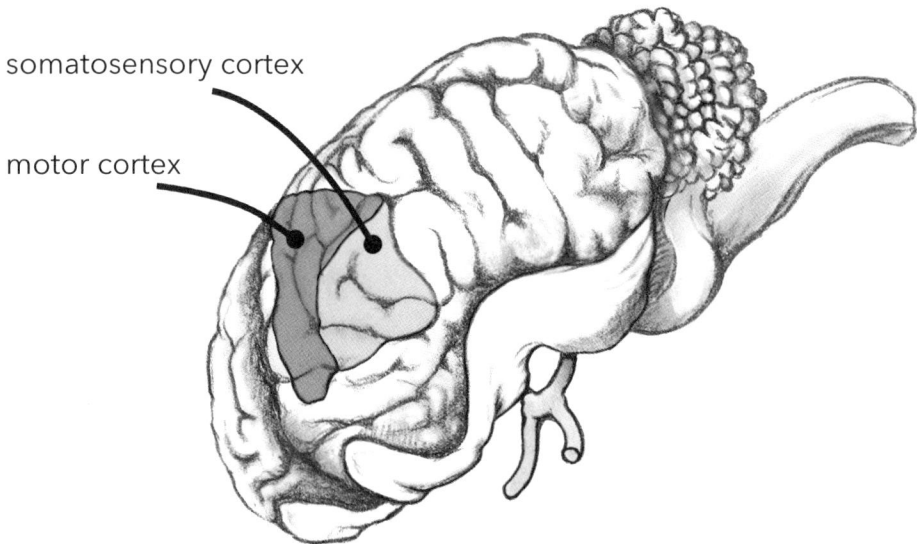

8.2 B In this view of the horse's brain, the motor cortex is shown in dark grey. The approximate location of the horse's somatosensory cortex appears in light grey.

representation in the equine motor cortex. This suggests that these areas are among the most sensitive.

Because it's difficult to explore the equine cortex, current knowledge of the horse's somatosensory area is based on research with sheep. A veterinary neurologist tells me that sheep brains are similar enough to horse brains that we can speculate about one from the other. Sheep brains are studied because the animals are easier and less expensive to handle than horses, and because the results can often be applied to human medicine.

To locate the somatosensory cortex, a paper-thin grid of electrodes is inserted into the sheep's brain. When the animal is touched in certain areas, the electrodes transmit audible signals to researchers, who then map the locations between brain and body. From their studies, I have approximated the location of equine somatosensory cortex shown in Figure 8.2 B. We will learn more as research continues in equine neuro-veterinary science.

Proprioceptive cells also send signals to clumps of neurons buried in the center of the brain, called the *basal ganglia*, which are responsible for learning, initiating, and performing voluntary movements. These structures are damaged in humans with Parkinson's disease, which causes an inability to move in a fluid fashion. In horses, the basal ganglia are harmed by the ingestion of toxic weeds, resulting in a fatal inability to chew.

After proprioceptive cells connect with neurons in the sensory or motor cortex areas and the basal ganglia, signals travel to the little ball of cauliflower called the *cerebellum* ("sare-uh-BELL-um"). The equine and human cerebellum time, coordinate, and remember sequences of movement. The horse's cerebellum is highly developed and very important for learning. Various areas of cortex have taken over much of its function in human brains. Problems in any of these areas can interfere with proprioception.

Proprioceptive Loss

After all this talk of people losing attached legs or falling like boiled spaghetti when distracted, you might be relieved to know that proprioceptive loss is very rare. Horses and humans have well developed peripheral nerves going to all areas of their bodies. When something goes wrong, it typically affects only one main nerve and is temporary. Most proprioceptive work for equestrian improvement consists of tweaking an area to bring it back into alignment and awareness.

Occasionally, a part of the human body is injured and cannot be moved. Immobility causes a temporary loss of awareness in that limb similar to the sensory adaptation that's caused by neural fatigue—the area might feel partly disconnected, or slow to respond, as if it's not there even though we know it is. When it is healed enough to wiggle around, proprioception returns gradually. Our brains have to retool the neurons that allow us to feel and move the injured area.

Horses have the same capacity to experience a temporary loss of proprioceptive awareness when injured. But in practice, it doesn't happen often because horses are almost never immobile. Plus, the mental experience would be mighty tough for a horse to describe to his veterinarian!

One of the million nice things about riding is that it offers a mild proprioceptive test every day. If you can walk, trot, and canter smoothly on a horse, your proprioception is pretty darn good. But to use your body to communicate brain-to-brain with a horse, it needs to be much better. In the next chapter, you'll see why proprioceptive errors are so detrimental to good riding, and learn how to correct them. Till then, I'll be standing on my head trying to touch my little toe to the back of my neck. Quickly.

CHAPTER NINE
Building an Equestrian Brain

Why do riders have to address small discrepancies in proprioception? If your brain thinks your left shoulder has moved back 1 inch, same as your right one, but in fact it's moved back 2 inches, so what? The answer is that we need to match our horse's proprioceptive sensitivity if we hope to achieve brain-to-brain communication. And horses are exquisitely sensitive animals when it comes to body awareness.

Flygirl is a Holsteiner built like a tank, black with a sprinkling of socks and some grey hair on her face. After a lifetime of Grand Prix jumping in the United States and Europe, she's now a late-twenties school horse who teaches equitation to beginning and intermediate hunt seat riders. One afternoon long ago I was working on flying changes with her and noticed how sensitive she was to my aids. To request a lead change on a straight line, all I had to do was shift my head slightly to the side corresponding to the new lead. She changed instantly. The same was true over fences. To turn left in the air, I just barely looked left.

Nearly every trainer will tell you that when riders look left, our hands, shoulders, hips, and legs unconsciously shift left. Horses could be picking up many bodily cues aside from head position—and indeed it's unlikely they would notice a 10-degree turn of the head. They can't even see us up there! So I experimented with Fly, holding every part of my body true north while shifting only my head slightly to the northwest. I tried this in all directions, at various locations, over fences and on the flat, at all gaits and unexpected moments over a month or so. She turned every time. She also matched the degree of her bodily turn to the degree of my head turn. Even if she was picking up some form of unconscious directional change in my body, that level of sensory discrimination is sick—in the very best way.

Can a huge animal be sensitive? Well, the average horse weighs 50 million times more than the average fly, but immediately feels the pest settle on his body. A hypothetical human with that degree of sensitivity would feel the weight of five unseen dandelion seeds—something real humans can't do. Trained horses can detect from two yards away a nod of the human head that measures only 8/1000 of an inch in displacement. That's two-and-a-half times more susceptible to visual displacement than we are. Faced with the same nod, humans wouldn't even know it had occurred. One more statistic: at the withers, a horse can detect 3/10,000 of an ounce of pressure from one nylon filament—the weight of about three grains of sand. Poke the same filament into a human fingertip, and we have no idea it's there.

With this level of sensitivity, horses notice the difference between 1 inch of shoulder movement and 2 inches. And they're trying to figure out what it means. If we fail to train our brains proprioceptively, our horses suffer confusion in the face of mixed messages.

A secondary issue is at work here, too: Vision, while a tremendous boon for daily life, often interferes with proprioception. For example, asked to walk at a normal pace and stop with both feet toeing an imaginary line, most people will look at their feet to accomplish the task. Just for fun, hop up and try that, then practice a few times without looking. You might be surprised at how close you come to the line that your eyes can't see. Our brains can direct our bodies without eyesight, if we let them. Vision cheats our proprioceptive system of the chance to do its work.

So, equestrians hone proprioception not only because our mounts are super-sensitive, but also because we can't watch our bodies or our horses while we ride. We have no choice but to ride by feel. Proprioceptive training teaches our brains to align our joints, maintain balance, isolate muscles for independent use, and regulate their flexibility and strength in ways that promote direct communication between horse and rider.

Under the Hood

Specific neurons receive and interpret proprioceptive signals from each area of the body. In most areas, this process works just fine. But we all have a muscle here or a joint there that is ineffective. With time, the brain cells that regulate those slackers also become lazy. They throw their little neuron arms up in despair and stalk off the job muttering about how the Big Shot Vision Neurons don't give them no respect. Or they slump down in a squishy corner and pull their caps down over their eyes for a nap.

Proprioceptive training has two effects on brain tissue: It forces sluggish neurons back to work controlling a given body part, and it recruits new neurons to help with the task. Neural recruiting helps blind people comprehend speech almost three times faster than sighted people do. That's because their brains take spare neurons from unused visual cortex and conscript them to auditory use. Likewise, a rider's goal is to commit more brain cells to body parts that are important astride a horse. The brain will only recruit under duress, as a teenager only cleans her room under threat of sanction. When we hold other brain cells back and insist that our proprioceptive neurons do their job, they're eager to work.

Train Your Brain

Head scans of guitar players and taxi drivers show that everyday training builds brain tissue. For instance, neural real estate that controls the left fingertips is much larger in people who play the guitar compared to those who don't. Keith Richards' brain bulges in this area; mine sags. London taxi drivers, who memorize over 25,000 city streets twisting in every direction, have more grey matter than average in the spatial memory zones of their cortex. Training—not innate talent or inborn anatomy—causes this effect. Just as guitar players and taxi drivers form musical and spatial brains, riders can build equestrian brains.

Because we improve proprioception through physical movement, people often assume that proprioceptive training is all about strengthening muscles and developing physical balance. But those results are merely side effects. Physical fitness is critical for good horsemanship, but today we are exercising nerves and neurons. To get them in shape, we place our bodies in varied positions, then focus mentally and make our brains do the heavy lifting. Ready? Let's get to it.

Joint Alignment

Joint alignment exercises follow a common process:

- Align a body part mentally
- Check it visually
- Correct as needed
- Repeat until your brain learns the position

This sequence works for all planes of alignment, so you can be creative in devising different actions with various joints. Pay special attention to the areas of misalignment that you identified in chapter 8 (p. 97).

- To start, stand in front of a mirror with your eyes closed. Square your shoulders so that each one feels the same distance from your ears. When your brain says they're aligned, open your eyes and look. Are they? If you're off by a smidge, close your eyes and readjust until both shoulders are in line. Try to memorize the aligned position. Use the same technique on your elbows, hips, knees, ankles, and feet. Align, check, and correct for a few minutes every day, and within a week you'll see results. When your mental alignment is accurate at a standstill, try walking or bending into each position. Preserving alignment while you move is especially effective at training the brain.
- Alignment techniques can be done standing, seated, lying down with bent knees, lying flat, or in the saddle on your horse. They can also be performed near a wall, so that you move joints one at a time

to touch the wall. Close your eyes and make your brain judge the distance, practicing until joints on both sides (for example, both shoulders, hips, or knees) move with equal facility and coordination. Have a friend take photos of you from various perspectives while mounted, then study them for misalignments. The position your brain says is square could be antigogglin!

Balance

Balance matters on a horse—a hint of unplanned forward or backward movement in a jumper rider's upper body can make the difference between a clean leap and a dirty stop. Have you ever flown off a horse after a hard refusal, with your skull playing the role of aimed missile? It smarts. It's not great for your neurons, either.

- To avoid the ballistic missile program, stand on one foot with your arms extended to the sides. Focus on an eye-level point in the distance, without using a mirror. When you can stand for 30 seconds on each foot, try it with your arms at your sides, then with your eyes closed. Advance to increasingly pliable surfaces like a thick mat or a balance disc. (It looks like a puffy dinner plate with rubber nubs.) When you've mastered those, stand one-footed on the round side of a BOSU half-ball. Eventually, proceed to the flat side of the half-ball, then to a balance board (a small platform mounted on a hard ball). Be careful as you try new surfaces; you want to build proprioceptors, not bruises.
- Leaning also tunes proprioception. Stand with your feet shoulder-width apart, about 2 feet from a wall. Keep your hands near your waist in case you need them for support. Lean forward (toward the wall) with your eyes closed until you are just about to lose your balance, then lean back into vertical position. Lean to the left and right sides, to all four 45-degree angles, and straight back, moving your stance each time so the wall is available to catch you. Lean farther to make your brain enlist extra neurons for backup.

- For equilibrium in a riding position, sit on a fitness ball large enough to lift your feet off the floor when you straddle it. Lean slightly to varied directions with your upper body, trying not to touch the floor with your feet. Instead, use your brain to readjust the balance point from moment to moment. Take it easy: big balls look solid, but they can squirt out from under you like a racehorse from the starting gate.

Balance on Horseback

Balance at a standstill is one thing—balance on a moving horse is quite another. Start to improve your riding balance by learning a solid two-point position. Raise your seat slightly above the saddle with your shoulders in line with your knees. This works in both Western and English saddles— you and your horse are seeking mutual balance regardless of the type of leather between you (figs. 9.1 A & B). You want to ride the horse, not the saddle.

Form matters here, because the body cheats to compensate for proprio-ceptive deficiencies. You can experience this phenomenon for yourself.

- Stand in a two-point position while mounted at a halt. Move your feet slightly forward, and your seat will immediately fall, swinging your weight back into the saddle. Move your feet backward, and your upper body will tilt toward your horse's neck. Notice that only a fraction of an inch of foot movement makes a big difference in your upper-body balance, even at a halt. Tall riders have even more trouble learning balance because there's so much length above the fulcrum of their knee joints.

There's no sense training your proprioceptors to hold an unbalanced position, so invest in a lesson to learn two-point or have your buddy snap a side-view photo while you maintain it. Use the photo to compare your position to the ideal. When you feel solid in a two-point at the walk,

9.1 A Two-point position in an English saddle.

9.1 B Two-point position in a Western saddle.

practice it at the trot and canter. Over time, learn to hold the position during curves, gait transitions, and lateral work, too.

Many riders assume the two-point position is the same as a half seat, but USEF makes a distinction between them. Two-point is an exercise. It requires the rider's seat to be higher off the saddle and less flexible than the half seat. Half seat is an accepted competition position used on course while riding hunters over fences. Equestrians of all disciplines—English, Western, dressage, trail, rodeo—can practice the two-point position to build balance and strength.

Bareback Riding

Bareback riding is not for beginners. If you cannot ride smoothly and confidently in a saddle for an hour at a walk, trot, canter, and gallop, please don't try bareback riding just yet. When you are ready to begin riding without a saddle, do so on soft footing with a quiet school horse under the guidance of a trainer or advanced rider. Safety first.

Sensing the Details

For intermediate and advanced riders on calm steeds, bareback riding helps the brain match your center of gravity to your horse's. It also teaches the proprioceptive signals our horses transmit—signals that are easier to feel without a saddle in the way. Sensing the details of a horse's movement is the first step on the road to effective two-way communication between human and equine proprioceptive systems. Practice in a confined area before moving to open spaces that invite misbehavior.

Use a lightweight bareback pad for friction if your horse has a slippery coat, and add a saddle pad underneath if he has high withers. Start at a walk, but aim in the long run to do everything bareback that you can do in a saddle: walk, trot, canter, counter-canter, transition, jump, race, halt, spin. Focus on the mental aspects of this work—think yourself into balance and alignment; make your brain choose accurate positions while noticing the motion of your horse's body.

Advanced riders can build balance by having a trainer longe a quiet school horse while you walk, trot, and canter without reins or a saddle. Eventually, you will be able to do all this with your eyes closed, to really make those proprioceptive neurons sweat. To maintain good proprioception, make a commitment to practice this exercise often enough to keep your equestrian brain sharp.

Top riders develop an independent seat by riding bareback in two-point position or jumping in a chute bareback and rein-less, with eyes closed. This is a supersonic level of proprioception and strength—if you shoot for it, be sure you are in excellent physical condition with advanced riding skills. Approach the goal gradually with an experienced trainer to reduce the inherent danger of the exercise.

Muscle Isolation

Most muscles work together in large groups, so the brain has little need to isolate a given muscle and use it independently. Until we become athletes, that is. Equestrians need control of specific muscles and often must flex one muscle while relaxing another within the same functional group. Our brains have to be taught to manage this, so isolation feels weak at first but rallies as the noggin calls in extra neurons to help with the task.

To get the idea of muscle isolation, lie flat on your back. Flex then relax your entire thigh. Not your whole leg and not your keister—just the thigh. Good job. Now, let's get down to proprioceptive business: Flex and relax only the inner thigh. That's harder, but keep at it even if your brain only allows a feeble contraction and release. At this point, we just want our brains to turn on a few fibers in the inner thigh and nowhere else. Do the same for the front, the outer side, and the back of the thigh in turn, trying to get a mental "grip" on each area. Aim for a delicate touch; we're toning neurons here, not crushing iron.

Play with muscle isolation all over your body, just to get the feel of how it works. Start with easy spots, like the calf. You'll notice that muscles differ in the position that allows isolation—for example, it's much easier to isolate the calf when your knee is bent than when it is straight. In each case, find the muscle on a diagram, experiment with various positions, will your brain to tighten that muscle just slightly, loosen and repeat. If it's hard to find a given muscle with your mind, exercise it physically until it aches. Ah, there it is!

As your proprioception improves, pulse the muscle by tensing and releasing rhythmically. Progress by isolating the muscle further—the calf, for example, is actually comprised of three muscles that can be controlled separately. Instead of housing a stable full of "calf" neurons in your head, you want to develop inner, outer, and middle calf neurons.

When you've got the general idea, teach your brain to isolate "slacker" muscles that are especially important for riding. Beginners need to sensitize the neurons that control their inner thighs from groin to knees. Muscles of the abdomen, lower back, and upper back are also very important at this stage, but it's hard to improve proprioceptive control of those areas until you've learned isolation on your arms and legs.

Advanced riders can double down on more specific riding muscles. Let's take *teres major* as an example. *Teres major* is the fancy name for a small muscle at the back of each shoulder just below the armpit. It opens and steadies your shoulders and upper back as you ride. Now, it's true that you can also steady those areas by flexing the entire shoulder and upper back, but this is one of many global tensions that causes the beginning rider to slap up and down at the trot like a concrete mannequin, while the school horse flattens in an effort to evade pain. You want to move with your horse, not against him. And you want him to stay loose, which he can't do if you're tight. Isolate *teres major*, and you'll be able to lift and stabilize your upper back while remaining relaxed. You can also rate your horse's speed with it, slowing your spunky fireplug without pulling on his mouth (fig. 9.2).

Other sleeper muscles include the *medial soleus* which, when controlled separately from the calf, can suck a horse's abdomen upward to

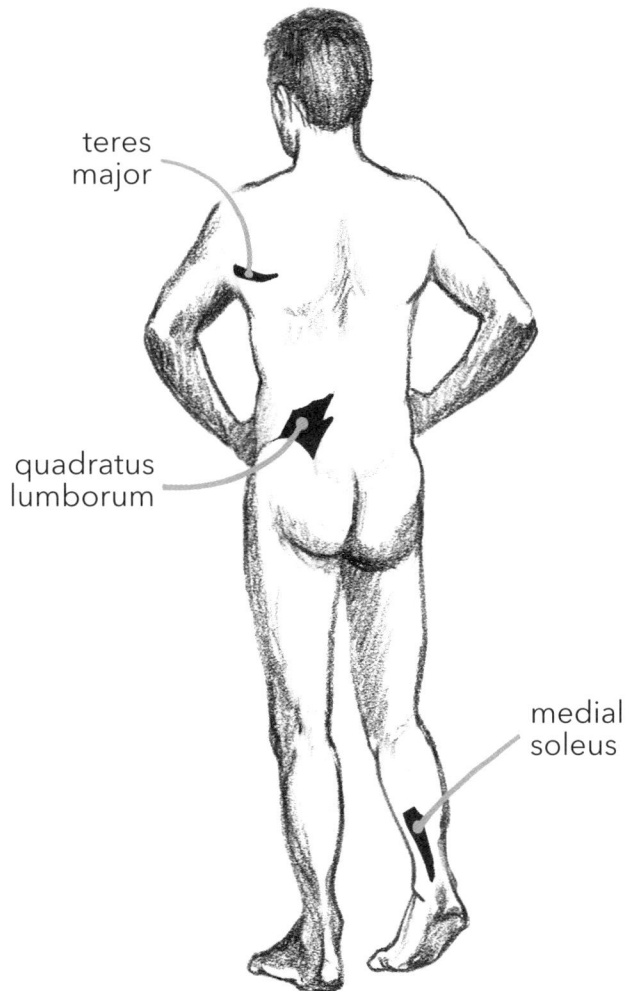

9.2 When you can isolate standard riding muscles like inner thighs, calves, and upper back, work on less common ones like these. They help the horse move in specific ways.

boost impulsion and enhance engagement. The *quadratus lumborum*, when isolated from the upper hips, allows you to sit deep in the saddle at the canter and swing freely with a horse's motion (fig. 9.2). Over-achievers can isolate the outer thighs from the gluteal muscles, to create an equestrian seat independent of the legs. This isolation places female seat bones on the horse's long back muscles for the perfect weight-bearing position that softens his back and increases his power.

Gradation of Pressure

Once a muscle is isolated, teach your neurons to contract it with precise gradations of pressure. Suppose you've schooled your brain to flex and relax the inner thigh independently. Now, try tightening the inner thigh very gradually. Instead of turning the flex faucet full on, ease it open one drop at a time. At first, the acceleration will feel jerky and sporadic as if the water line is spitting air. But with practice, the change becomes smooth and refined. Perfect this technique on horseback, and you can almost hear your horse's muscle spindles and Golgi organs say, "Ahhh."

You can use gradation to slip the horse into a new movement like silk, rather than clamping him into a tsunami of motion. Practice creating the entire range of pressure, from none to the tightest contraction possible and back again to none. Most equestrian brains need greater work in the lighter half of the range.

If a proprioceptive neuron doesn't have to be precise, it isn't. It will fire in response to a large range of tensions, like flipping a crude on/off switch. To foster precision, we have to expose those neurons to gentle muscle pressure. They'll calibrate their sensitivity to match your needs, each becoming tuned to an exact range of flex and stretch. They're specializing themselves for horseback riding and enlarging brain regions that control equestrian muscles and tendons. And—good news—with daily practice, noticeable improvement shows up in a few weeks. You can continue beyond that as far as you like because the brain's capacity for improvement is endless.

Transfer of Proprioception

Because well-trained, horse-and-human teams communicate brain to brain, each species' proprioceptive powers transfer to the other. But their weaknesses transfer, too. If you ride with your left shoulder lower than the right, your horse will compensate by moving with his left shoulder lower than his right. If you tip forward, he will move in a downhill fashion with his hindquarters higher than his shoulders. And so on, from one body part to another.

Flygirl, the Holsteiner I mentioned earlier, provides an excellent example of proprioceptive transfer. Her owner is a good lifelong rider whose leg was injured permanently in a car crash when she was in her forties. Because of the injury, she now rides with varying degrees of imbalance and weakness on one side. The horse compensates for her. When the two of them work together as a team, they are in good balance. But when a rider with centered balance hops on Fly, she feels lopsided.

During the time I rode Flygirl, the effort of straightening and balancing her body caused one side of mine to work harder than the other. My muscles became sore on that side, and one knee began to squeal. Fly's proprioceptive compensation for her owner was transferring to me. It caused my own body to become misaligned—a three-part transfer! And to make it four parts, I went to a massage therapist to free up the knots that had transferred to me from the horse. The massage therapist worked on the locations in which my body was compensating for Fly's—who was compensating for her owner's—who was compensating for an injury. It's like that old saying, "What goes around, comes around."

Take the Time to Tune Up

With better proprioception, you'll have faster reaction times, greater coordination, and superior balance—both on and off a horse. The sense of where your body is in space declines with age, by as much as 50% from age 30 to 60 in some studies. It's not necessary to perfect your proprioception in order to ride, but you might want to do it to preserve your balance and save yourself a fall. Your horse will appreciate the fringe benefits.

You'll also begin to feel your horse's body, noticing with the muscle spindles and joint angle receptors of your seat, for instance, the relaxation or tension in his back. You'll feel where his legs are and how they move under you. Feeling the action of your horse's legs, back, and sides is the precursor to controlling them, especially in complicated maneuvers.

These improvements enhance equine proprioception as well. Your horse's brain will become more sensitive to your aids because they are now easier for him to recognize. He will respond more quickly yet remain calm as your aids become gradual. Best of all, the two of you will begin to communicate through the medium of your bodies, with your movements travelling straight to his brain and his to yours.

Direct Cross-Species Communication

It's hard to overstate the rarity of mutual brain-to-brain communication between a predator and a prey animal. We do not see this level of communication between people and their dogs or cats, nor do we see it in such direct form without the mediation of language, symbol, gesture, or equipment.

Brain-to-brain communication is very difficult even within our own species—we all know what it's like to wrangle with tech support, automated voice systems, or family members talking politics at holiday dinners. We have trouble expressing problems, understanding accents, hearing past background noise, comprehending other people's wishes, and knowing in the end whether they ever addressed the issue or understood our point of view. To connect so directly with a different species—especially a prey species that has evolved to evade our predatory instincts—is far more challenging.

Let's look at a specific illustrated example, just to firm up the concept. In Figure 9.3 A, a good rider presses inward with her lower leg and that pressure is transmitted to the horse's side. It's picked up by sensory organs in the equine skin and muscles. Local proprioceptors then transform it into an electrical signal. From there, the impulse travels to the spinal cord and on to the somatosensory cortex of the horse's brain. The horse becomes aware of the rider's pressure.

In Figure 9.3 B, the horse's brain analyzes and interprets the rider's leg pressure as a cue to move forward. From the somatosensory cortex, neural signals travel to the basal ganglia and motor cortex, where movement is planned and initiated. The equine brain executes that movement by sending neural impulses to the horse's cerebellum and spinal cord.

In Figure 9.3 C, electrical signals travel down the horse's spinal cord to peripheral nerves that cause joints and muscles to move his leg. He steps forward, just as the rider has silently instructed him to do.

9.3 A Brain-to-brain communication is not mediated by language, symbol, gesture, or equipment. In this example, the rider is using leg pressure to ask the horse to step forward. Sparks represent neural activation in the horse's side, running through his body to his spinal cord, and from there to the somatosensory cortex of his brain.

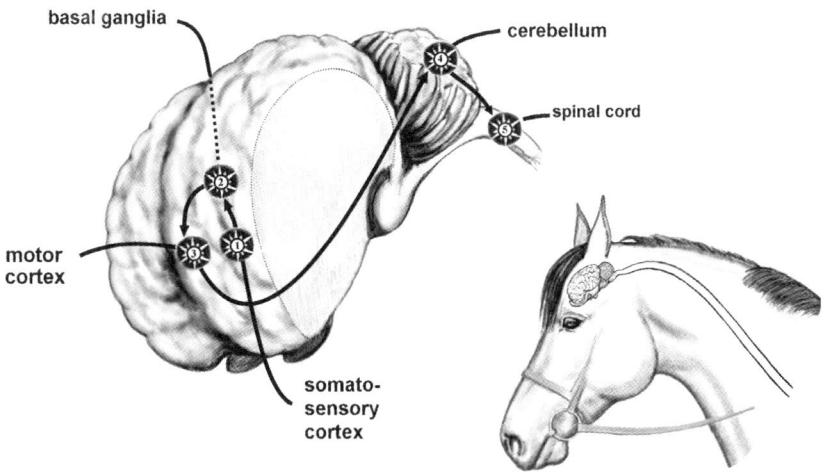

9.3 B In this simplified view, neural activation regarding the rider's signal travels from the horse's somatosensory cortex (1), to the basal ganglia (2), motor cortex (3), cerebellum (4), and back to the spinal cord (5). The horse's brain has processed the rider's signal and is now responding to it.

Building an Equestrian Brain | 125

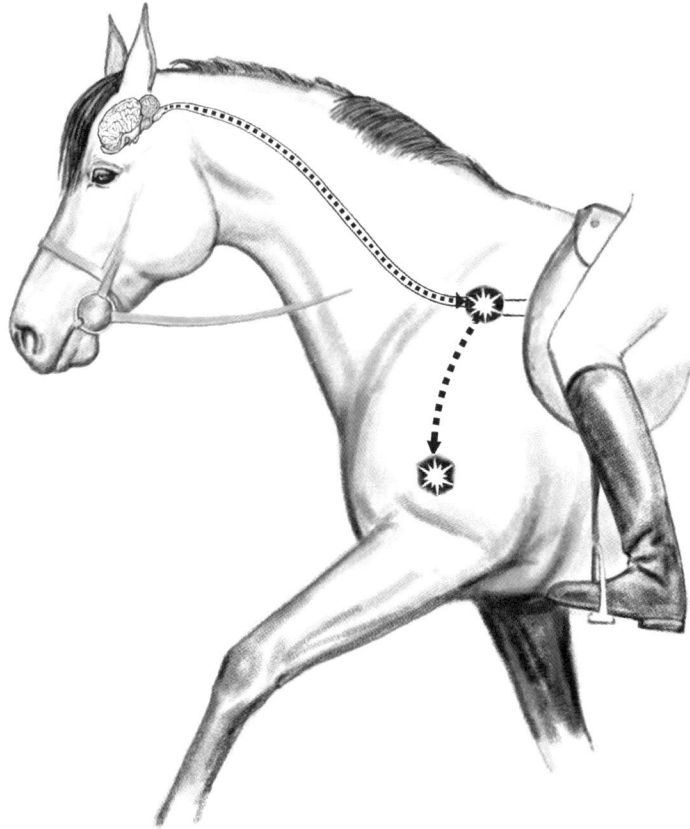

9.3 C Activation travels down the horse's spinal cord, then through peripheral nerves to his front leg, which now moves forward.

Finally, Figure 9.3 D shows the rider's body receiving signals from the horse, telling her that he has moved forward. She senses this movement in the proprioceptors of her lower leg, thigh, and seat. In addition, of course, she senses the horse's motion throughout her body and on her face, where a slight increase in air movement now touches her skin. All of these signals arrive at the rider's spinal cord and travel from there to her somatosensory cortex. It is only at this point that she becomes aware of the horse's action.

A neural communication loop between two species has just been completed. And with an experienced team, it happens in about two seconds. When that neural interaction occurs once, it's like a miracle of communication. The neurons between prey animal and predator are talking to each

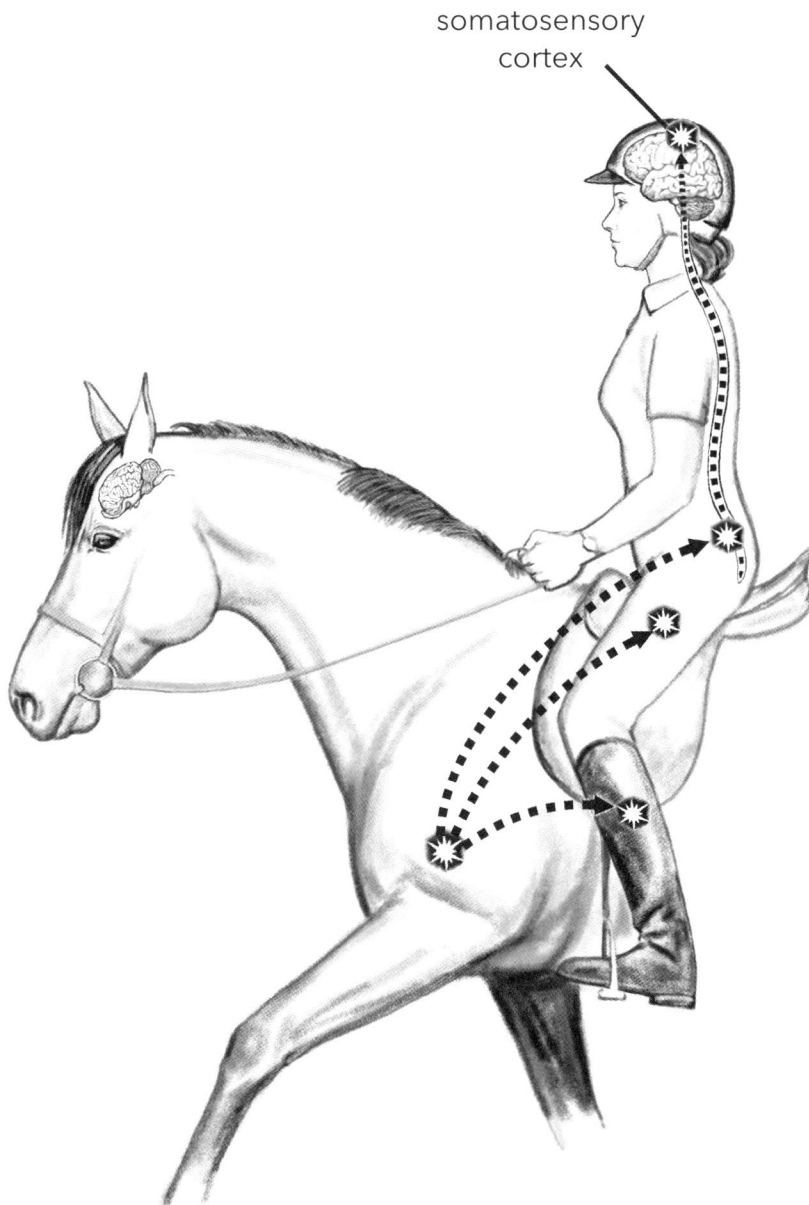

somatosensory
cortex

9.3 D The rider senses the horse's forward movement through nerves in her lower leg, thigh, and seat. Her spinal cord sends that information to her somatosensory cortex, and she becomes aware that the horse has met her request.

other with no mediation! But it doesn't happen just once. In a masterful ride, it happens a million times using most areas of both bodies. The team's two brains are in full neural communication. We talk of highly trained horses and riders becoming one, but really it is their *brain function* that integrates to become one.

The fact that horses and humans can communicate mutually from brain to brain, and sharpen direct communication with practice, is truly a remarkable feat. In time, ethologists, neuroscientists, and comparative psychologists will come to view proprioceptive interaction between horses and humans as a standard by which other forms of cross-species communication can be measured.

PART THREE

Learning to Be a Human's Horse

CHAPTER TEN
How Horses Learn

A 15-hand palomino mare, Princess, was the best of my lesson horses at accommodating many different riders. She was perfect for hunt seat equitation, Western Pleasure, and beginner jumping. Most schoolmasters operate by anticipation or habit, guessing what a green rider wants them to do. Princess did only what you asked. If you leaned left by accident, she turned left. If you sat forward, she sped up. If you hadn't wanted to go left or go faster, well you shouldn't have said you did. This reliance on human cues is a valued skill in a school horse because it teaches riders to refine their aids and take leadership.

Most people assumed that Princess had been a school horse all her life. But in fact, she was 14 when I met her, obese and unfit. She wheezed even at a walk, and her muscles flopped like jelly. She had a grand total of three under-saddle skills: tail another horse on the trail, run full-out in a straight line, or neck-rein tight and fast around stationary objects. Walking with steady leg pressure on both sides, she weaved back and forth like a drunk leaving a bar. Her balance was tipsy carrying a rider at a trot or canter. She had no idea how to jog or lope and leaned inward around every curve, no matter how wide. She was petrified when we walked alone in a nearby field. And if you rode within 50 yards of the barn door, she'd pretend to ignore it until the last possible minute…then whirl and dash in, scraping you against fences, cars, or anything else in her way. I probably still owe a friend a side mirror.

What imbecile would want this misfit for a school horse? As crazy as it sounds, I believed Princess had promise. She had a nice Quarter Horse body and a good mind under all that flab, and she deserved some attention. A barrel racer in her former life, most of her problems were rooted not in mischief but in ignorance—an excellent basis for education. Like a disadvantaged child, this mare simply hadn't been taught what she needed to know.

Horses learn in many ways and Princess used all of them. Understanding how she learned helped me tailor my training to her needs. In two months, she could walk, jog, trot, lope, and canter on straight lines and balanced curves at a consistent pace. She learned to direct-rein and bend into her turns. In one 15-minute lesson, she agreed never to run to the barn. Little Blondie slimmed down, muscled up, reclaimed her lungs, and became one of the best school horses I've known.

"Teach Me"

Horses are not just smart; they are learning *machines*. They scout for cues everywhere and soak up information. Once acquired, new knowledge sticks to a horse's brain like superglue. If there's a problem with equine learning, it's that horses learn too quickly—and forget too poorly—to accommodate human errors.

In equine environments, horses remember where fresh water and grass are located, what times of year such resources are available, where the best shelter is found and how to get to it. They learn the hierarchy of every horse in their group and know complex kin relationships and behavioral rules within an entire herd. They recognize the distinct smell of each animal in their environment, not just different species but also different individuals within a species. They recall which situations to avoid, and they don't forget events that caused them fear.

In human environments, horses learn the sounds and sights of various car engines and horse trailers. They show anyone within view whether they're accustomed to ramp loading or step-up entry. They recognize our faces and voices and clothes, they learn to associate verbal commands with specific behaviors, they know their own tack, they remember the meaning of 10,000 almost imperceptible body aids. Greet a horse you haven't seen in 10 years, and he will remember you. For many of these feats, no instruction is needed: Just stand back and watch the flypaper of a horse's mind capture everything that rubs up against it.

But when it comes to mutual performance within a horse-and-human team, animals need help. Each one is saying silently, "Please, teach me what I need to know, show me what you want." By nature, they use their heightened sensitivity for body language to seek the tiniest signals. They assume each one has meaning if only they can crack the code. Given a handler who uses the same cues consistently to achieve a given response, horses parse out human expectations the way bears find honey.

The trouble is that we humans are not as precise with our cues, or as clear in our expectations, as horses need us to be. We send mixed messages and reward bad behavior inadvertently, not realizing that our mounts just made a permanent connection between, oh say, rearing and resting.

We often fumble with which cue to use or how to produce it. We don't remember exactly which behavior it instigates. We generalize far more than our horses do—to us, the almost correct cue is close enough. But horses don't have human levels of categorical perception, remember? They learn each cue and response as a separate instance, with exacting detail. To horses, little differences have big meanings.

Many people think they've got to change course if a horse doesn't respond to a signal the first time. But more cues, different cues, only make the problem worse. Instead, just ask again in the same way you have asked before. The cleanest and most consistent cues work best. If the horse is paying attention, knows the signal, and can perform the requested behavior, he will. If not, you need to take a step back and teach the horse more clearly what you expect. If he doesn't catch on after repeated tries, something's wrong. And usually it's the lesson, the timing, the teacher, or the task.

Vetting the Task

It's important that a horse can physically complete the behavior you request. This sounds obvious, but it's a very common problem. Trot poles are a great example. You've probably seen them—usually four poles laid on the ground, spaced so that the horse places one foot between each pole at a smooth trot. These poles can be used at a walk or canter as well, but the spacing is crucial—it varies from 3 feet to 14, depending on the horse's size and gait. And 3 inches of variance in spacing can spell the difference between failure and success.

Riders often attempt to trot their horses through poles that are too close together. The horse either fumbles or balks—of course! An impossible task has been set: What else can he do? Unaware of the problem, the rider raises the poles—or gets larger ones—in an effort to make the horse pick up his feet. Some use crops or spurs to move the horse into the ill-set poles more rapidly, as if that will help.

When you have trouble with a horse, ask why. Maybe he didn't notice your cue, failed to understand it, or can't physically perform the task you requested. Have consideration for the horse who won't hop a cross-rail because the soles of his feet hurt when he lands, the cob who isn't long enough to canter a 12-foot stride, and the gentle giant who can't possibly trot through poles set for a Shetland pony.

Basic Requirements for Learning

To learn well, a horse must:
- Feel calm and secure
- Pay attention to you
- Be able to identify the cue clearly
- Suspect the meaning of the cue
- Be physically able to complete the task

Types of Equine Learning

Learning—to many of us—is just that. We learn. How? Most people don't know. Maybe because we have stuff between our ears. But when we try to teach a flighty beast manners or maneuvers, it helps to know how his brain learns. We can then teach in the way that best matches the brain processes at work.

In general, the basis of all learning is neural connection. Allow me to over-simplify: A group of neurons that represents water activates at the same time as a group of neurons that represents lever-pushing. They form a weak connection that strengthens with use. Soon the horse knows that pushing the lever on an automatic waterer makes water arrive. In brain science, we say, "Cells that fire together, wire together." Eventually the connection gets so strong that learned behavior becomes automatic (fig. 10.1).

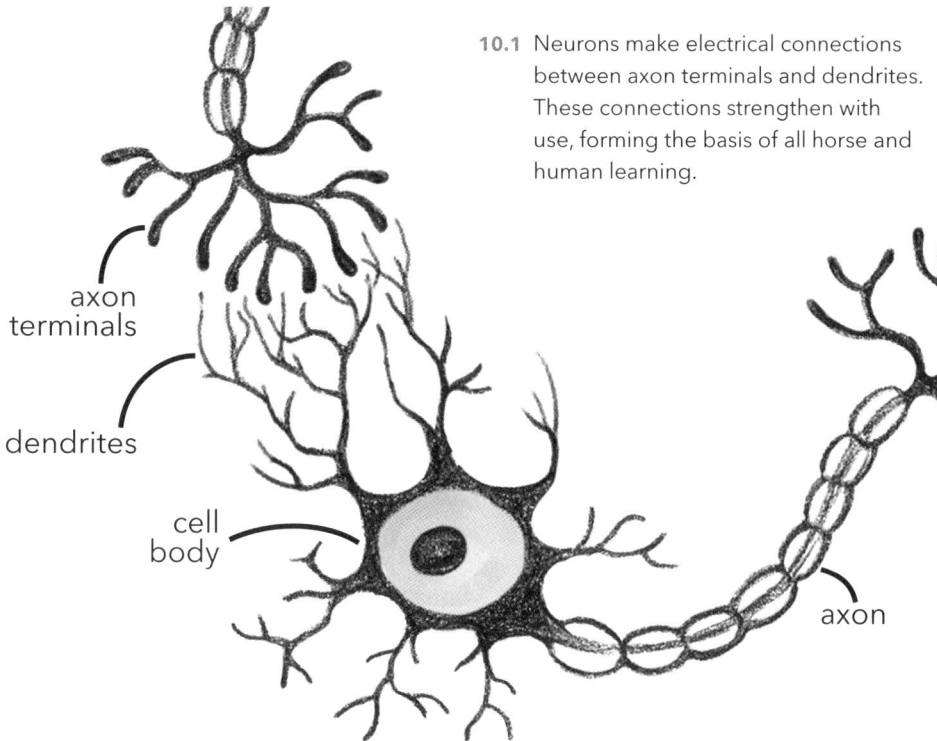

10.1 Neurons make electrical connections between axon terminals and dendrites. These connections strengthen with use, forming the basis of all horse and human learning.

Using neural connection as a physiological basis, horses pick up knowledge by:

- Association
- Consequence
- Observation
- Emotion
- Problem-solving
- Testing

Humans use these types of learning, too, but we add to them the powers of cognition, planning, reasoning, forethought, and judgment, along with doubt, bravado, arrogance, and fear of embarrassment. A whole lotta extra baggage, in other words.

Horses are fast learners partly because they don't carry that baggage. They're pure learners, too. A horse's behavior is a mirror of his past: It is not diluted with his parents' expectations, boss's demands, or children's needs. A primary joy of living with horses is that they never lie about who they are. Good trainers can work with a new horse for a week and know exactly how he has been handled—including the indiscriminate carrots an owner offers in secret or the weekly groundwork she claims to practice.

Learning of any type can yield both positive and negative results. Horses and humans gain knowledge that accrues to our benefit, but with equal proficiency we gain knowledge that is detrimental. We have to be careful what we teach a 1,200-pound horse, because he has such a great memory that we might not be able to unteach the lesson for a long time. It's cute when a frisky young mount bounces with happiness under saddle. But it won't be so cute when he's bigger and bouncier.

Learning by Association

Learning by association occurs whenever we link two events or ideas by space or time. Lightning immediately precedes thunder; for that reason, our minds connect thunder and lightning. A hay truck precedes hay in time, so horses relate the truck to the hay. From simple association, we get to classical conditioning: By nature, dogs salivate just before receiving food. Pavlov rang a bell with the food, and the dogs learned to salivate to the bell alone. Praise to a horse in the form of a phrase like, "Good boy," precedes a stroke on the neck, so the horse learns to link the words to the pleasant stroke.

Learning by Consequence

Learning by consequence takes classical conditioning a step further. Sometimes it's called *operant* or *instrumental* conditioning, but don't let the terms scare you away. Think back to Psych 101. Do you remember B. F. Skinner—the guy who experimented with rats and pigeons to explore the science of reinforcement? Reward a rat for pushing a lever when a specific noise occurs, and the rat learns to slap the lever whenever it hears the noise. Horses who happen to paw the ground when the hay truck arrives then get fed, learn to connect pawing with a reward—and there ya go: "Houston, we have a problem." Horses who learn that stopping to rest is linked with the phrase, "Good boy," will soon slam on the brakes whenever they hear that term—or a similar one like, "Goodbye!"—and presto, another glitch is born.

Learning by Observation

Observation is a powerful tool that should be used more often in horse training. Humans observe and follow suit every day—witness all the research showing that children imitate their parents and peers along with their favorite television and video game characters. Among the earliest demonstrations were the Bobo doll studies, in which children watched an angry adult punching, kicking, shoving, and striking a 5-foot inflatable doll. Left alone with a similar doll, the children did the same things.

Adults watch and copy, too, as if one person's misbehavior gives the rest of us permission to act up. Likewise, we learn positive skills when we watch a friend negotiate a conflict successfully then try the technique for ourselves the next time we're in hot water.

Household pets imitate—many people let their older dogs teach new puppies to come, stay, jump into a car, and walk down the stairs. Working dogs teach youngsters how to herd sheep, forage for food on sled trips, and work cattle. Saint Bernards learn from each other to rescue lost hikers in teams of three. Two of the dogs lie on each side to keep a victim warm, while the third dog goes for help. No training is supplied by humans. Wild animals learn by observing. In Australia, a wild dolphin was hospitalized in a training center where she watched her counterparts practice unnatural behaviors for exhibition. Upon the wild dolphin's return to home, she taught her pals how to walk on their tails.

Horses are experts at learning by observation, especially when watching equine buddies who are superior to them in age or rank. Foals who watch their dams being groomed and shod are much easier to groom and

10.2 Horses learn well by observation, especially when watching an older, familiar, higher-ranking equine friend.

shoe later in life. Stroke a mare, and her foal will soon come to you asking for similar treatment. Foals who watch their mothers accept frightening objects become more calm themselves around those objects. Young or old, horses can learn to open gates and stall doors by watching their peers.

Horses copy "join-up" behavior by watching their friends approach and follow humans, and they learn to load into a trailer more easily after they watch other horses saunter in without a fuss. If you have the Loader from Hell, let him watch a dominant horse from his own group hop on, get praised, petted, and rewarded with a yummy treat, and get back off. Make the observations comfortable, with no strings attached. (Don't show him loading problems—remember, horses learn whether the ultimate result is bad or good.) Observations of polite loading will allow your horse to accept future trailer lessons with greater attention and composure (fig. 10.2).

When horses live in indoor/outdoor stalls or paddocks, I sometimes teach them to urinate outside by rewarding that behavior. Their stalls stay fresher this way, and with long-term shaping they learn not to pee in barn aisles or show arenas. One of my horses was undergoing this work in a paddock/pasture he shared with a bay Thoroughbred hunter called Zeb. For several days, Zeb watched me reward my horse for urinating in certain locations.

So what did he do? Yep, you guessed it. Whenever I arrived, Zebber marched over and peed, watching my eyes and face carefully. He didn't seem to grasp the details of the lesson, in terms of where or when to urinate, but he got the general idea, "Okay, my friend here pees and gets a yummy treat. So, I pee and get a treat, too?" There it is: learning by observation and imitation!

Many trainers use an older horse while starting a new one under saddle. The wise sage shows the young buck how it's done, as if to say, "Here, see? They sit on top and you go around like this." Having a buddy nearby calms the newbie, of course, but it also shows him what's going to happen, how to handle it, and what sort of treatment to expect if he handles it well. Everybody needs a friend sometimes, right?

Even in natural settings, horses watch each other work. I used to ride in an arena bordered by pastures on both long sides. The pastured horses frequently came to the arena fence to watch the action, swiveling their heads back and forth as if watching a tennis game in slo-mo. When a mounted horse in the arena jumped a course of 8 or 10 fences, the equine peanut gallery tracked his loops, circles, and changes of direction, watching the horse clear each fence. The spectacle was hilarious—the pastured horses and the arena trainers looked as if their heads were yoked—but it was a great example of the equine desire to learn from watching others.

The equine brain also learns by observing humans. In one study, two groups of horses were given access to a feeding box that opened when a switch was pressed. "Observers" watched a human press the switch to open the box. "Non-observers" received no human demonstration—they were simply allowed to investigate the box and figure out how to open it. Four times as many Observers learned the task, and they learned it faster than the Non-observers did. Young horses were especially good at learning by human observation. Interestingly, horses who did not learn the task well— whether Observers or not—approached human experimenters more often, as if they were seeking help.

Horses have far greater ability to learn by observation than we give them credit for. We don't step back often enough to say, "Just let him watch, and let's see if it helps." Chances are, it will. Try teaching a young horse to tie, clip, lift his feet, drive in long lines, or stand for grooming by watching older horses model those activities. Pony a horse who lopes too fast off one who lopes at just the right pace. When your horse is ready to hop poles, pull logs, or open gates—whatever—let him watch a dominant herd mate demonstrate the maneuver. Then ask him to try. You'll need to repeat this show-and-try scheme several times, but brain science suggests that the technique will hasten training.

Until 1998, brain scientists didn't know the basis for observational learning. Then surprised researchers discovered brain cells known as *mirror neurons*. Here comes the neuro-speak, so bear with me for a minute. Mirror neurons are brain cells that code action. They do not cause our muscles to execute the action—neurons in the motor cortex do that. Instead, *mirror* neurons prepare *motor* neurons to perform specific tasks, the way a symphony conductor lifts the baton before the music begins. For example, when I pick up a cup, my mirror neurons tell my motor neurons to be ready to alert my muscles to execute that action. Fair enough.

But here's the shocker: When you watch me pick up that cup, the mirror neurons in your brain fire the same way and at the same strength as they do in mine. In other words, these microscopic mirror cells do not distinguish between my action and yours. If you think about this, it's pretty remarkable—my action is represented by *your* neurons!

Loading with Mirror Neurons

When a horse watches an equine friend load into a trailer quietly, his own mirror neurons fire. Both the friend and the observer are calm, so neither horse's neural firing includes fraught emotion. As the observing horse sees this tranquil activity repeated, his neural connections for "loading-minus-fear" strengthen. Later, when the observing horse tries to load on his own, his brain will help him do so calmly. Fear has been etched out of the neural equation.

Mirror neurons are equally helpful to riders. Developing riding skill is largely a matter of honing the activation patterns of a bunch of motor neurons in the brain. Mirror neurons allow us to activate the coding of those cells merely by watching someone else ride. So, when you can't participate, at least get out there beside the arena with the pastured horses and watch.

Learning by Emotion

Brain chemicals cause emotion to create especially strong memories. When an event occurs that triggers fear, for example, the brain releases stress hormones of corticosterone, vasopressin, and epinephrine. These chemicals prepare the body for a fight-or-flight response and set the memory of that event in neural concrete. Why? Because to survive, we must remember fearful experiences—they're dangerous and need to be avoided in the future.

Although fear consolidates memory, it's not a tool for learning that we wish to use. It's too strong. It stamps an event into brain tissue, but without discrimination. So the horse ends up saddled with both the helpful and the harmful lessons within a given incident. By contrast, consider an experience that occurs without strong emotion. The beneficial parts of that memory won't stick with as much instant power, but neither will the detrimental parts. For horses and humans alike, teaching good behavior is always easier than unteaching bad behavior.

For optimal learning, try to cultivate in your horse the emotions of tranquility, curiosity, and trust. Encourage the horse to look to you for reassurance and leadership. These emotions allow human and equine brains to function at their best, and they give us more control over the horse's learning environment. When fear enters the mix, consider hiring a professional trainer to set your team back on track.

Learning by Problem-Solving

Southwestern Colorado is home to an 80-square-mile national park that preserves ancient Pueblo ruins. It inadvertently hosts a group of almost

100 abandoned horses who roam free and seek their own food, water, and shelter. The land usually offers limited sources of water and enough greenery to keep the horses alive. But drought conditions in 2014 caused the horses to ramp up their problem-solving skills.

The horses, called "trespass livestock" by frustrated park rangers, learned that there's little need to trek through steep rocky canyons in hot weather searching for muddy droplets of water. After all, the park's bathrooms and restaurants have water! Let's just go there. And that's exactly what they did—hanging around near faucets and puddles outside snack areas and museums, waiting for a drink. Of course, the rangers seldom allowed visitors to turn on faucets for these horses, but that didn't slow them down. The horses learned to dig for water lines and break them open. They learned to open ice machines near snack areas and help themselves to the contents. Nothin' like a cool cube on a hot day!

Now, before we leap to the conclusion that these equines sat around a conference table and discussed various strategies of water production, let's use our own noodles a little. There are a lot of things going on here: With their excellent capacity for smell, the horses would have sniffed out the most plentiful sources of water. Natural instincts for easy travel would lead them to civilized areas—why skitter around over boulders when you can just saunter down a road? They would have been rewarded on rare occasions by humans who turned on a hose—and they would have watched people turn on the water. They would have seen visitors opening ice machines. That's several forms of learning combined, as is common in real life.

Hmm, a horse operating a water faucet? Sounds sketchy. But journalist Wendy Williams writes of her experience as a young owner whose horse had watched her fill water buckets at an outdoor spigot near her house. One winter morning, the water in the horse's stall had frozen—a horseman's nightmare. Watching from the kitchen, Williams saw her horse solve the problem. He jumped his pasture fence and jogged directly to the water spigot. He smacked the handle with his hoof a few times to turn it on, formed his big horsey lips into a cup, and took a long drink. Satisfied, he then moseyed on back to the barn.

Learning by Testing

Don't be surprised at the beginning of a ride when a trail horse grabs for grass, an arena mount cuts corners, or a field hunter hesitates to trot. These horses are testing, and experienced riders answer by correcting with their bodies. Novices don't even realize they are being tested, so the horse ups the ante. Soon, our trail stinker is grazing belly deep in clover while the rookie tugs uselessly on the reins, and the eventing jughead remains behind the leg at a four-beat canter while approaching a big log jump.

Most people interpret testing as misbehavior. But brain science tells another story. Testing is one of the most effective means of learning in all mammals. To improve human memory, we test ourselves as we study, answering our own questions by retrieving a given piece of information repeatedly. We then lengthen the interval between retrievals until we can go for a week or a year without forgetting the answer. This process isn't limited to academic study; it works with procedural memory as well. Every time we post the trot, we are retrieving information about how to coordinate our bodies for that movement.

A certain subset of neurons activates every time we pull knowledge from our brains. This neural subset can represent anything from a simple yes/no answer to a complex sequence of sophisticated behaviors. And whenever it activates, the connection among those neurons becomes stronger. Soon it is strong enough to last. When we have a neural network that is triggered reliably by a test of some sort, we say we have "learned" that response.

Horses never stop testing because they never stop learning. Pay more attention to your horse's testing behavior. Reward him when he accomplishes a desired behavior or fails to perform a common misbehavior. Remind him of your expectations when he asks whether he can get away with a naughty trick. And be grateful that your horse tests you—it's his way of figuring out what you want.

CHAPTER ELEVEN

Negative Reinforcement

The phrase "negative reinforcement" is usually greeted with wrinkled foreheads and glazed eyes. Yeah, we know the term—but please don't ask us to define it. Many people say it's "punishment" or "reward," ending with that uplift in the voice that signifies a question. So, let's start with a clear definition: *Negative reinforcement* is a form of training in which we apply painless pressure until a horse responds as we wish. This pressure ranges from barely noticeable to moderate, depending on the situation, and often falls into the category of encouragement. As soon as the horse responds, we remove the pressure. Negative reinforcement is *not* punishment.

An easy non-equestrian example occurs when our cars train us to fasten our seatbelts. The seatbelt alarm applies pressure to our ears, stopping only when we buckle up. In equine terms, it's used when we press our legs against the sides of a walking horse then release that pressure as he begins to trot. Learning by consequence, the horse links equal leg pressure on both sides to the action of picking up a trot.

Shaping performance by releasing pressure is not often the best way to teach horses what we want. But it is the most common, and very likely the method you were taught when you began to ride. Because of that long history, it's our natural default mode, one that we fall into with little thought. Let's take a closer look at its strengths and weaknesses, and see how it alters the equine brain.

Displacement

Negative reinforcement works best when it's applied in a form that corresponds to the horse's nature. Horses use displacement in their natural lives every day—a dominant mare pins one ear to get a disobedient subordinate to move away from the food. If the ear isn't enough, she bites or kicks, and the other horse gets out of her way. Horses displace people by swinging their heads or hindquarters toward us, stepping into us, pushing against us, biting, or kicking—just as they move other horses. Sometimes they are gentle in these actions, sometimes not. But there's no doubt that horses know how to move us around if we let them. Because displacement is a natural equine tool, we can harness it for greater learning.

To meet the horse's displacing nature, we choose a type of pressure that accommodates it. Take leg pressure, for instance. Why don't we use eye blinks, bicep curls, or words like, "Hurry up, slowpoke!" to get a horse to speed up? Because leg pressure mimics the horse's natural means of displacement—he moves away from pressure no matter who applies it. If you apply pressure to a horse's left side, he moves to the right, and vice versa. Equal pressure on both sides sends him forward. Theoretically, he could choose to move backward (even on a loose rein), but backward motion is much less natural and consequently rare in a green horse.

As soon as the horse responds in a natural way that fits a rider's desire, like moving from a walk to a trot, we remove the pressure. Ahh… to a horse, that feels good. Horses do not like pressure and will work to avoid it. If you release immediately, the equine brain will connect its action with your response. Next time you press with both legs, the horse will speed up again, hoping to achieve the same release.

Nuts and Bolts

The association between pressure and release occurs when two neural networks become linked by simultaneous activation. One group of neurons in the horse's brain represents the sensation of your leg pressure. You press, certain brain cells light up, and he feels. A different set of neurons represents forward movement. When the two networks—pressure sensation and forward movement—fire at or near the same time, they are linked through a chemical process we call *long-term potentiation*.

Timing by the Brain

Long-term potentiation is a form of priming. Active neurons remain more fully awake for a while after they first fire. During this time, they fire more quickly and intensely at any event that stimulates them. Releasing pressure during these first few seconds of long-term potentiation causes two networks to become connected in the horse's brain. Release your pressure too early, and the first network isn't activated yet. Too late, and its priming is weak. Equine brain function demands careful timing to create the link between your pressure and your horse's response.

Trainers use negative reinforcement to teach the green horse to respond to human pressures of all sorts. A young horse's first mounted canter is usually confusing for him, even if he knows the voice command from groundwork. He has been ridden at a walk and trot, learning the basics of stop, go, turn, circle, and loop. But cantering with a rider is something new—suddenly the trainer is using the pressure of only one leg, yet her upper body position and light rein suggests that she wants him to speed up. If horses used conscious thought, they might wonder, "Hmm, that's different from the usual trot cue. What does it mean?"

With steady pressure from one leg, and some awkward moments at a jarring super-trot, the green horse will eventually try a canter. Imagine him saying, "Okay, it's not the fast trot she wants because her leg is still pressing my right side. I can try throwing my head…no, that's not it. How about a stop? No, she pushes with both legs when I do that. Well, let's try some canter…" The moment this baby starts to canter, the trainer releases leg pressure and moves comfortably with the horse. The horse now knows,

"Aha! That's what one leg means." His brain uses long-term potentiation to connect the two networks and learn the lesson. Over time, of course, we will sharpen that horse's perception of our cues in many ways. But at the very beginning—after suitable groundwork—one leg, a light rein, and some stick-to-it-iveness is all the mounted canter takes.

Later Stages

Negative reinforcement works best in early stages of horse training, but it is used commonly at later stages as well. The half-halt into a downward transition is a case in point. Suppose you are trotting and wish to walk. You hold your seat in a stilling tempo that resists the horse's back movement. He feels that pressure and responds by slowing down to accommodate your rhythm. When he walks, you release seat resistance and move with him once again. He learns the half-halt in this way and will respond more effectively each time, as the two neural networks wire together through practice.

The equestrian seat is a critical source of training pressure. A good rider's seat variations change by many units of physical force and in all different directions—up, down, left, right, forward, back, diagonal, and circular. (Researchers actually measure this stuff with seat pressure sensor pads attached to saddles.) Eventually, a highly trained horse will respond to seat variations of every angle and force within 360 degrees per vector. When this happens, a skilled rider can place each of the horse's shoulders, hips, and feet at any location with her seat, in real time—at a walk, trot, or canter. Squeeze the outer corner of one glute, and the horse changes leads. Lift a quarter-circle with the adductors, and he jumps an inch higher to clear the hardest obstacle on course. Drop a quarter-circle, and he spins faster.

Using Negative Reinforcement to Correct Misbehavior

Work is another form of pressure to a horse, and rest releases that pressure. Alternating work and rest is a gentle way of using negative reinforcement to correct problems. Suppose your horse occasionally bunny-hops under saddle. If bronc riding is not your forte, hire a trainer to correct this behavior. But if you have the skills to manage it, don't stop or slow down when the tricks begin—instead, put your little rascal to work.

As soon as he bucks, push him forward, trotting hard and fast until he flows forward easily without hopping around. Release the pressure by letting him walk. Then try the initial maneuver again. Each time the horse begins to buck, push him forward into harder work. You are not trying to tire or punish the horse; you are teaching him that he will be relieved from the pressure of work as soon as he stops bucking.

Negative reinforcement works with more serious problems as well. Shadow is a lovely Quarter Horse mare, almost liver chestnut with a long strip and kind eyes. She had been trained as a reining horse when I found her for a client who wanted a hunter. Shadow had never jumped or even worn an English saddle, but she was an excellent mover, calm, smart, well-priced, six years old, sound, and local. I rode her several times and tested her over fences on a longe line, where she tucked her little knees up tight and rounded her back into a perfect arc.

When we got Shadow home, it became increasingly clear that she had been trained with an iron hand. She was accustomed to harsh spurring, and she had been drilled on a small number of reining patterns to the point of following them in her sleep. When Shadow didn't want to canter, her primary form of evasion was to run backward. And I mean, *run.* Our veterinarian found no lameness, so we knew her reluctance to canter wasn't a physical problem—besides, she was perfectly sound when running the wrong way!

Usually, this isn't a huge problem to overcome. But the backing cues Shadow had learned as a reiner were the ones we normally use to move a horse forward—a forward shift in weight; a forward movement of the hands, arms, and upper body; less contact with the horse's mouth; an application of leg pressure. The more you used these aids on this horse, the faster she'd go in reverse. Add spurs or a crop, and she'd win the Belmont Stakes backward! I had to give her credit for such a clever trick.

Shadow's misbehavior changed by virtue of four combined-training techniques:

- Encouragement to develop trust that her new people wouldn't hurt her
- Efforts to forget rather than practice backing of any kind
- A very consistent technique of negative reinforcement
- A reward beyond the release of pressure following each instance of that negative reinforcement

Each time the mare shifted into reverse gear at the cue for a canter depart, I held a neutral body position but tapped her rhythmically with a crop. These were not painful smacks; they were audible taps on her hindquarters spaced about one second apart, more for sound than pressure. They continued with the same timing and pressure until she stopped running backward. As soon as she came to a halt, the taps stopped. I rewarded her with a stroke and a moment of rest, then walked forward and asked for the canter depart again.

Shadow was earning an "A" in all other aspects of her training as a hunter, but it took six months to un-teach this one misbehavior. She followed the typical unlearning pattern: At first, she increased her evasive backing, as if to say, "This trick has always worked in the past and if I just ramp it up, it'll work again now." Then she began to respond in fits and starts, backing shorter distances. The next stage involved fewer attempts to back at all: true progress! Every now and then, she would test me—"Backing used to work; does it still?"—and I answered that it did not. Gradually, Shadow stopped testing her usual riders, but would occasionally test someone new. This pattern is very common in humans and horses who are unlearning entrenched misbehavior.

Finally, Shadow's reverse-gear evasion was completely extinguished. Today she is a relaxed, well-behaved, and cooperative mount for her happy owner. They compete in hunter classes, where Shadow is eager to pick up her canter and jump around a hunt course any time. Negative reinforcement was the perfect tool for this mare.

The Downsides to Negative Reinforcement

Despite its effectiveness in many instances, negative reinforcement can also hit snags. For one thing, *it has to be done on the fly*. Most amateurs have trouble coordinating their movements with a horse's movements in real time. Think back on your first canter, pounding along at a bone-jarring trot that threatened to shake the teeth out of your head, wasted muscles flapping in the breeze. About that time, the instructor says, "Press lightly with your left leg, just behind the girth." Oh, sure. I'll get right on that. Many riders at such moments aren't even sure their legs are still attached to their torsos.

Second, *coordination becomes even more difficult* while simultaneously timing the application and release of negative reinforcement. Because the height of long-term potentiation lasts for only a short period, timing must be very precise. Imagine you are teaching the leg-yield, in which the horse stays straight head-to-tail but moves diagonally away from leg pressure. To teach this maneuver, you apply your inside leg during the swing phase of the horse's inside hind leg. The "swing phase" is that teensy micro-moment when the horse lifts a leg off the ground but before he sets it down again. So, you apply inside pressure behind the girth as the swing phase begins, and if the horse responds by moving his inside hind diagonally, you release your pressure just as the swing phase ends (fig. 11.1). This interval lasts for less than half a second at a medium trot. That's precise timing!

Accidental unintended reinforcement is a third problem. You're flying along at a gallop and need to touch the left rein lightly to begin a large circle. Whoops! You "touch" too hard, the horse turns on a dime (exactly as you unwittingly requested), and you are sitting on the ground where the horse used to be. By coming off, you've relieved pressure in abundance, providing a potent lesson. If the horse could speak, he might say, "Holy wow! She wanted me to turn right out from under her. I did, and she released all pressure instantly. I'll do that again next time."

Strong equitation skills reduce this sort of unintended reinforcement. By riding with weight in our heels, upper bodies straight, arms and hands soft, legs and seat moving with the horse, we can deliver clear cues. We can repeat those cues consistently time after time, giving the horse practice at a new lesson. (We can also save on medical expenses!)

Fourth, and perhaps most important, negative reinforcement teaches a horse to obey and respond, but *it doesn't build much trust between horse and handler*. It leads a horse to seek, identify, and use human cues—all very important abilities—but it does not offer the added benefit of teaching the horse that you're on his side. That belief can make all the difference in a horse-and-human team.

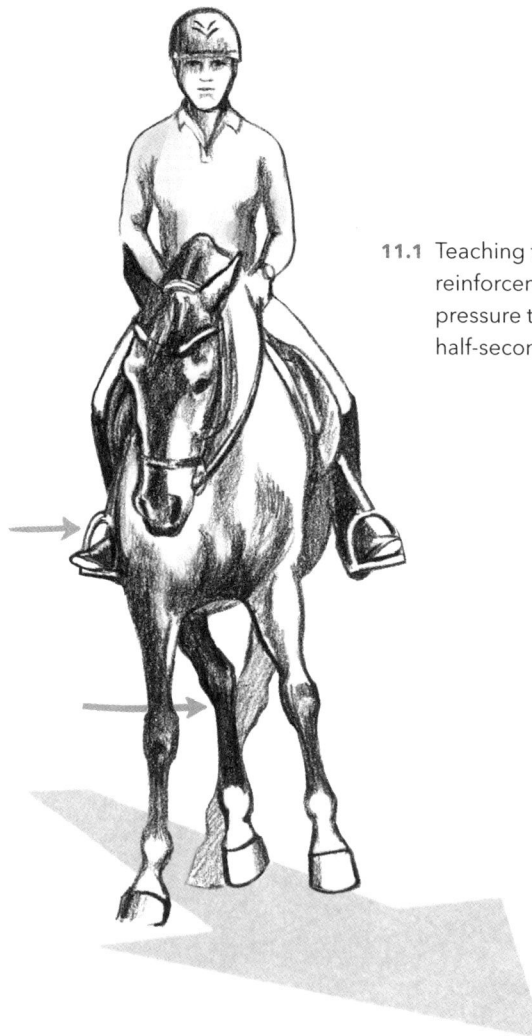

11.1 Teaching the leg-yield by negative reinforcement requires human leg pressure to alternate at less than half-second intervals.

Release

We've seen that neural fatigue prevents horses from sensing constant pressure. Negative reinforcement is used incorrectly when riders apply pressure but fail to release it as the horse responds. This is a frequent error. Horses do not respond well—in the wild, on the trail, or in the arena—to constant pressure. Some stop trying to please; others become too jittery to perform; a good number act out by bucking, rearing, freezing, or bolting; a few will fight. Pressure release is the most critical part of negative reinforcement.

Release works for all forms of equine performance, from leading to the levade. Holding a correction—like when a *touch* becomes a *steady pull* on the bit—impedes learning, annoys or frightens the horse, and places human strength in competition with equine power. No matter how strong you are, you will never out-pull a half-ton horse. Instead, your horse will develop a hard mouth, an inverted neck, and a sullen attitude—and you will develop some very sore arms.

To avoid steady pressure, try using the series of touches I described in chapter 7, releasing the horse when he responds correctly (p. 92). Remember the seat-belt alarm? It doesn't need to play continuously to cause us to buckle up; it can exert pressure just by beeping on and off repeatedly. Incorporate other aids as well, to help the horse decipher your cues. For example, if you are trying to slow a horse:

- Lower your body weight
- Bend your elbows
- Soften your legs
- Open your shoulders
- Post more slowly
- Provide less movement in your seat
- Adopt a more vertical upper-body position

If necessary, use your voice while the horse is learning; soon, he won't need it. Touch his mouth repetitively only if these other cues don't work.

Punishment

Riders sometimes mistake "pressure" for punishment. The pressure of negative reinforcement might be annoying or displacing at first, but it should never be painful or damaging. Many people also think of "correction" as punishment. This too is not accurate. To correct horses is simply to show them a better way of responding.

Chili, a chocolate Rocky Mountain Horse with a flaxen mane and tail, persisted for 10 years at trotting into the canter instead of cantering from the walk. When he finally came to me for training, I corrected him by lifting my upper body and his forehand before asking for the canter. I also corrected him by backing a few steps prior to a canter depart to transfer weight to his hindquarters. If he picked up a trot upon being asked to canter, I corrected by halting then tried again. With these corrections, Chili learned the canter depart quickly. No punishment was involved. It's like correcting a toddler's direction of movement by placing a gentle hand on her shoulder now and then.

Problems with Non-Abusive Punishment

Although punishment can be a short-term fix, it causes long-term problems even in its non-abusive form, especially when used frequently. Animals and children for whom punishment is the standard means of learning are often scared into anxiety, including lifelong "fight-flight-or-freeze" reactions. Many experience learned helplessness, a state in which they lose all motivation to perform. Some become aggressive or violent. A 2017 review of the effects of equine punishment adds several items to the list. These include reluctance to try new actions, decreased learning ability, and hostility toward the punisher. No one learns well under these conditions.

Even as a non-abusive educational tool, punishment is the least effective means of training a horse. We can define it as anything the horse finds unpleasant. Unlike negative reinforcement, it is applied *immediately after* misbehavior. It's a lesson we plan in advance, not an emotional reaction, and it should surprise the horse.

Extreme misconduct sometimes warrants non-abusive punishment if all other techniques of training have failed. I'm talking about severe transgressions in horses who know better. When a trained horse whirls and kicks you 50 feet through the air, runs you down from behind, strikes at you while rearing, or bites through your arm—all without cause—then non-abusive punishment would be necessary. But here's the thing: 99% of the time, a horse like that needs to be replaced rather than punished.

Finally, some "punishments" are flat-out abuse and must never be condoned: spurring a horse hard enough to draw blood; withholding food, water, or equine interaction; snubbing to a post; repeatedly whipping or striking a horse; working or chasing him to exhaustion. These actions are not only cruel, they are also counter-productive because they flood the animal's ability to learn. They should never be used.

Negative reinforcement is the most common form of equine learning by consequence, but it requires superb coordination, timing, and equitation. It teaches a horse to respond like a good soldier, but it rarely motivates him to want to please through excellent performance or to build a bond of trust with his handler. For that, we train by reward. In the next chapter, I'll explore the ways in which a horse's brain learns by reward and apply that knowledge to everyday horse handling. Now, if only cars would stop beeping and just drop a bite of cheesecake from the ceiling as we fasten our belts!

CHAPTER TWELVE
Training by Reward

Reward is the most effective means of encouraging horses to learn by consequence. Upon hearing this news, most people smile broadly and bust out the carrots, peppermints, and horse cookies. Whoa, there…not so fast! *Training by reward* doesn't mean shelling out treats. In fact, it works best without food and even then, it's tricky. That's why you need to understand how the brain uses reward to form connections. Then, you can apply that understanding to daily work with the horse, creating opportunities for success.

Training by reward demands more attention to equine behavior than negative reinforcement does. You have to notice the horse's subtlest tests so you can honor good conduct. Offering rewards at the wrong time or for the wrong reasons inadvertently teaches bad habits. And edible treats are especially prone to misuse because of brain function. You don't want to link the wrong actions with delightful consequences or waste the special power of a surprising treat by making it commonplace (see Reduce Edible Treats, p. 161).

Let's suppose a new friend hands Monty a carrot because she wants to be nice. He happens to gently bob his head over the stall door at the same time. Yum! A mental association has formed—bobbing equals carrots. Next thing ya know, Monty's smacking his head up and down harder, more often, and in other contexts, trying to win another treat.

Edible treats are like power saws—they work very well, but only when you know what you're doing. One or two instances can be enough to create a new behavior. When it's a behavior you want, this associative clout is wonderful. But you're less pleased when it's a behavior you don't want, like a horse bobbing his 100-pound head into somebody's face.

Chemical Associations

In the last two chapters, I looked briefly at the nuts and bolts of activated neural networks. Here, we need to slide into a little more detail. Most mammals learn by association and consequence. Some are much better at it than others, and horses land near the top of the class, thanks to their brain function.

Basically, a group or network of neurons represents an action. Think of a simple equine action, like bobbing a head. The brain controls the motion of lifting the head up slightly then allowing its weight to fall as the neck stretches downward. Certain neurons fire electrical signals simultaneously to cause that action. Each time the network fires, the head bobs.

Next, the electrical signals fired by this neural network become associated with an external event. This occurs by virtue of timing. You might recall that when neurons send out an electrical impulse, their capacity to fire remains strong for a while afterward. The associative engine is primed. During the initial activation or the primed state that follows, any external event can become associated with the network. If a carrot arrives while the head-bobbing network's potential to fire is still high, the horse will form a link between the two. Long-term potentiation is the Ferrari of horse training—but to train well, you have to learn how to gun the engine without making it backfire.

Let's add one more shot of physiology to the process. When a neural network fires in association with a new event, chemicals made in the brain are released to strengthen the bond. Some of them shoot across tiny gaps between the two associated networks; others well up in clumps of brain cells that are designed to accept them. We can think of these chemicals as a kind of glue (fig. 12.1).

So, neurons representing an action (head-bobbing) fire when a different set of neurons representing a reward (carrot) also fire. Like magic, the paired activation of these two networks creates an association. The brain's own chemicals glue the new link together, helping it remain strong over time. Bobbing now equals carrots in a physical connection that is as real as the spark that moves a piston.

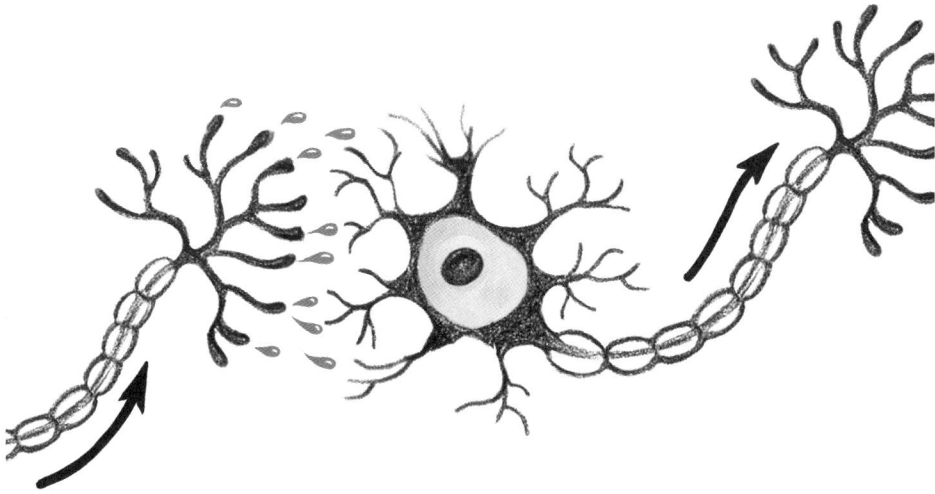

12.1 Neurons making a chemical connection. Neural activation in humans and horses is both electrical and chemical.

Dopamine Release

The glue that makes reward so powerful is *dopamine*. Dopamine is a natural chemical made by the brain that makes us feel good. Food when we're hungry, water when we're dry, the pleasures of sex, and the goosebumps of a perfect musical chord progression—all these feelings of satisfaction come from the jolt of dopamine that is associated with them.

In humans, dopamine forms a basis for addiction in which we repeatedly evoke pleasure through drug or alcohol use. It's so potent that many humans knowingly destroy their health to achieve dopamine release. Lab rats refuse water, ignore sexual mates in heat, abandon their newborns, and starve themselves to death in favor of pressing levers that provide dopamine stimulation. It's strong stuff!

Training by reward activates much greater dopamine release than training by negative reinforcement does. So, lessons are literally more pleasurable to the horse and more salient to his brain. Add dopamine release to long-term potentiation, and you've got a level of learning that's off the charts. Mammals don't forget these lessons quickly, so you want to be sure you're forming the right associations instead of the wrong ones.

Associative Learning in Humans

Humans also learn by rewards that are timed to coincide with the long-term potentiation of a neural network. But human minds trowel many layers of modification over the top of their learning. We're bogged down with cultural standards, social mores, general knowledge, personal hopes, familial expectations, past experiences, procedural memories, perceptual filters, ethics and values, cognitive controls, attention, peer pressure, the weather, and all the muscle of varying emotions. Okay, maybe not so much the weather, but you get my point: our minds stir a thick brew that often overrides the automatic force of a reward. Not so for our four-legged friends. Their learning is more pure than ours.

Mature adults are motivated more by a sense of self-regulation than a desire for reward. We want control of our fate, responsibility for our successes and failures. Even when personal control is limited, the human brain is motivated by believing it exists. Horses don't care if they are manipulated into a behavior by their desire for sugar. Humans do. Excessive praise backfires with us, especially when proffered for mediocre skills or easy tasks. Over-praised riders, for example, are often discouraged by minor failures and stop trying to improve. Receiving too many extrinsic rewards damages people's sense of responsibility for achieving their own satisfaction.

Abundant rewards can backfire with horses as well. The unexpected reward for a given behavior is the strongest—it adds an element of surprise, which boosts dopamine release. But rewards have less power to shape that behavior when they are doled out frequently. Why? Because overuse diminishes surprise and reduces the amount of dopamine that is discharged. Soon, the neural power of strong rewards is lost. There's a fine line here—you want to reward the horse for lessons learned, not for just being a horse.

Keep your mount's interest by rewarding when a new action needs reinforcement or a complex maneuver is finally achieved. The definition of "complex" depends on your horse—something that is difficult for that horse to do, at that time, in that setting. Up the ante as your horse learns: Two steps of backing are praiseworthy at first, but eventually it takes 20 steps—smoother, straighter, rounder—to earn the same prize.

Reduce Edible Treats

To horses, edible rewards—treats—are *crème brûlée* in Waterford crystal. They become associated with good or bad behavior instantly. When a horse performs a rare and much-desired act that is complicated, goes against equine nature, or has in the past been a source of deep resistance, he deserves a treat. The rest of the time, use non-edible rewards. It's too easy to reinforce bad behavior by accident. The yummier the treat, the more powerful the learned association. To train well, we must use that power with care.

Treats have another drawback: the horse always wants more. He'll mug for a second tidbit then touch your arm to remind you of your obligation. There's nothing awful about a touch, but horses escalate quickly in the face of a scrumptious nugget. Most horses who receive treats become more "mouthy" and less respectful of human space. Over the course of time, they can go from nudging to knocking you down, from lippy little nips to skin-tearing bites, and from delight in a baby carrot to demand for a carrot cake. Horses don't know they can hurt you—they just want the candy machine to work.

What Counts as a Non-Edible Reward

Most people assume that a reward is something very special, and unfortunately—for our own waistlines and our horse's training—most Americans prefer to reward with delectable tidbits of food. But in fact, a reward is anything desirable. Here are a few items that most horses like:

- Rest
- Known locations
- Quiet surroundings
- Equine buddies
- Familiar people
- Calm voices
- Gentle handling
- Soft hands
- Clear direction
- Strokes on the neck or shoulders
- Scratches on the crest or withers
- Muscle massages
- Soothing words
- Consistency
- Routine
- Chance to play

- Downward transitions
- Light rein
- Conditioned verbal praise
- Gentle handling

Add to this list any extra items your particular horse enjoys. Then rank them based on your horse's desires and on your ability to deliver the reward at the right time. For example, most equines find withers scratching and neck stroking much more pleasant than patting. Stroking a horse's neck reduces his heart rate—and yours. It's easy to deliver, too—it can be done within a second or two of good behavior using the back of your knuckles while holding both reins. This is a distinct advantage when you need to reward at a gallop and prefer to avoid a face plant.

Verbal praise is also effective while mounted because you don't have to change your body position to provide it. Pair it first with known rewards, so the horse learns that "good job" is a form of praise. After that, the words alone will do the trick. Just avoid the common error of associating verbal praise with slower motion—you don't want your harness trotter to put on the brakes every time he hears an, "Attaboy!"

Non-edible rewards allow you to pamper your horse, offer pleasure or appreciation, and aid learning. Better yet, they do not come with the problems that treats create. Often, we give animals goodies only to make *ourselves* feel better. But there are a million ways to show a horse your love. Spend five minutes scratching the "love spot" on his crest a few inches in front of his withers. He'll show you where it is! Offer calm reassurance in the face of fear; that's better than food. Tend gently to his wounds when he's injured; take him for an easy walk or a visit with his horse friends; massage his muscles for a while. Food sparks a horse's momentary attention, but non-edible rewards build longstanding bonds of trust (fig. 12.2).

Timing

Mammals associate a reward with whatever happened immediately preceding it. We have high expectations for equine behavior, and horses are usually alert and active when working in their horse-and-human team. This means they are likely to produce a series of behaviors in rapid succession.

12.2 Rely on non-edible rewards: relaxed gait, loose rein, physical stroke, and verbal praise make a strong combination.

For these reasons, we have to reward within two or three seconds of a desirable behavior, before the horse does something we don't want to reinforce. If you're slow to notice a desired behavior, it's too late. The spark has missed the piston.

The most robust instants of a training session (what I call "power moments") occur just before cooling the horse out, just before you dismount, and just before you return the horse to his stall or pasture. Why? Because these rewards create great equine comfort. Use power moments wisely. When you get the perfect slow lope, end your session and cool the horse out. He'll want to lope like that next time, in hopes of winning the cool-out lottery again. If your horse dislikes backing, have him back one or two steps just before you dismount. Your dismount is the berries. If your horse gets ahead of you when you're leading him, stop him at the stall door, wait, *then* put him away. Entering his stall is the Nobel Prize. Whatever simple action your horse avoids, get him to perform a bit of it during a power moment, and you will be teaching a potent lesson.

Unfortunately, an equally potent lesson is learned when you accidentally reward a negative action during a power moment. If you quit a session in frustration because your horse refuses to lope slower than 30 mph, you have just rewarded excess speed. When you dismount while the horse is dancing around, you have rewarded unsafe behavior. And when the horse hurries you into his stall, you have taught him that "pushing" is acceptable. Think about how the horse is behaving from moment to moment to be sure you are not rewarding bad conduct.

Pairing success and reward with split-second timing might seem like an impossible standard of perfection. Just try your best, and with practice you'll improve. Eventually, training by non-edible reward becomes second nature. The best trainers manage such unions all day long with little conscious planning.

Basic Principles of Training by Reward

- Rely mostly on non-edible rewards
- Seek moments of long-term potentiation (p. 147)
- Reward during or immediately after desired behavior
- Use power moments wisely
- Save the best rewards for the most difficult tasks
- Prohibit indiscriminate rewards

Ground Manners and Mounted Performance

With the well-timed use of non-edible rewards, horses learn many positive behaviors. Ground manners can be taught by reward, so horses learn to stand quietly, allow ears and underbellies to be groomed, receive injections, and lift all four feet. You can teach them in groundwork to stop, turn, slow down, speed up, wait, or back up—all without pressure on the halter. When you have his attention, a horse will cue off your unmounted body language quite well. Ground manners prevent injury to horse and handler, teach the horse to respect human leadership, and allow veterinarians and farriers to provide emergency care. Non-edible rewards can even reduce, though seldom eliminate, genetically based vices like weaving, pacing, and stall-kicking.

Mounted learning by reward works from basic boot camp to elite international competition. Let's return to those trot poles, spaced out properly this time. Hunters and jumpers don't just automatically trot through those babies. They've been taught not to touch the poles. You introduce the exercise at a walk. When the horse is comfortable with that, you space the poles for a trot—if he bumps one, you continue trotting and try again. As soon as the horse trots through without touching any poles, you praise, stroke, and drop to an easy walk. A triple reward! Later, budding hunters are taught in the same way to hop cross-rails and jump solid fences. Someday, with a strong dose of talent, training by reward can teach them to leap obstacles that stand 6 feet tall and 8 feet wide.

Keep in mind when training by any method that you have a neutral gear. Suppose the horse doesn't succeed at the task you request, but you're pretty sure he knows what's expected. Just continue working and try again. Reward success, but don't punish failure. Sometimes you have to ignore failure, regroup after the ride, and think of ways to break the task down more clearly so the horse can learn what is expected.

Generalization

Horses learn to generalize by reward, too. Suppose you've taught your horse to avoid touching trot poles in the arena. Without generalization, a horse sometimes associates place or time, rather than action, with a given behavior. He could come to believe, for example, that he is not to touch poles when they are painted yellow or located in the covered arena. He'll need to learn that the lesson holds for all poles in all places. Generalization occurs by practicing new moves in other locations, or with different equipment, using mild rewards.

Rewards don't always come from humans, at least not directly. Many horses learn to escape their stalls through rewards they deliver to themselves. This is still reward-motivated behavior rather than rational strategy: there is something desirable outside the stall that the horse wants—a basket of treats that smell like molasses, a well-traveled path to tasty dandelion greens, maybe a cute mare down the aisle. It's also dangerous behavior: horses who escape to the grain bin or the spring pasture can founder or die.

Incentives Are Not Rewards

Contrary to a thesaurus, *incentives are not rewards*. Rewards *follow* good behavior, but incentives *precede* good behavior. The classic example is holding out a carrot or shaking a can of grain to lure a reluctant horse from a pasture. He might come to get the grain, but he is associating that behavior only with the lure. If all you want is today's capture, incentives work. But if you want to teach a horse to continue to come to you, use reward instead. Reward is more effective for long-term performance because it builds rapport between horse and handler. You want the horse to respond to you, not to the pogey bait you're holding.

Training by Lure

Many current techniques of "training by positive reinforcement" involve holding whole bags of edible treats while asking horses to perform certain behaviors. The trainer then doles out the goodies, maybe 20 or 30 treats in 5 minutes, while Sugar Pie alters her behavior slightly until it reaches the trainer's goal. To an extent, this works, but not as well as training by reward. Why not? Because Sugar knows the lures are there.

Dopamine release is strongest with surprise, remember? So, when a horse is rewarded unexpectedly, his brain produces a huge surge of dopamine that cements the association between his most recent behavior and the arrival of that unforeseen reward. Successive expected rewards get less dopamine, and in turn produce weaker associations.

Many of my recommendations in this chapter are based on preserving the element of surprise. Over-treating a horse makes goodies commonplace. This is especially true when copious treats are given indiscriminately, but it also plays a role when specific desired behaviors are rewarded too often or too strongly. Instead, work with your horse's brain and use dopamine release to your advantage by avoiding lures and prohibiting indiscriminate treats. Make edible rewards rare, and offer them only when the horse achieves a difficult task. These suggestions will help to save your training power for those moments when you really need it.

Extinction

Anyone who has allowed a trail horse to snatch long grass while mounted knows that once taught, a given behavior can be very difficult to un-teach. *Extinction* refers to the effort to eliminate a learned association. As you saw with Shadow's runaway backing in chapter 11 (p. 149), there's a typical pattern to extinction: with retraining, misbehavior increases before it begins to fade. People who are not aware of this pattern assume their retraining method isn't working—it's making the problem worse!—so they change it. Instead, stick to the plan and give it time.

Rewarded misbehavior can be especially difficult to extinguish, for two reasons. First, many misbehaviors are based on instinctual movements developed over millennia of evolution. Pawing, for example, is a natural activity for a bored, hungry, or thirsty horse who is restricted. Teaching the horse not to follow this natural instinct will be a challenge.

Second, horses rarely forget a lesson that was once accompanied by an extremely desirable outcome. When a horse paws in cross-ties, what often happens next? The owner becomes exasperated and puts the horse away. That's a five-factor reward: food, water, rest, comfort, and buddies! Next time Mr. Ed wants to speed the journey to his stall, all he has to do is start digging a hole to China.

To reward well, it's important to make opportunities for horses to succeed, then watch carefully to see what they do. But there's a human brain bias that often gets in the way. I'll tackle that in the next chapter. Meanwhile, the next time a new friend offers to give your horse a treat, invite her to pet him instead. It's a higher level of care.

CHAPTER THIRTEEN
Seeking the Good

Bookie is still learning to respect human space and stand quietly while being tacked up. A bay Appaloosa with the perfect sprinkling of white over her croup, she's only three but has the conformation of an adult champion. She has a world of knowledge to achieve before she can turn a calf, negotiate a bridge, or hop a low hunter course.

Among her errors, Bookie sometimes tries to rub her face against people while being bridled. I don't want to make a federal case out of this when there are more critical lessons to teach. At least she's dropping her head and accepting the bit! So, each time Bookie turns to rub, I push her face away gently but firmly. Good training doesn't punish misdemeanors, but it doesn't allow them to continue either. For several days, I bridle from the left, she turns and tries to rub, and I push her face back to center. Human brains are designed to notice the presence of her misbehavior.

One day, Bookie holds her face forward while being bridled. In effect, she is asking a question, "Is this what you want?" The horse has been shown the one thing not to do, but she's not sure which of 10,000 alternate behaviors to offer instead. But because she is offering the *absence* of misbehavior, the human brain is likely to miss it. We don't realize we've been asked a question, so we don't reward the filly with a resounding, "Yes!"

Most people assume that the failure to notice Bookie's effort is merely coincidental, but it's not. The human brain is designed to perceive presence automatically, but perceiving absence requires time, effort, and attention. This innate brain bias causes us to miss chances to reward a horse when he does well.

Attention to Presence

Human brain bias toward presence is easy to demonstrate. On page 172, there are two diagrams containing a bunch of horse heads. Please don't look yet! When I give you the signal to turn the page, look at Figure 13.1 A and find the horse *with* a forelock as quickly as you can. Then look at Figure 13.1 B and find the horse *without* a forelock as quickly as you can. The captions will remind you what to do. Okay, turn the page and give it a try.

Because of the way brains are built, *it takes longer to search for the absence of something than to search for the presence of that same thing.* Consequently, people require more time to find the horse whose forelock is absent, even though he should stand out by virtue of his unusual look. For a stronger demonstration, show each array to friends who haven't seen this chapter and time them while they search.

The process of finding the horse without the forelock feels more difficult, too: You have to search Figure 13.1.B more carefully than Figure 13.1 A. These differences in time and effort occur because your brain is working against itself to search for absence. Seeking presence is automatic: The presence of one forelock pops out of the array with no effort. Seeking absence requires work.

This result is so robust that we use it in teaching the basics of brain science and research methods to college students. It's every lab professor's dream—forgiving enough to accommodate a budding experimenter's mistakes, but strong enough to yield a statistically significant effect. Most psychological effects are tiny differences measured by high-precision millisecond timers, but this one is large enough to show up with the second hand on a cheap wristwatch.

The high-dollar term for our slant toward presence is *visual search asymmetry*, but I prefer the plain old nickel talk: "pop-out." Discovered during the 1980s, pop-out occurs across ethnicities, social backgrounds, age ranges, incomes, and education levels. It persists regardless of the number of items in a display. In other words, you will find the horse *with* the forelock (in fig. 13.1 A) in the same amount of time whether it is embedded among 50 horse faces or 500. It's an unconscious and involuntary process.

On the other hand, finding the horse *without* a forelock (in fig. 13.1 B) requires attention. You must search the display item by item, taking time to inspect each face briefly. Because of that effort, finding the absence of a forelock takes more time as the overall number of items in the display increases.

What I'm getting at is this: Human brains use different brain processes for the two types of search and are biased powerfully in the direction of presence. For this reason, we must train ourselves to identify *the absence of misbehavior* that horses use when they ask whether they are meeting our expectations. To use the horse's natural tendency to learn by testing, we have to be prepared to notice and answer his questions.

Reasons for Search Asymmetry

Why do our brains rely so much on presence rather than absence? The two most credible possibilities are evolution and memory. Brains evolved over time, with greater survival among individuals whose noggins could find food and notice threats. There is little evolutionary use for speed at identifying the absence of berries on a bush. Instead, it is the presence of berries that keeps us alive. Likewise, in an equine world where predators chase you down and eat you, it's much more important to notice the presence of a predator than to get all riled up about its absence.

In addition to the evolutionary argument, the presence of an event acts as a reminder to brains that are focused on other activities. Let's return to Bookie for a moment. We are bridling the horse because we are preparing her to be ridden. We are busy grooming, tacking up, considering the more critical lessons to come over the next hour or so. If Bookie-baby doesn't rub today, we forget that it's an issue. To overcome this brain-based slant, we have to study the horse's efforts to communicate. Once you bring absence of misbehavior into your training radar, you will expand your ability to identify and reward it. Seek the good!

Our inclination to ignore the absence of misbehavior is relevant not only to interactions with our horses, but with everyone we know. Close family members hear little from us when they are behaving well, but all too much

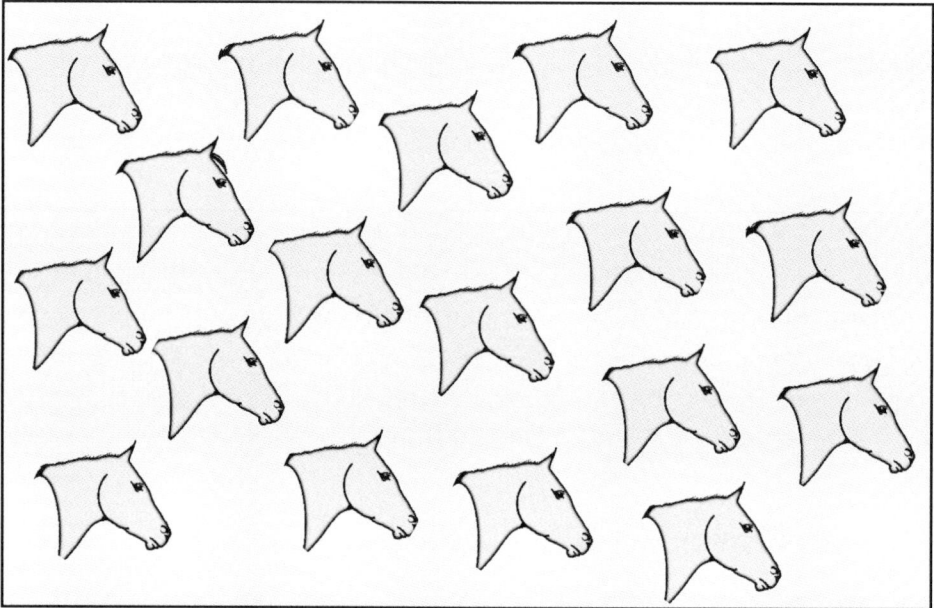

13.1 A As quickly as possible, find the horse *with* a forelock (used with permission from *EQUUS* magazine).

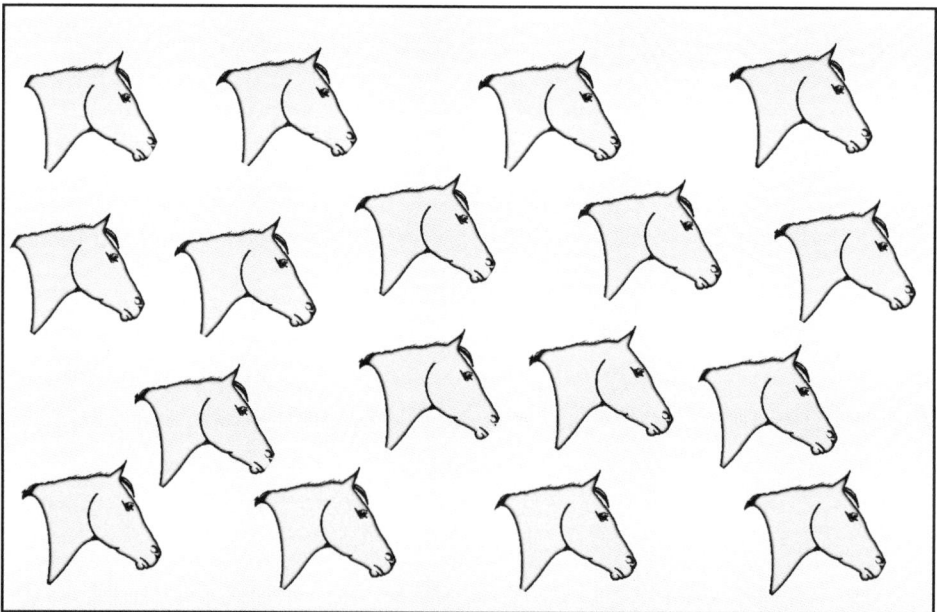

13.1 B As quickly as possible, find the horse *without* a forelock (used with permission from *EQUUS* magazine).

when they do something wrong. Turn that equation around, and you'll have much better luck—happier interactions and more positive behavior.

Equine Pop-Out?

If human and equine brains evolved over time to find food and notice threats, shouldn't horses also experience search asymmetry? That research has yet to be done, but I'm willing to guess that they do. Mammalian brains share much physiology, and perception is critical to all of them. Items that pop out automatically in the human brain include presence, color, shape, movement, and tilt.

Certainly, movement must pop out automatically to the equine brain. You've already learned that the horse's eye is specialized to perceive tiny rapid movements that the human eye can't see, so it stands to reason that the equine brain would be specialized to use that information.

Presence is also likely to pop out to horses. After all, it would be the very rare equid who might shy from an object that is suddenly missing! Knowing this, overrule your own search asymmetry and watch for instances in which the horse does *not* shy from a scary sight or sound. Then praise him for that absence of misbehavior.

Do or Don't

One of the biggest obstacles to successful horsemanship occurs when our animals do not know what we expect. This happens more often than most of us realize. We can reduce equine confusion by sharpening our ability to identify the absence of misbehavior. Horses are trying to crack the formidable code of human expectation—let's help them out.

Frequently, we communicate which behaviors we don't want but fail to communicate which ones we do want. We tell the horse, in effect, "Don't wiggle, don't buck, don't jig, don't shy, don't bolt, don't go too fast, don't go too slow, don't, don't, don't." It's like a broken record—for those of us who remember records—in which the horse is constantly being scolded rather than encouraged.

The horse learns quickly what we do not want because we show him. Yep, no bucking under saddle, got it. But think of how much more complicated it is for a horse—or a dog, child, friend, spouse—to suss out what we *do* want. The possibilities are endless! With animals, we have to use nonverbal communication including reward to convey our expectations.

Teach the Positive

Begin to think in terms of what you want from your horse: "Do stand still, do move forward, do walk on, do observe scary things calmly, do slow down when asked, do rely on me." Turning your mindset upside down—from don'ts to do's—is not as easy as it might seem. But thinking in this way increases your reward opportunities. Suddenly, the horse is being taught how much he does well, what a good horse he is, how easy it is to be successful at meeting human expectations. As your attitude becomes more positive, your horse relaxes and learns in comfort. You'll feel better, too!

Add Chances for Success

Another way to seek opportunities to reward your horse is to break the task down into smaller increments. Humans often give a horse tasks that are too big for his brain. For example, when teaching a horse to open and close a gate while mounted, we don't just march up and shout, "Open Sesame!" to the horse. First we teach him to halt and stand. Then we teach him to accept the jangling of a gate chain and the bending motion of a rider who needs to reach the latch. After that, we teach him to step sideways, later to turn on the forehand and haunches, then to neck rein a bit so that we'll have a free hand available. Only then is the horse ready to begin working with an actual gate (fig. 13.2).

One pleasant side effect of breaking tasks down like this is that each component provides another chance for the horse to succeed—and to be

13.2 Learning step by step. Gates are great mental exercise for horses in every discipline.

rewarded. In the gate example, I've created eight opportunities for reward instead of one. It should come as no surprise that the horse with eight chances to hear, "Good boy," will be more motivated to learn.

Equine Guessing Games

Horses who are praised for multiple behaviors will sometimes "guess" what you want in the hope of receiving a reward. Remember Cory, the off-track Thoroughbred who freaked out when a friend set a chair against the outer wall of the indoor arena? He underwent major surgery a few years ago and was not permitted to eat for 12 hours prior to general anesthesia. Now, this bruiser measures 17.1 hands in bare feet, with a super-stoked metabolism and four hollow legs—in other words, after 12 hours of fasting, he was *hungry!* When I arrived the morning of the operation, he performed his entire reward repertoire, one action after another, in hopes of receiving food. I use edible rewards sparingly, as you know, so he had to choose from only a few behaviors but he reached back a decade in his mind.

He started with a big "down dog" yoga stretch, forelegs straight out in front of him, nose between his knees, croup high. No luck. He stared at me, then tried it again, legs almost parallel to the floor this time. He held the pose and looked up at my face. I began to feel guilty. He moved on to popping his lips together, a substitute action I had rewarded years ago to counter-condition pawing. That didn't work. He touched my arm, then walked to his empty feed bucket and turned to me. He touched the feed bucket with his front hoof. Nope. He raised his head and stared over the top of the stall door at a bale of hay across the aisle, then moved his huge eyes from the hay to me and back again. Nothing worked—I praised and stroked him, but anything edible would endanger his life during anesthesia. At the risk of suggesting animals have human characteristics, I swear Cory seemed disappointed with my slow intellect.

Anybody who says horses don't communicate hasn't spent much time around them. They communicate with us all the time, just not in the way humans communicate with each other. Watch for your horse's guesswork—if he throws varied behaviors at you in succession, he could be trying to figure out which one you want. When he stumbles on the right one, tell him! Let him know through gentle strokes or a return to his stall that he has succeeded.

Set Him Up to Succeed

Every time you work with your horse, find something to praise. If necessary, set a task that you know he will do, just so you can reward him. Because your brain is biased against absence, try even harder to find some typical misbehavior that the horse has not done today. Reward him for not making that usual mistake—within a few seconds of his inaction, of course. Watch for his silent question, "Is this what you want?" and answer it. Soon you will have a horse who rewards you with the absence of misbehavior all the time.

Another way to improve equine conduct is to remove temptations to bad behavior and increase temptations to good behavior. For example, if your horse routinely turns to nip you for no reason while tightening his girth in the cross-ties, shorten up the off-side tie. If he is afraid of a saddle pad, place it near some green grass or his supplement bucket while he eats. Sometimes, you can alter behavior naturally just by managing the horse's temptations.

Counter-Conditioning

Many equestrians believe that long-term bad habits can only be trained away by punishment or negative reinforcement. But there is a way to put reward back into the mix, and it's called *counter-conditioning*. Watch the horse to see which behaviors accompany a bad habit. For example, pawing, lip-popping, head-shaking, and weight-shifting are all expressions of nervousness that often coincide. The expressions that are not yet entrenched will be easiest to extinguish when the time comes. So, to counter-condition pawing, reward one of the other behaviors as a substitute. Don't worry, your pawer won't become a lifelong lip-popper—when the bad habit has been extinguished, you'll stop rewarding the substitute.

Training for Better or Worse

Over these past couple of chapters, I've heard soft whispers in the background, little goblins in my office saying, "Okay, but um…I don't really want to *train* my horse; I just wanna ride!" So, let me address that concern. Many people own horses for pleasure riding and do not feel the need or desire to teach them anything new. And many people own competition horses and hire professional trainers to take care of the learning component. I understand and value both groups.

The thing is, though, the equine brain is built to learn. It's an ability that horses are very good at, for natural reasons, and cannot simply turn off. Whenever horses are near humans, they are making associations, picking up nuances, seeking information. So, in a very real sense, horses are always learning, which means that we humans are always teaching, whether we want to or not.

Whenever you interact with your horse, you are teaching him something, for better or worse. Hand him a treat just as he happens to swish his tail, and you've just taught a lesson. Put him away when he paws, and you're teaching "pawmania." Try a flying change by cuing with the wrong leg, and he'll be confused. His trainer won't be too happy with you either, because you're undoing her work. And so on.

We've considered the details of learning by association, consequence, and testing in the last three chapters. No one of these is best for all horses in all circumstances all the time. Instead, use training tools in a blend that works best for you, your horse, and the task at hand. Usually there are many different ways of teaching a horse the same thing. You have options!

Some people are better at using one training mode than another—this, then, is the one they should rely on most of the time. Likewise, some horses take to a specific form of learning by virtue of their temperament or past experience. And certain tasks call for the use of one training technique over another. Try to understand how each mode of learning works, then mix and match to suit the team's needs.

Horses look to us for leadership and lessons. When we drop our responsibility to lead, we leave our horses without a safety net in the human world. They need reassurance and education. So we have to play the part. Horses don't need us to be their friends or equals—they already have friends in spades within their equine herd. They need us to be caring leaders, to show them how to manage loose dogs standing at eye level in a viewing box, or to teach them to allow a veterinarian to explore painful spots on their bodies.

With some knowledge of how the horse learns and how to train him to cooperate with you, you'll be able to lead your horse to good safe behavior. That's what a horse-and-human team is all about.

CHAPTER FOURTEEN
Indirect Training

We've all been there: at the crossroads of the behavior we want and the behavior our horses provide. They're cooperative, even generous, most of the time. But sometimes horses say no. And when a half-ton beast says no, we aren't always sure what to do. We insist, they resist; we demand, they deny. A bit like raising teenagers, right? There's a reason for that similarity, and it's tucked inside the differences between human and equine brains.

Just above our eyes rests a mass of brain cells called the *prefrontal cortex*. This area is responsible for *executive function*, which includes planning, organizing, and evaluating. It allows you to identify realistic goals and plan step-by-step actions to meet them. Without executive function, you would have little capacity for forethought, time management, decision-making, or risk determination. Your attention span would be short, and you'd have trouble changing your behavior to meet new demands.

Teenagers have immature prefrontal cortex; horses have none at all. Don't despair: kids' brains will mature by about age 25. (No joke—the human brain is not fully developed until then, and cannot be expected to function as if it was.) Your horse's brain grows a few cells in forward areas, but those meager neurons aren't devoted to executive function. Instead, the equine brain allocates space to perception, fear, agility, and learning.

We can't expect the horse to learn in ways that require executive function, because his brain does not have that capacity. Yet, when a horse acts up, we tend to insist and demand. Why? Because human brains are built for goal achievement. Trainers often have luck with direct commands because their cues are clear, their balance is sharp, and their riding muscles and mental strategies are toned. But most amateurs don't have years of experience managing bad actors. And many horses build trust more easily through the use of indirect techniques that match the machinery of the equine brain.

Direct Training

Scout is calm in the arena but nervous walking away from the ranch. The usual route traverses a 20-foot-wide passage, narrow relative to the open spaces nearby. A three-story hay shed looms on Scout's right, throwing shade on the whole enterprise. To the left is a parking lot for heavy equipment: snow plows, field plows, 14-foot wheel rakes, oversized snow blowers, and a sickle bar hay mower whose edges glint like knives in the sun. Two steel drags the color of dirt lie camouflaged on the ground, gaping with holes that are ideal for catching a hoof.

Then there's that "impaler" guarding the entrance to this gauntlet. Oh, all right, it's actually a rotary tedder: 7 feet tall in upright position, when stretched out the tedder turns cut hay that's drying in the field. About 50 steel tines protrude 12 inches outward from its upright body, each the diameter of a sharpened pencil. A shying horse could jump sideways and tack himself to the impaler, then try to run from it. A bucking horse could throw you upward, where you might dangle on top with 20 steel tines through your backside (fig. 14.1). Boo-yah!

Many horses balk when the gauntlet comes into view. They tense their muscles, crane their necks upward, and big-eye the towering hay shed. The hot-bloods blow loud enough to be heard downtown—an explosion is imminent. The question for us is how to handle the problem most effectively.

Scout's trainer prefers the *direct* method: She pushes him forward without letting him pause. When he resists, she clucks and pushes harder, eventually adding spurs and then a crop. When he attempts to turn his head, she counters with a thump on one rein. Often, this direct technique becomes a spectacle of grand proportion as the horse struggles to get away and the trainer flaunts her determination.

A month after he began, Scout walks the gauntlet, not because he trusts his trainer but because he is afraid of her. He tightens his back, locks his

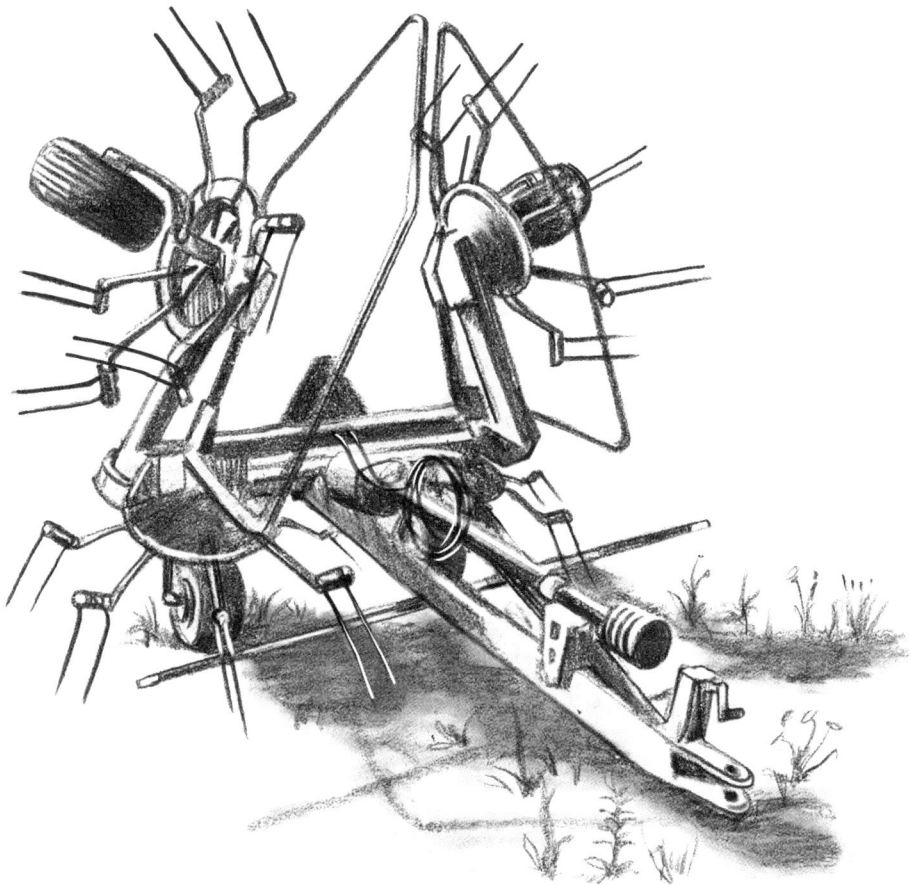

14.1 A miniature version of The Impaler. The real one is 17 feet tall–oh, okay, 7 feet–and contains a lot more spikes.

jaw, inverts his neck, and maneuvers his shaky feet at a mincing walk—but he goes through.

Scout has learned to fear his rider in addition to his environment. The added fear will cause him to become doubly nervous next time he's in a scary location. With practice, he has also become more agile at whirling, bolting, bucking, and rearing. He has learned that bad experiences happen in narrow places, and he will need retraining to surmount that. But he walks the gauntlet, so his trainer believes she has won.

Indirect Training

On Day One, Rico's trainer feels him begin to stiffen up as he approaches the area near the gauntlet. She angles the horse away without fanfare and finishes the session with other tasks. She wants time to turn her prefrontal cortex toward a strategy tailored for the equine brain.

On their next ride, Rico's trainer takes him an eighth-mile away, where she has discovered long-distance access to the gauntlet from its opposite end. Other horses graze nearby. There are no ominous hay sheds or heavy equipment. Long views open in every direction. Entering the gauntlet from this end, Rico will be facing his barn, moving toward friends and familiar places. The trainer knows, but the horse does not, that this side route is only temporary—a teaching tool to be discarded once the lessons are learned.

When Rico is comfortable near this easy end of the gauntlet, his trainer dismounts and leads him into it. He can focus more effectively on the task without carrying a rider at the same time. She strokes Rico's neck and praises him after 10 or 20 steps, wherever he is still calm and she has met her goal for the day. They turn back before he misbehaves and at her request, not his. She adds a few steps each day, turning back before he tenses. If she misjudges and Rico suddenly stops, she encourages him to take two or three steps forward and praises him when he does, then turns back.

Occasionally, something frightens Rico. A bird flies up, or a distant neighbor fires a gun. His trainer spends a day or two hand-grazing near the scene of his fear. It's amazing what a frightened horse will ignore when fresh grass is available! When Rico regains his readiness to learn, his trainer continues the step-by-step process until she can lead him all the way through this path of least resistance. Now she can mount up and begin riding Rico along this path. Soon he will negotiate the gauntlet calmly from either direction.

After a month of easy practice, Rico strolls past the "impaler," through the shade of the hay shed, and away from his stall. He does so without concern. His low head bobs in natural rhythm, his body is fluid, feet steady, ears soft and forward. This horse has developed trust in his trainer, learning that she will not ask him to overcome all his fears in one gulp. In the future, he will be more likely to go where his riders wish, even if the neighborhood seems questionable.

Why Indirect Training Works

The frontal physiology of our brains is what makes direct thought so easy to produce, and so hard for us to supplant. Frontal cortex makes up 41% of the human brain, more than any other area. Unless we grab on and hold it back, the prefrontal portion of this brain tissue takes over automatically—setting human goals, creating human strategies, planning human steps to goal achievement. It demands direct results from direct techniques.

Unfortunately, we tend to fall back on this default mode of direct thinking at exactly the worst times for our horses (as well as our teenagers)—when we're hungry, tired, annoyed, afraid, or distracted. At these moments, it's doubly difficult to wrench ourselves away from the brain's status quo and lean toward an *indirect* technique that's more likely to succeed.

Two additional brain regions work with the prefrontal cortex in humans to evaluate new information and decide how to respond. I'll use their anatomic names, but it's the process that we want to focus on. First, the *thalamus* (T) collects incoming information—sights, sounds, smells, tastes, touches, verbal, and nonverbal cues. Second, the *basal ganglia* (B) prepare the body for movement in reaction to that information. At that point, the *prefrontal cortex* (P) intervenes to consider the new data and determine whether and in what way to act (fig. 14.2 A).

In a horse, T collects information, and B prepares the body for instant movement. But there is no P to hold reactions back. So the horse perceives something and reacts instantly without thought (fig. 14.2 B). This ability has kept *equus caballus* alive for the last five million years. Horse training is partly a process of teaching your mount to depend on you for prefrontal decisions.

In teenagers, whose prefrontal cortex is not finished growing, a similar process occurs. Teenaged brains have some capacity for executive function, but it's slow and inconsistent. So, T collects information, B prepares the teen to react, and P might or might not evaluate. Enter the accidental house parties and drinking experiments.

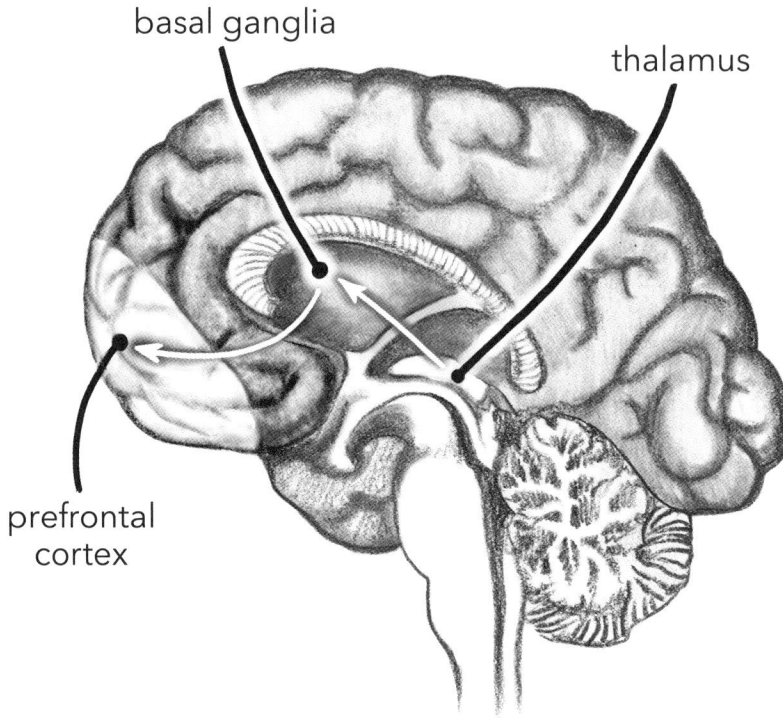

14.2 A The human brain collects sensory information (thalamus) and prepares the body to move (basal ganglia), but decides whether to move using the prefrontal cortex.

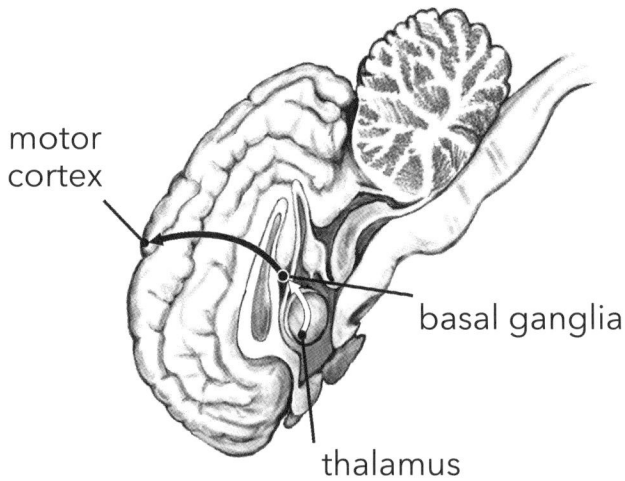

14.2 B The equine brain collects sensory information (thalamus), prepares the body to move (basal ganglia), and sends movement commands directly to the motor cortex. There is no prefrontal cortex to evaluate the movement.

Human Executive Dysfunction

Adults whose frontal lobes are not working well have the same problems our horses do when it comes to executive function. Such damage can occur through brain injury or natural deterioration. Fronto-temporal dementia is a good example. A disease of the elderly that is distinct from Alzheimer's, this form of dementia is caused by the shrinking of the human brain's frontal and temporal lobes. Memory, language, and intelligence remain normal until the end stage. But executive function is severely impaired from the start.

Individuals with fronto-temporal dementia cannot set goals, manage their time, plan actions in advance, adapt flexibly to new demands, make reasoned decisions, organize their own behavior, or anticipate the consequences of their actions. (These symptoms should sound familiar to horse handlers and parents of teens alike.) Often, brain damage precludes their awareness of these difficulties—they think they're just fine! Patients become frustrated easily and act out with inappropriate, aggressive, or even violent behavior. People don't like to be treated as if their memories, language skills, or intelligence are impaired when in fact they are not.

Victims of *executive dysfunction* also have trouble ordering the steps of a task and telling stories in sequential narrative. Think about describing to a beginner how to put on a horse blanket: "Hold the blanket at the center of the neck and place it over the horse's withers. Straighten the blanket over the horse's hips. Fasten the front buckles, then the belly straps, and finally the hind leg straps." One, two, three. Normal human brains automatically think of the procedure sequentially. Unless our prefrontal cortex is impaired, we do not say, "Fasten the belly straps," before we have told our friend to place the blanket on the horse's back.

Horse brains focus on one thing at a time, like a bite of grass or a haunches-in, not on an ordered sequence of steps that lead to a long-term objective. In addition, just as our brains are built for executive function, equine brains are engineered to pay special attention to fear. Indirect techniques work partly because they identify one task at a time, helping horses to overcome their fears.

The same techniques work for fronto-temporal dementia victims—set a realistic goal for them, create a strategy, plan small steps, respect their intelligence, and communicate clearly. Try similar techniques with difficult teenagers, whose pride and intellect preclude direct confrontation. They might be the smartest kids in the world, but their frontal lobes, and executive function, are not finished growing.

Other Applications

Because the indirect technique is foreign to human minds, let's explore a few more examples of how it can help you and your horse. Have a veterinarian check your horse's soundness first if resistance could be linked to pain or illness.

- Lefty won't pick up the correct lead? Urge her into a canter, then change direction to accommodate whichever lead she chooses. I know—that's heresy! But remember, the indirect method is only a temporary tool. When Lefty learns that you want her to canter on the proper lead for each direction, then you can begin training her to depart into that lead from your outside leg.
- Pokey drags around the arena? Let him "draft" a few horse lengths behind a faster buddy…or a mare. He'll want to pick up his pace. Once he has it, circle him away from his friend and praise his speed. Follow the buddy again as needed. It's much easier to maintain pace than to create it in a sluggish horse. After a few weeks, you won't need to follow.
- Smarty swings her hips away from the block, or walks off, when you try to mount? Practice mounting at the end of the session when she wants to stand still, rather than at the beginning when she's rarin' to go. Stand her next to a fence so she can't move her hindquarters away from you. Face her into a corner so she can't walk away with you in midair. Later, you can transfer her success to the beginning of your rides and to open spaces.
- Stormy's lathered up within 60 seconds of hyper-jig? Get off and lead her for a while, encourage her to relax on a longe line, or put her to

easy work like a steady trot and ignore the fussing. In other words, back off—added stress doesn't relieve nervousness. If the arena's a madhouse, wait till tomorrow or ride at a quieter time. Encourage Stormy to move calmly rather than adopting the notion that you are "working her down" to a state of rideable exhaustion. Give Stormy tasks she does well, so she has a chance to succeed every day. Resume her education when she is quiet and ready to learn.

Indirect Techniques with Groundwork

The indirect technique works well on the ground, too. No horse likes to be approached head-on with a brisk Type A advance. Instead, walk confidently but easily toward the horse's shoulder to halter him. When administering medications, try approaching from the side rather than the front. It's less confrontational, safer for you, and your horse can see you better over there, too. Instead of yelling, "Whoa!" 10 times while longeing or round-penning, slow your horse's movement by breaking eye contact, slouching, or squatting down; speed it up by engaging eye contact and standing tall.

With all training—direct or indirect—praise often for good behavior, so that your horse discovers what you want. You can use direct and indirect training in a thousand creative ways once you know the basic rules of each game.

Rules of Direct Training

The direct method is so human that we know its tenets by instinct. We ask a horse to perform a new task. If he does, we're golden! The direct method has worked. Praise the horse, practice the task on upcoming days, and pat yourself on the back.

But what happens when the horse resists? With the direct technique, we do not allow the horse to evade a major goal. We demand relentlessly until the horse performs as desired. We do not acknowledge the horse's fears. Such sessions are usually long and sweaty—often dangerous—because each party refuses to settle for less.

Settling would be "letting him get away with it." Some readers will have been thinking of that throughout this chapter, so let's pause to unpack the idiom. What exactly are we letting the horse "get away with"?

- Taking time to observe?
- Mastering natural fear?
- Learning how to perform a task?
- Developing trust?

Yes! These qualities are exactly what the best trainers are trying to teach.

Direct training often prioritizes human commands above a horse's fear. The horse must do as we ask. Why? Because we asked. Now…um, I don't know about you, but every time I demand behavior "because I said so," the results stink. It doesn't work on anybody—children, teenagers, adults, or horses. Even the dog sulks. On the very rare occasion that this attitude appears to solve a problem, it creates many new ones.

I'm not suggesting that the direct method be discarded. There are times when a horse obeys a light but direct request right off the bat. Congratulations! There are also times when a troublesome mount must learn to obey. Period. Powerful animals need to be brought up short when they mow you down at the stall door, run for the barn while you cling helplessly to the saddle, buck and rear when asked to move forward, or bite to get attention or treats. Such horses need professional training, and sometimes it will have to be direct.

Rules of Indirect Training

The indirect method counters automatic operation of the human brain. If your horse's behavior is not dangerous, and if you have the necessary equestrian skills to correct it, then train your mind to consider indirect techniques.

Start by refining your sensitivity toward the horse until you can feel upcoming problems before they begin. Notice the horse's muscle quality, head position, eyes and ears, tail. Listen for changes in his breathing. Allow your legs to seek the earliest stage of lateral evasion, a slight bending away from the area of concern. Teach your seat to detect stiffness in the horse's back.

When you've identified an early concern, move the horse gently onto a different trajectory before the concern morphs into a problem. The indirect method is not effective after the horse has blown up. We would be rewarding bad behavior if we were to turn away at that point. Instead, move to a task your horse performs well, then praise him and put him away.

Now, here's the hard part—sit down and think: Why is my horse evading this task? Is he sound and pain-free? What exactly is he afraid of? How does he perceive the situation? How can I break the task down into smaller steps that will be easier for him? Put yourself inside your horse's mind and imagine how you would feel if you were forced to attempt a task that scares you.

When you've analyzed the situation from an equine perspective, set a goal and plan the sequence needed to achieve it. Small goals are best for horses—you're not trying to cure cancer here. Fear is every teacher's enemy, so your plan must reduce the horse's fear one small step at a time. The most common error with indirect training is making the steps too large.

Develop your plan on an equine timeframe. Step 3 begins whenever the horse has mastered Step 2, and you have no way of knowing when that will be. If you ask the horse for too much one day, go back to the previous step. Give him a chance to succeed at something he has already learned. Remind yourself to slow down. It's not a race.

Revise your plan freely, but not during a moment of equine resistance. Remember the definition of insanity often attributed to Albert Einstein, "Doing the same thing over and over again and expecting different results." Note your horse's responses to your efforts, and change your steps as needed after you've had a chance to reconsider them. If you listen well, your horse will tell you what you need to know.

Indirect Training in Steps

1. Anticipate upcoming problems.
2. Redirect to a different task, then put the horse away.
3. Analyze the problem and develop a plan.
4. Start with a small goal.
5. Train on equine time.

To train well, by any method or means, honor the equine brain. There's no use demanding that our horses think like we do. They can't. Next time your horse says no, try an indirect solution and see how it works. Sometimes, in the words of the poet Emily Dickinson, "success in circuit lies."

Effective horse training is a long haul, day by day, little by little. The process should be as enjoyable as the final product, though there is that feeling of pleasure each time you succeed. When you're at the crossroads between good and bad behavior, adopt the mindset that your horse is *trying his best*—because usually he is. Praise for good behavior, ask for only a little more at each step, offer the time he needs, and he'll give you what he can. Maybe next month he will be able to give you what you want.

CHAPTER FIFTEEN
Easy Does It

Whew! I've been talking about a lot of activities—tasks, lessons, exercises, goals, projects, missions. A heap of effort all piled up in a small space. Your horse might be rolling his eyes, "Oh, no, it's worse than a clinic. Every time my people read a new chapter, I have to do more work!" So let's pause for a moment and think about that. All living things—horses and humans alike—need some down time.

Let me introduce you to Marie and Misty. Like many riders, Marie can't get to the barn every day. She knows that interaction is important for horses, so she spends a lot of time with Misty on the weekends. She's a kind intelligent person and a capable rider. She's surprised how time flies at the barn, but there are so many things that have to be done.

Marie arrives early on Saturday morning eager to enjoy the day. First, there's the grooming and tacking up. Misty stands for a thorough grooming, then chills out while Marie takes phone calls and chats with friends on site. Busy talking, Marie doesn't notice that Misty frets about the people hustling past her hindquarters on their way to the tack room. She expects Misty to stay calm while dogs dance around the grooming area or toddlers squeal up and down the barn aisle.

After an hour of preparation, it's time to ride. Misty strives to detect every cue Marie provides, an indiscernible orchestra of gentle pressures and tiny weight changes. When Marie wiggles a finger, Misty tries to soften her mouth or reposition her head. When Marie moves one leg back half an inch, Misty changes gaits. All parts of her body are held in the positions Marie dictates, yet she is expected to move in a fluid manner. Marie—like most of us—also insists that her horse remain attentive and obedient under saddle at all times.

Sweating after an hour of arena work, the pair cools out on a five-mile walk along a nearby trail, stopping occasionally to admire the view. Arriving back, how about a bath? Now entering her fourth hour of human interaction, Misty stands fast while Marie pours water all over her and soaps it up. Since nobody else needs the wash rack, let's do her mane, tail, and face, too—and how did those white socks get so dirty? Rinse well. Lather some antiseptic soap into small wounds. Scold the horse when she wiggles. Chat with the barn buds some more, and check for texts. Maybe a bit of thrush medicine in a hoof or two. Trim that fur in her ears; well, gotta let it dry first. Oops, almost forgot the dewormer!

We all know Maries, good people who can't stop ladling out the love. Any of us could fall into the same pattern, because that's how human brains are built. But by now, the horse is tired, hungry, and thirsty. She needs to pee. She tries in her patient equine way to say, "Isn't that enough for today?" But we're busy thinking that this morning has been fun. Our frontal lobes are hyped and happy, zinging along at top speed. Maybe this afternoon we'll practice trailer loading or participate in a friend's groundwork class. Or both! The weather's gorgeous, good for body clipping....

If we asked this much of our human friends, they'd never put up with it. By handling our horses for hours on end, we are creating physical and mental stress that's likely to result in conflict or injury. We ignore the clock until finally the horse has little choice but to escalate into bad behavior.

Human Goal-Driven Brains

What are you planning to do tomorrow? I've got to revise the first half of this chapter and work on Superstride's right-lead canter, then start on that relentless equestrian laundry. Even the least ambitious people have goals of some sort for a given day. Human brains are hard-wired to set goals and execute them with plans, even if the plan is nothing more than slumping on the couch with a box of cookies. Planning is what humans do, just like fish swim.

We've seen that the prefrontal cortex of the human brain is responsible for planning and organizing goal-oriented behavior. It identifies and sorts options, prioritizes objectives, forms strategies to achieve those objectives, initiates action, monitors our accomplishments, and shifts behavior when circumstances change. The prefrontal cortex is located in the brain's frontal lobes, which are so good at their job, we don't even realize how intensely they're driving our activity. That lack of awareness makes it easy for us to overdo. About the only way to stop goal-oriented planning in the human brain is to damage the prefrontal cortex—a solution I really don't recommend.

Lobes

The *cortex*, or surface, of a brain is divided into *lobes* so that scientists can refer to locations with ease. By convention, the human brain is divided into eight lobes, four on each side (fig. 15.1). The left and right *frontal* lobes extend from your eyes to the crown of your head. In very rough terms, they govern speech, movement, personality, and executive function. From the crown back several inches lie the two *parietal* ("puh-RYE-uh-tuhl") lobes, which are critical for somatosensory and spatial information. Drill inward just above each ear, and you'll find the *temporal* ("TEM-pur-uhl") lobes. They rule hearing, speech perception, and music processing. The left and right *occipital* ("ock-SIPP-it-uhl") lobes are in charge of vision and sit at the very back of the skull.

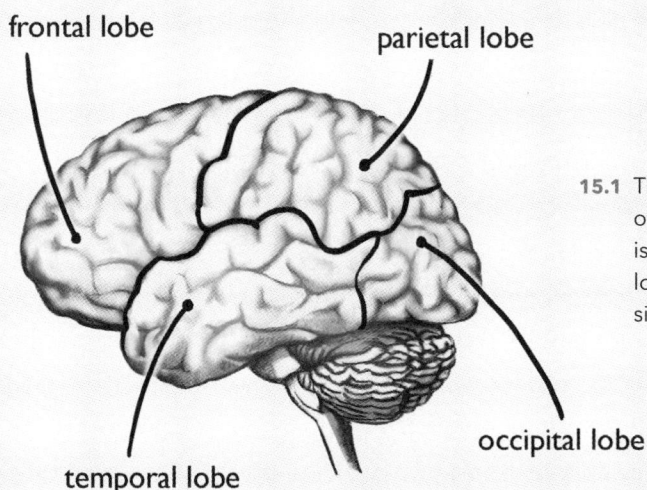

frontal lobe

parietal lobe

15.1 The cortex, or surface, of the human brain is divided into eight lobes, four on each side.

occipital lobe

temporal lobe

Of all mammals, humans have the most highly developed frontal lobes, making up how much of the outer surface of the brain? Right, 41%. By contrast, only 18% of our cortex is used for vision, and only 19% for movement and tactile sensation. So the frontal cortex is our Goliath; it hogs power even when we'd rather see it sit down and shut up. That's why sometimes we forget that we're expecting too much from our horses all in one day. We've got goals to meet even though we aren't fully aware of them.

Goal-oriented behavior feels good because it's socially acceptable, merits praise, and leads to success both personally and professionally. But it also feels good because the brain's most rewarding neurotransmitter—dopamine—is released and received when we meet our goals. Dopamine is chemically similar to mood-boosting drugs like opiates and cocaine, having much the same effect on the brain. When we form plans and execute them in service to desired goals, our neurons are floating in dopamine, slurping it up like liquid joy.

Equine Stimulus-Driven Brains

Our equine friends do not have goal-driven brains with bloated frontal lobes. Horses' brains are stimulus driven. In other words, instead of being motivated by internal plans and goals, horses are motivated by the sights, sounds, and smells in their immediate external environments.

Several distinctions between equine and human brains are relevant here. First, horses' brains are much smaller than human brains when body weight is held constant. The average equine brain comprises .1% of a horse's weight, whereas the average human brain makes up about 2% of our weight. Size isn't everything, but a 20-fold difference is probably meaningful.

Second, nearly half of our cortex is located in the two goal-oriented frontal lobes, while the remaining six lobes limp along underfunded. In contrast, horses have almost no tissue in the frontal regions of their brains and have no delineated frontal lobe. Equine cortex is devoted primarily to sensation and movement. Horses don't need frontal lobes: Why out-think a predator if you can out-run one instead?

Third, the human brain processes goal-driven and stimulus-driven motivation in two different locations: the frontal lobes and the temporal lobes, respectively. To speculate, it's likely that the horse's reliance on stimulus-driven motivation is due to the fact that equine brains do not contain frontal lobes. If so, it would be physically impossible for horses to motivate their activity through planned long-term goals.

Fourth, it's very likely that equine brains produce less dopamine than human brains do, even when the two are controlled for size. This claim is based on the fact that chimpanzee and macaque brains contain less dopamine and fewer dopamine circuits than their human counterparts. In addition, dopamine in human brains drives higher-order functions of cognition and attention that horses do not display.

Less reliance on dopamine in the equine brain would be good news for horses because along with dopamine's many qualities comes a critical weakness. It limits the amount of sensory information entering awareness. Dopamine helps human frontal lobes ignore stimuli that distract us from our internal plans—like the pesky clocks that tell us we've been fooling with our horses too long. But horses' brains are designed to be aware of external stimuli that might signify a lion's approach. To survive, horses need all the sensation they can get.

Highs and Lows with Dopamine

Although there is a normal range for the amount of dopamine in a horse's brain, individual horses also vary within and outside that range. In general, high dopamine within the normal range is connected with anxiety; low dopamine within normal range is linked to docility. Horses with levels of dopamine above the normal range are likely to exhibit stereotypies like cribbing and weaving. High dopamine levels in humans are associated with schizophrenia. On the other hand, horses with especially low levels of dopamine tend toward Cushing's disease. Their human counterparts are likely to suffer from depression or Parkinson's disease.

All of us are more or less captive to our brains, but horses have little choice in the matter. Human frontal cortex allows us to imagine various options and select the one that's best under existing conditions. We have the brainpower to think, "Gee, maybe I've done enough with this horse today." We can then ponder the tasks we have left and ask ourselves whether some of them could be postponed or omitted. Our horses cannot do this—their brains don't allow them to, and we don't either.

Over-Handling

The best horse-and-human teams enjoy daily interaction rather than weekend warrior schedules. Daily interaction achieves many goals. It:

- Builds a bond
- Allows both parties to learn subtle cues that improve two-way communication
- Provides a frequent check on our horses' welfare
- Forms new skills one small step at a time

Almost every horse benefits from an hour or two of daily human contact, assuming they're spent with a knowledgeable humane individual.

But current equestrian culture suggests that if some handling is good, more handling is even better. Training websites offer thousands of activities that a horse and human can share, and many online discussion forums push the idea that "there is no such thing as over-handling." Some equestrian disciplines claim that the more hours spent with a given horse, the better.

Most trainers and equine researchers disagree. Animal scientist Temple Grandin notes, "A basic principle is that animals with a flighty, excitable temperament [i.e. horses and cattle] must be trained and habituated slowly, in small steps over many days…." Equine scientist Jane Myers points out, "A young or old horse should not be expected to work for long periods." Professor of ethology Martine Hausberger provides results of several equine studies showing, "'Excessive' handling may well bring aversive responses."

Scientific data support these statements. In one of the largest studies, 170 young horses were tested on 21 breeding farms. Some farms handled their foals occasionally and only for brief periods between 6 and 18 months of age. As they grew up, these horses approached humans readily, accepted novel situations, and learned quickly without fear.

Other farms provided far more handling. Their horses were imprinted from birth and encouraged daily to accept halters, walk around the farm on lead ropes, allow their hooves to be cleaned, and stand for grooming. These over-handled youngsters learned slowly, showed fear of new stimuli, and remained wary of humans even at age three. In general, they were significantly more fearful than the horses who received less human interaction. So, there's a balance that's necessary here between too little handling and too much.

Horses can also develop nervous behaviors from the frustrations of excessive handling. Stall weaving, in which a horse shifts weight incessantly from side to side, increases with hours of weekly work. Pawing intensifies with the amount of time a horse is required to stand tied. Psychological stress can even exacerbate physical problems like hives.

Usually we define "work" as physical labor and assume that a horse tied in a barn aisle is not working. But mental work is taxing, too—especially for horses. We know what we expect, but our horses don't. Even just standing around, they have to decipher our cues, interpret our demands, ignore their own needs, and acquiesce—and they have to do all this with brains that were designed to run away.

How Temperament Affects Expectations

Every horse has a unique personality but also falls into a more general set of temperament categories. Temperament is inborn and includes dimensions of fearfulness, gregariousness, reactivity to humans, sensitivity to touch, and motor activity level. We can match certain temperaments to specific training techniques. For example, horses who are more socially oriented and less fearful tend to be highly sensitive to reward. They'll take risks in performance if there's a chance that it might lead to something positive. This group does well with training by reward (see p. 157).

Nervous Nellies are usually more focused on avoiding negative events than on seeking positive rewards. Because of this temperament, they usually respond best to negative reinforcement (see p. 145). There's less risk involved. That doesn't mean we have to use it all the time, just that we need to know it's a good base camp for them on difficult days.

Lowered expectations and less handling can be especially helpful for fearful horses who are highly reactive to human interference. Zoni is a perfect example. He's a small, middle-aged Appaloosa, strawberry roan through his forehand but spotted on his upper hindquarters. By the time he came to me for training, his brain was riveted to the faintest movement of a hair on your arm, and he flinched at every touch. Talk about overreactive!

Zoni was a good basic dressage, low jumper, and trail horse when his owner purchased him. He wanted to do his work, follow precise aids, and otherwise be left alone. Instead, this horse of textbook neurotic temperament was overstimulated by trainers who believed he needed stronger demands, harder work, more activity, and daily desensitization. As his overtraining continued, Zoni became increasingly skittish.

Desensitization is a practice that needs to be used with care, by professionals, only when necessary, and only on horses who have the right temperament for it. Zoni fit into none of those categories. You could see the worry steaming off his skin as trainers kept flooding him with one novelty after another in rapid succession. And most sessions lasted for hours. The result was that he became over-sensitized to everything.

What Zoni needed was *less*. I started by having him stand still in the cross-ties for five minutes. That's it. Stand still, stroke his neck, put him away. We worked up from there as I showed him what I wanted little by little. Beneath the fear that over-handling had caused, Zoni was a smart boy. He was hypersensitive to aids and tried hard to please. Ironically, this was his downfall. He was trying so hard and listening to his rider so carefully that he over-analyzed human expectations. His rider's aids weren't too precise in the arena and that confused him, too. An animal who's trying to be perfect needs to receive perfect signals. And if the signals can't be perfect, they must be minimal. Otherwise, the sensitive horse burns out from the stress.

With an hour of indirect training every day, Zoni settled. At the same time, his owner worked hard to refine her aids in lessons on one of my school horses. A few months later, when she and Zoni were paired again, they made a much calmer team.

Matching Human Goals with Equine Needs

In addition to creating performance problems, over-handling steals time from a horse's basic needs. A healthy well-adjusted horse spends 70% of the day munching forage and sipping water. Reduction of that time causes chronic low-level stress and increases the likelihood of stomach ulcers, cribbing, and colic. Equine bellies can hurt when they're missing food for hours.

Horses sleep off and on through the day and night, sprinkling naps into time spent chewing. They need to lie down and rest their feet a while, soak up some sun or shade, or stand silently and muse over the moment. They crave casual movement at their own pace. Healthy horses wander all around their paddocks, not only out of curiosity but also because digestion requires easy motion. Under natural conditions, horses graze and saunter most of the time.

While nibbling, our horses keep an eye or ear on surrounding events that might become important, "What's that handsome gelding doing over there in turnout?" "Hey, there's a trailer coming down the driveway—who's in there?" By attending to each small event as it comes, horses regulate their tranquility. Too many stimuli arriving at once are overwhelming.

Anyone who's fed a big barnful of horses half an hour late knows that they expect their feed on atomic time. For mental health, horses need routines. Feeding times should be consistent. Turnout should begin and end at roughly the same time every day. Performance horses need regular exercise on a steady schedule. An animal whose muscles, ligaments, and tendons are fit is less prone to injury and more likely to recover quickly when an injury does occur. Exercise is also good for the mind.

Finally, horses need social interaction with their friends, no humans invited. We egocentric *homo sapiens* think we are facilitating social interaction by hanging around the equine group, perhaps even "introducing" one horse to the others. In fact, we are usually interfering with communication and companionship among the horses themselves. I don't suggest we throw a new horse into an established herd where space is limited, but neither do we need to act as if we're hosting a child at a cocktail party.

Horses cannot meet their basic needs if they are busy with human activities all day. When their needs are not met, our animals become tired, uncomfortable, and anxious—perfect emotions for creating bad habits. Some horses become distraught. Even the sweetest children's mount can go from tired to terrifying in a heartbeat, causing damage to himself, his owner or rider, barn, and bystanders of any kind. The outburst seems unexpected only because we weren't listening to the horse and managing our expectations ahead of time. When horses finally do lash out, they are blamed for being "vicious" even though we were the ones who expected human perfection as the hours rolled past.

Avoiding the Marathon

The stimulus-driven equine brain isn't made for daylong marathons of goal-driven human expectation (figs. 15.2 A & B). What to do? If possible, interact with your horse for an hour or two, five or six days a week. If that's not possible, carve out one mid-week slot to supplement weekends, so you can space visits more evenly. To reduce daily grooming time, hire competent help for a weekly deep-cleaning. Find a good rider who can exercise your horse once a week. Or alternate rides with a trusted friend whose barn days are different from yours—you can work his horse and yours on one day, and he can do the same on another day.

Identify tasks that are particularly stressful for your horse. Some horses don't like to be groomed, even if it's a soothing activity for you. Others are simply impatient—they'll stand for grooming after a ride but not before. Remember that body-clipping produces anxiety even in horses who are too obedient to display it. Your horse might dislike deworming or bathing. Whatever it is, keep these tasks short. Body-clip gradually over several days; teach trailer loading a few minutes at a time.

15.2 A The horse's brain is stimulus driven, so items in the immediate external environment receive primary attention. The owl, bird, branch, leaves, and deer in this drawing occupy the horse's mind.

15.2 B Human attention is driven by internal mental goals, like reaching the house. The rider's brain pays little attention to items that the horse's brain cannot miss, and vice versa.

Look for tasks that can be simplified or omitted. Trim manes in 15 minutes with razor tools and knowledge rather than jerking roots out of an animal's neck for two hours. Reconsider the number of shampoo baths that are needed. To assuage your own need for extra horse time, offer to groom or hand-walk a mount whose owner is away.

If you must extend horse-human interaction past three hours, split it up. Put your horse away to eat, drink, and rest, then come back five or six hours later and finish the task that can't wait till tomorrow. Be considerate of your horse's generosity and patience. Save phone calls for later; speak calmly; keep pets and children at bay; watch the clock. Focus on the horse and heed signs that he's had enough.

Lighten Up!

- Limit yourself to roughly two hours a day with a given horse
- Shoot for five to six days a week with that horse
- Omit or reduce the frequency of stressful tasks
- Spread stressful tasks over several days
- Borrow a horse who needs some TLC
- Provide long rest breaks during a mandatory task

Trail riders often ask how to manage their work in short periods of time. If you're hauling trail horses to a distant trailhead, try to arrange overnight stabling so you can depart a day before the ride and return a day after. Break the ride into segments to allow the horses to eat, drink, meander around, or snooze for a while. Pay attention to footing, altitude, and slope—scrambling up shale on a 12% grade at 10,000 feet can't last for long. Be sure your horse is fully conditioned for the ride you have planned. Match the size of the horse to the weight of your body. Don't schedule an eight-hour ride all in one day—it's too much. ATVs can do that, but horses are living animals who get tired and sore. With this kind of care, your horse will remain sound, healthy, and motivated longer into the future. And you will be much safer while he carries you around.

Fitting human plans to equine brains improves communication and advances the horse's physical and psychological health. So, by all means, interact with your four-legged friend! Then bid him an early farewell and come back tomorrow.

PART FOUR

Attention, Emotion, and Forethought

CHAPTER SIXTEEN
Earth to Horse: Capturing Attention

Horses are butterflies sometimes:
"Ooh, what's that?"
"Look! A trailer!"
"What a pretty mare…"
"Hey, the feeeed truuuck."

This distractibility cramps the horse-and-human team when it occurs during work. To learn their disciplines, horses must pay attention. And there's plenty of attention to be had from a horse—but we have to capture it for human use.

Brain scientists study attention in species from honeybees to humans. We find that similar processes direct most mammalian brains to peel an eye or put a nose to the wind. These parallels let us speculate regarding the horse, whose powers of attention are hard to test. Go ahead, try sweet-talking an unsedated horse into a pounding brain scanner while predators stalk the room. See what I mean?

In horses and humans, "attention" refers to many different skills. Equine brains are engineered for vigilance. They notice new sights, sounds, smells, and touches; identify changes that breeze by most humans; and switch focus from one item to another—all at lightning speed. Human brains are much less vigilant, but they're better at shutting out distractions and concentrating on lengthy tasks.

Because we excel at the types of attention that horses muff (and vice versa), together we have far greater powers of engagement than either species has alone. If you understand your mount's attentional strengths, sharpen your own, and foster brain-to-brain communication, the two of you can expand your integrated powers of awareness. That will lead to increased learning for both of you.

In this chapter, I'll explain how human and equine brains stoke vigilance, alert to warning signals, and orient mental capacity toward potential dangers. I'll apply this knowledge to the task of capturing a horse's attention so he can learn with greater ease and mastery. Let's get started, "Earth to Horse! Come in, Horse!"

Inattentional Blindness

Being egocentric creatures, we humans tend to assume that our cognitive powers lie at the top of the heap. Are horses truly more vigilant than we are? In 1999, cognitive scientists created a short video in which two basketballs were passed among six players. Observers were asked to count the number of times the balls were passed among three of the rapidly moving players. While each observer was counting passes, someone dressed in a gorilla suit walked through the game, standing at the center of the action for five seconds.

A gorilla is impossible to miss, right? It's novel, unexpected, large, and covered in thick dark fur for goodness' sake! Yet almost half the observers never saw it. In disbelief, the researchers created a follow-up study in which the man in the gorilla suit pounded on his chest during his five seconds at center stage. Again, half the observers missed the gorilla. Humans can focus so intently on one aspect of a task that we become blind to more obvious parts of it. Horses? No way.

In a related study, viewers watched a short video in which two people were chatting over a meal. Details in the video changed inexplicably: The scarf one person was wearing suddenly disappeared then reappeared. The plates on the table changed color from red to white. And 90% of viewers failed to notice these changes. A second set of viewers were warned that the video contained changes in "objects, body position, or clothing." Even with this heads-up, people identified fewer than 25% of the vanishing scarves and chameleon plates.

Perhaps the most intriguing aspect of *inattentional blindness* is that our confidence remains strong despite our errors. When asked ahead of time whether they would notice scarves disappearing or plates changing color, 83% of people said yes. Yet only 11% of those confident viewers actually did.

Humans are likely to miss distractions that are not critical to performance on a focused task. But horses won't miss a gorilla suit! They won't ignore sudden changes in the color of a jump pole or fence rails that morph from white plastic to brown wood. Horses constantly notice small variations that people do not perceive.

Taking It In

Attention helps all species sort incoming data. Bombarded by our environments, we need to know which items are important and which are not. Horses' sensory organs take in copious data and their brains automatically sort it for danger.

As this barrage of incoming data enters the equine brain, it is filtered by specialized neurons. Is it food, water, danger? Let it through. Otherwise, block it. Such decisions are unconscious, a function of normal attention rather than premeditated thought. To stay alive, horses must alert to a warning signal instantly and flee the area *tout suite*. Mistakes are fine; it's better to run from moving grasses that harbor no predators than to wait for more information while the cougar launches his game of chase-and-pounce.

This bias in favor of mistakes allows equine neurons to be tuned toward very tiny changes in the external world. The equine brain considers every distraction potentially important. The human brain can afford to miss a few distractions in favor of stronger tuning for concentration.

Neural Tuning

Attention depends on *neural tuning*, a process that can occur most anywhere in the brain with the help of natural chemicals. Our noggins mix up these chemicals using recipes written in our genes. Various aspects of attention are mediated by our old friend dopamine, but also by acetylcholine, norepinephrine, cortisol, and nicotine. Yes, you read that right—your brain and your horse's brain make nicotine, just like the kind found in tobacco. Brains use it to provoke vigilance.

Suppose you and Star are out on a mountain trail. It's narrow, wooded, and rocky, flanked by a vertical drop of 50 feet on one side and an inclining cliff on the other. The pair of you are vigilant, paying close attention to the trail, right? Natural nicotine is coursing through your brain, and—because she's a horse and has greater vigilance—even more so through hers. This nicotine supercharges the firing potential of neurons that represent items of danger.

Suddenly in the tense silence, a grey squirrel chatters. Dopamine floods several areas of Star's brain and your own, flipping switches that alert you of peril. Neurons that are sensitive to dopamine boost their firing rate, in effect jumping up to get to work. Shots of norepinephrine and cortisol prepare your bodies to run. Acetylcholine orients the team to switch focus to a particular location. Star shies away from that location and tries to run because her brain has a direct connection to cells that cause rapid movement. You swear, using a direct link to the vocabulary niche in your brain that is saved for obscenities. Your melon then has to slog through a bunch of cognitive processing before the "run" command is initiated.

The Supplementary Motor Area

The human brain really does contain a special storehouse for obscene words. By physical separation in distance, it often survives when brain injury damages standard language areas. For this reason, people whose brain damage prevents them from speaking normally can still make a crusty horse trainer blush with their cursing. The same area is implicated in Tourette's Syndrome, in which uncontrollable swearing can be a symptom. Do horses have the equivalent of a supplementary motor area? A place for obscene four-letter whinnies? I have no idea, but if they do I'm sure they've used it on me once or twice.

In this moment of shying and swearing, neurons in areas devoted to perceptual information tune themselves up. Those that signal any color of "grey" now restrict their vigil to the specific shade seen in most grey squirrels. Neurons that are sensitive to other colors remain snoring on the couch. Brain cells for shape limit their firing patterns to curved tails and bulging eyes. Auditory brain cells are primed for the rapid-fire sound of squirrel chatter. Neurons in conceptual areas are hyped to convey the meaning of a chattering squirrel. All of these highly specialized brain cells become excited, seeking very specific information and firing much harder and faster than normal when they find it (figs. 16.1 A & B).

As these "squirrel neurons" boost their firing strength, they also inhibit the strength of irrelevant neurons nearby. The neurons for squirrel grey

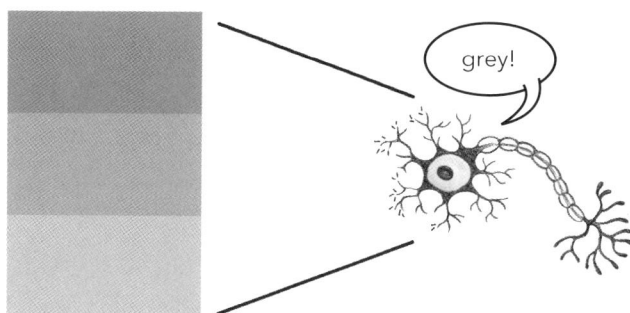

16.1 A This untuned neuron is specialized to detect the color grey.

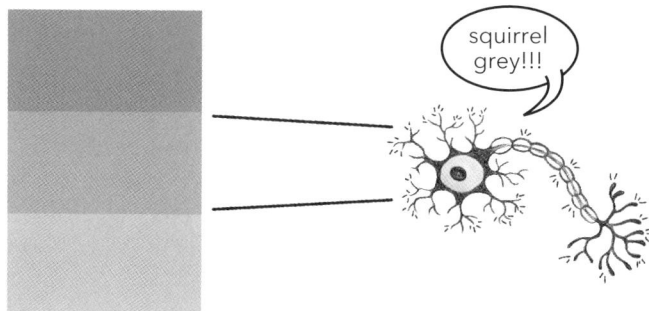

16.1 B The same neuron, now tuned by attention, will detect only the most relevant shade of grey. It will also fire harder and faster than normal when that specific shade appears.

tell the neurons for battleship grey to mind their own business. Those for a fluffy tail tell the cells for a short-haired tail to stand down. Imagine a group of 20 colleagues being silenced by an over-excited bully, "You all be quiet because I have something important to say!" Usually we ignore or shut down bullies. But if the message is likely to prevent death, in a real or evolutionary sense, everyone will listen.

From just before the instant of squirrel chatter to the instant of squirrel recognition, Star's brain and your own have been:

- Nicotined for vigilance
- Dopamined for an alert
- Norepinephrined and cortisoled for action
- Acetylcholined for the location of danger
- Neurally tuned to precision levels
- Suppressed for irrelevant noise

And all of that in one to two seconds.

Now, if you and Star haven't fallen down the cliff yet, your prefrontal cortex will begin to quell your fears, "Oh, it was only a squirrel. I'm okay, Star's fine, let's go on." (Alternatively, your brain might say, "Holy crap, it's scary out here, let's go home!" Either way, it is allowing you to make an informed decision.) Star's brain has no prefrontal cortex; it's made for action, not thought. She needs to borrow your prefrontal cortex for a minute, soaking up composure through your ability to make a decision, steady your mind, and relax your muscles.

The upside of equine attention is that horses notice most things that are different, unusual, or unfamiliar. Their brains are designed to pick up the minutiae of change. Ours are designed to categorize objects by similarity instead of difference. The downside is that the horse's attention is easily diverted and anatomically joined to instant response. Training a distracted horse whose fear is linked to thoughtless action is almost impossible. So, to teach your horse how you want him to behave, you have to capture his attention. Distracted horses tend to fall into one of two categories: busybodies or daydreamers.

The Busybody

Busybodies are usually nervous, looking in all directions except the path ahead. Their eyes and ears are in perpetual motion, their heads raise suddenly and swivel often, their muscles stiffen, their pace changes frequently, and unexpectedly they halt at high alert. Like a teenager texting himself into a light post, Busybodies are likely to stumble because they're so distracted. Watch for these signs, noticing where a horse's focus is located, so you can distinguish equine attention from distraction.

Your goal with a Busybody is to reduce his vigilance. You also want to redirect his alerting and orienting reactions from the external world to the handler—that's you! Because his hyped-up reaction is innate, a Busybody demands time, effort, and patience. Work slowly and calmly, making progress in small steps. His brain needs a lot of practice to alter the distribution of all those natural chemicals, especially the stress hormones norepinephrine and cortisol.

Start by placing the Busybody in a location that includes only a small amount of distraction. Ask for brief moments of attention during groundwork with just a halter and lead. Is the horse pivoting around like a chacha dancer? Lead him at a walk rather than trying to make him stand still. When his attention moves to an external event or object, gently bump the halter back toward you and keep walking. This touch is a brief reminder, not a pull or a punishment. Tap repeatedly if necessary. When the horse turns his attention to you, reward him with a stroke or a word of appreciation.

As the Busybody becomes less distracted at a walk, ask him to stand for a few seconds, stroking while he remains attentive to you. Over time, teach him to walk forward or backward, halt, turn right or left, with just a light touch-and-release on the lead. Move up to busier locations that offer more distraction. Devote about 15 minutes a day to *attentional exercise* until your horse redirects his busy mind to you reliably. You're not expecting sustained attention yet; just brief redirections.

Now it's time to hop on. Under saddle, the Busybody's eyes, ears, and head will be oriented to all sorts of external events. Pay no attention to them—remember, the two of you are in mutual brain-to-brain communication, so anything you attend to, your horse will also attend to. Vinca, a grey mare I trained for Western Pleasure, reacted to everything in and outside the arena during the first few weeks with her new owner. The pace of her gait changed every few seconds, she oriented toward every car that drove in and every person who walked past, there was no event trivial enough in the environment for her to ignore. But she had never displayed this behavior with me during several months of training.

Vinca's newfound distractibility was produced by her new rider. Sue is an outgoing, highly social person, your friend for life—and truly a good one—upon first meeting. She's a social genius, spotting every nuance in human interaction. She would never ride past an incoming car without looking to see who it was, or ignore someone standing at the rail in favor of maintaining the rhythm of Vinca's jog. Sure enough, as soon as Sue turned her focus to her horse, the two of them were able to resist diversions. The horse wasn't highly distractible, but her teammate was.

So, when you ride your Busybody, disregard external forces. Take one rein lightly in each hand at a walk. When your horse's engagement flits away, redirect it by touching the rein opposite the direction of his interest (fig. 16.2). He looks left, you touch right. If the horse ignores you, bump again—a little stronger—and release, like you did with the halter. No luck? Turn his head away from temptation and circle. He'll bumble around the circle and stumble over his feet, discovering for himself that he needs to pay attention. As he improves, practice at different gaits.

If your horse is not responding, try these tips. First, in any training program, you can always return to the previous step: groundwork, a slower gait, a quieter location. Second, use a round pen to limit distractions. Round pens with high solid sides reduce the horse's view, but even an open fence has some psychological effect. Redirect the Busybody calmly; the object is not to run the horse in circles with sliding stops and half spins. Third, speak a word or two to the distracted horse while bumping the halter or rein. Voice is especially effective if you don't often speak to your horse under saddle—he will likely divert his attention to the surprise.

16.2 Redirecting the horse's attention with the opposite rein.

The Daydreamer

Daydreamers plod along devoting little awareness to the outer world. They're especially indifferent to your riding aids—legs, hands, seat, weight distribution—and would prefer a long snooze. They take a passive approach when something captures their interest, bending toward the arena gate, slowing as they pass the barn, leaning toward a bite of grass.

With this type of horse, your goal is to stimulate attention without causing fear. One way to attract a Daydreamer's attention is to ask for rapid forward movement. If this expectation comes as a surprise, so much the better.

Begin off-lead in a round pen or circling on a longe line, and ask the Daydreamer to walk. Praise immediately if he steps out like he's headed to the treat aisle at the tack store. But if the Daydreamer lags, tap his hind-quarters with a longe whip. Teach him that "walk" means WALK: a fast four-beat gait with shoulders and hips swinging forward, head bobbing in time. Practice rapid walking, trotting, turning, stopping, and backing in the round pen and in hand. Encourage the horse to realize something new is happening—we are no longer lounging in the recliner with a bag of chips!

Under saddle, Daydreamers usually need more activity from the legs than the hands. So instead of touching a rein to redirect their outward attention, bump or tap them forward with your legs. Provide clear cues and insist that the horse obey them right away. Follow up with a spur or crop if the horse offers his middle hoof in response to your efforts. And of course, whenever you get momentary attention, reward the horse.

Another technique for inspiring Daydreamers is to place them in busy settings. When nearby events attract their attention, use the techniques described for Busybodies, gently bumping the rein opposite the attraction. Often it's easier to redirect a horse's attention from an external attraction than to dig it out from within his internal world.

Capturing Attention

- Calm the Busybody; awaken the Daydreamer
- Find a location with suitable levels of distraction
- Start with groundwork
- Use hands to touch the Busybody back to you
- Use legs to touch the Daydreamer into awareness
- Touch briefly and release, tap repeatedly if necessary
- Use circles, round pen, or voice as needed
- Practice at various gaits and locations
- Reward redirections of attention to you

Cautions

In the early stages of capturing a Daydreamer's attention, artificial aids (crops, whips, or spurs) must sometimes be used. These aids require skill and should be used as humane extensions of your hands and legs rather than tools of punishment. Avoid the horse's desensitization to these aids by using them firmly but not often.

Busybodies can be very nervous, with jet-like reactions and agile bodies. When a leaf rustles in the wrong place, they can jump in your lap. Such horses often need professional training and advanced riders, at least for the first few years of their education. With any horse, you might need qualified help. Hire a professional trainer, if only for short-term work on specific topics. Lessons are cheaper than hospital bills and a lot more fun than bed rest.

As you teach moments of attention, your Busybody will become less distracted and your Daydreamer will wake up. They are learning that when the two of you work together, you devote your attention to each other. This discovery will be the foundation for teaching your horse to focus on you at greater length. So, head out to the barn and practice capturing your horse's interest! Then you'll tune his neurons for concentration and lengthen his attention span.

CHAPTER SEVENTEEN
Stay with Me: Keeping Attention

"La, la, la, la, la!" Picture a horse with his hooves clapped over his ears, singing loudly to avoid the lesson you're trying to impart. Without his engagement, even the best training goes unheeded. Without yours, there is nothing he can teach you—and horses have a lot to teach. To foster learning on both sides, we must sustain focus within the horse-and-human team.

Human "attention" usually denotes the ability to focus our mental capacity on one task, to concentrate. This is an accurate definition within brain science, but it's also important to weigh popular connotations of the word. A thesaurus offers these synonyms: care, courtesy, consideration, kindness, devotion, helpfulness, thoughtfulness, responsiveness. Let's keep these concepts in mind when asking horses to focus on us. If we wish to foster trust in prey animals, we cannot demand their attention. We must earn it.

Everyday practice and scientific research agree that focused attention is the basis of animal training. Even the fruit fly learns faster when engaged. To learn to perform effectively, you and your horse must concentrate on each other. Each of you provides cues that the other must discern. Each of you has expectations and drives that must be addressed.

Mutual Attention

A handler's attention to the horse is critical for several reasons. For one thing, two-way communication with another species requires effort.

(Skeptical? Try getting your dog to longe at liberty sometime, or do tempi changes on command!) It might look easy to handle a horse well, but in fact it's very complex and requires years of daily practice with multiple animals. It's an exercise in the Italian art of *sprezzatura,* making the difficult seem simple. A figure skater flies across glare ice, leaps into the air off the edge of a quarter-inch blade, and turns four revolutions in less than a second before landing smoothly and gliding away. It looks easy, as if any of us could be so graceful.

Sprezzatura is exactly what causes non-horsey people to assume that riders just "sit up there and look pretty" and that "the horse does all the work." Some seem to think they could hop on at the drop of a hat and cut the fastest cow out of a herd, post without stirrups for an hour, or race a Triple Crown winner around the clubhouse turn. Developing mastery requires focus—not to mention discipline, effort, strength, knowledge, skill, endurance, and endless motivation—from both horse and rider.

Another reason for human attention to the horse is the fact that equine brains are built for vigilance rather than concentration. We must teach our mounts to overcome their natural instinct to dart from one distractor to another. Focusing at length on human cues is a skill that horses learn with time and training, just as it is refined developmentally from child to adult. Horses can never achieve the same degree of extended concentration that humans can, but they do improve with education.

In addition, horses mirror their handlers' moods and body tone. If you are distracted or impatient, your horse will be distracted or impatient. Many good riders who are not calm in their own minds have trouble getting their horses to jog or lope slowly or to jump quietly. If you are tense, tightening your muscles or gripping with your leg or hand, your horse will display tension too. Performance horses and riders must be relaxed yet attentive to function well.

Where's Your Focus?

So…uh, how can I say this gently? In a work session with your horse, how often do you give him your full attention? And how long does each of those moments last? If you expect a horse to listen to your cues, you must listen to his. Let's say you ride for an hour, including a 10-minute warm-up and a 10-minute cool-down. Of course, you will include short breaks during the heart of the session. But it's not unreasonable to suppose that there will be some 10-minute chunks of time during which you and your horse need to focus on each other.

People rarely focus on their horses for 10 minutes at a time. Many riders daydream or rehash office politics and family dramas in the saddle. External interruptions occur—the wind picks up, a loud motorcycle roars to life, another rider won't stop clucking. Cell phones ring, friends wave, and the barn manager has a question just when you're working on a sticky lead change. Interruptions distract both members of the team. Riding is a two-way street: If you expect your horse's attention, you have to give him your own. He will reflect it back to you just like he reflects your fear, impatience, or generosity.

Multi-Tasking

I hate to break the news, but multi-tasking is a myth. Human brains cannot divide attention equally across simultaneous tasks, although mental illusions allow us to imagine that we do. Our brains can switch attention rapidly between two tasks, but doing so degrades performance. And not just by a little bit. On average, human brains require 50% more time to complete a project when switching tasks. When the work is finished, the result contains 50% more mistakes. With these reductions in speed and accuracy, multi-tasking decreases overall productivity by about 40%.

Let's apply these time lapses and error rates to horse sports. The average horse weighs 1,200 pounds and moves like lightning. He can kill you accidentally in a fraction of a second. In fact, horses and cattle account for the largest number of human deaths-by-animal each year in the United States. Equine handlers can't risk a 50% error rate by trying to do two things at once. It could literally kill us.

Most people who hear these statistics claim they are immune. That's because our brains don't have enough *attentional capacity* left over while multi-tasking to notice that we're wasting time and messing up. In addition, every normal human brain is biased in favor of believing that its owner is a genius. If only! This incorrect belief protects us from the mundane reality that each of us, no matter how smart, can only do so much at one time. Attentional capacity in the brain has a physical limit.

The Locus of Concentration

The hunt for concentration's substructure has a long history. Cognitive psychologists began by identifying the mental processes that occur when we focus on solving problems. The advent of brain imaging led us to seek the location at which concentration was stirred up like a salve and buttered on to some external task. Answers flew in. Attentional processes were seen in the prefrontal and medial frontal areas of the brain. Oh, and the ventral frontal, superior parietal, lateral parietal, midline, anterior cingulate, insular, right cerebral, and frontoparietal cortices. Did I forget the thalamus, midbrain, forebrain, basal ganglia, frontal eye field, tempoparietal junction, hippocampus, lateral geniculate nucleus and superior colliculus? The locus coeruleus? The reticular activating system?

Don't worry—there's no pop quiz coming! My point is that attentional processing has been found almost everywhere in the brain. And everywhere, in scientific research, is the equivalent of nowhere at all. We already know that attention is mediated by stuff that happens above the neck. Like love and fear, the experience of concentration lights up almost all of the human brain.

Paradoxically, about the only location that can be ruled out is the one that clinicians sometimes mention as the heart of equine attention. The reticular activating system is a nucleus of cells at the base of the brainstem. It keeps mammals awake but not necessarily alert. When it is damaged, we do not only lose the capacity for attention—we lose consciousness, fall into a coma, or die. There is much more to attention than just being awake, right? We are awake while cleaning tack, shoveling manure, or reading *Paradise Lost*—but are we alert? Vigilant? Spellbound? Not likely. The reticular activating system plays such a minimal role that it's not even mentioned in current textbooks on attention.

Von Economo Neurons

Instead of hunting down the holy grail of an "attention center" in the brain, we now study specific neurons that facilitate concentration. *Von Economo neurons (VENs)* are spread throughout the brain. About four times larger than the much more common multipolar neuron, VENs have a long distinctive shape with only one connection at each end. They're named after a Romanian neurologist, Constantin von Economo, who first observed them in 1926 and spent his life examining them.

Types of Neurons

Mammalian brains contain many different types of neurons. The *multipolar neuron* is one of the most common and can receive and transmit electrical impulses in various directions using a large number of connected cells. *Von Economo neurons* are a type of *unipolar neuron* (fig. 17.1). They receive and transmit impulses in only one direction, stretching long distances to communicate with widespread parts of the brain.

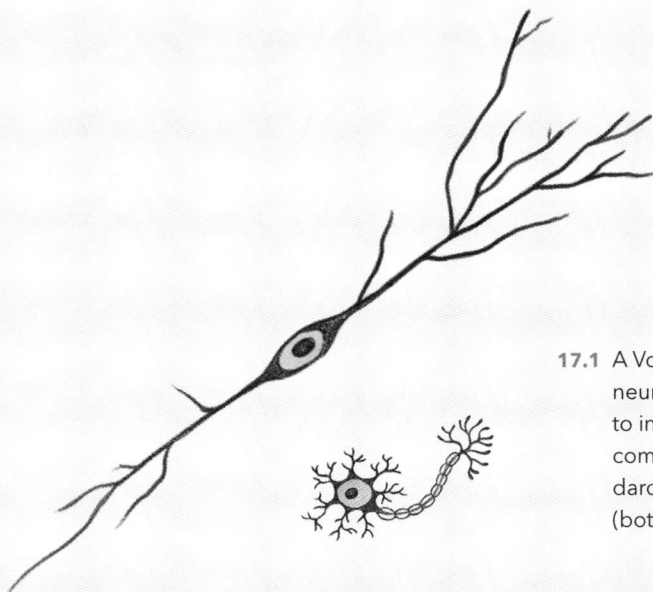

17.1 A Von Economo neuron (top) is used to increase attention, compared to the standard multipolar neuron (bottom).

When activated, VENs send messages stimulating other areas to become especially alert. This action primes multipolar neurons in each area to fire hard and fast for information pertinent to a given task. For example, let's just suppose you are reading a fascinating book on brain science in horsemanship. (A purely hypothetical example, of course.) As your interest grows, activation is pumped through your brain by Von Economo neurons, then sharpened by the neural tuning of multipolar cells.

Now, getting back to the horse. For decades, VENs were thought to exist only in primates with large brains and rich social lives. But science never stands still. As research progressed, we discovered VENs in dolphins, whales, elephants, monkeys, pigs, sheep, cows, and deer. In 2015, researchers found them in the anterior cingulate cortex of the horse, an old part of the brain in evolutionary terms. In humans, this location is rich in VENs that mediate concentration.

In a minute, you'll see how these attentional cells help you and your horse focus on each other. But first, you need to know how to identify the spotlight of equine engagement, so that you can praise the horse who turns it on.

Identify Equine Attention

How do you know if a horse is paying attention to you? On the ground, an attentive horse will watch, sniff, lick, nuzzle, and/or turn his head toward you. When something new occurs, his feet will remain still, but he will study your face and feet for clues to the mystery. He might then explore your body with his eyes or nose. He is actively seeking information, which is the perfect mindset for learning.

Under saddle, an attentive horse responds to a rider's cues right away. The response might be incorrect at first, but that's all right—your four-legged friend is still learning what the cue means. First he has to notice it. From there, you can adjust his response. A knowledgeable horse who simply ignores your leg, hand, or seat is not giving you his attention. He's giving you guff.

Ear movements also tell you where a horse's attention is. Are they pricked forward? He's interested in something up ahead—maybe a jump or a cow, but it could also be a distraction. Are his ears flicking gently toward you when you cue him? Good! He's listening.

Horses distinguish between familiar and unfamiliar humans, and they know when you're paying attention to them. They learn quickly which humans require their attention and which do not. That's why many horses concentrate on their trainers but lollygag with their owners.

Keep Your Horse's Attention

I've explored several means of capturing your horse's attention for brief moments. This capture fires VENs to prime many areas of the horse's brain, tuning multipolar neurons to seek information relevant to the task. Once you catch a horse's interest, you can begin to extend his moments of concentration.

Next time you redirect your horse's attention to you, immediately assign a task that is a little different than normal. This task is your VEN generator. What it will be depends on your horse: A baby can begin with a circle or figure eight; an intermediate horse might do a shallow serpentine, or some canter–halt-canter transitions; an old hand could try some half-passes or turns-on-the-forehand. A jumper might be asked to open a gate, a trail horse to negotiate trot poles. Choose something your horse has done before, but not often. You want him to have to think about your aids and what they mean. Pretend you're a teacher calling on a sleepy student in class—or a bunch of sleepy Von Economo neurons dozing inside your horse's head.

Praise your horse for extended moments of attention, and let him rest between brief successes. Build concentration time gradually. Maybe today you only get 10 seconds before his mind wanders. That's fine! Tomorrow you might get 15, and in a month maybe you'll have a minute. Keep the horse calm, and redirect as needed.

Another way to teach sustained attention is to prevent the horse from anticipating the next maneuver. Instead of planning ahead, the well-trained horse listens to his teammate for direction. This process revives his VENs periodically and gives the horse's multipolar neurons frequent opportunities for tuning. Remember neural fatigue from chapter 7 (p. 89)? You don't want cells to tucker out and stop functioning; you want to keep them alert.

Choose Your Location

To teach a horse focus, it's important to choose the work location that provides the right amount of distraction. You want enough distraction to make attention a goal, but not so much that your horse is overwhelmed. The time will come when he will focus on you even in the hoopla of a rodeo, but you have to build that ability. Remember, your horse has no prefrontal cortex to slow his instinct to divert, and his brain chemicals have not yet been altered enough for extended concentration.

To prevent anticipation, make random transitions during your ride—unexpected stops, starts, turns, and changes in pace, gait, and stride length. When the horse begins to figure out a pattern and lose focus, change it. Write messages in the dirt with his feet. Dismount and reverse in hand. Do whatever the horse does not expect. While jumping, reining, or barrel racing, set the course as usual but ride it in a new pattern. Practice dressage tests in many random orders. In every discipline, teaching by attention is much more effective than repetitive drilling—and a lot less boring! Your horse will listen carefully to see what comes next.

Create a series of random loops and turns, some tight and some loose, in all directions, halting and backing occasionally. Imagine embroidering an intricate pattern on the ground. Some trainers use this technique to supple horses, but it also focuses equine attention because they can't predict the next move. Start at a walk, and work up to performing this attentional exercise at any gait, adding diagonal and lead changes as you go (fig. 17.2).

When the horse notices something distracting, ride past it—not toward it—in multiple patterns. Keep focused on your work without glancing or leaning in the direction of the distractor. Tell your horse

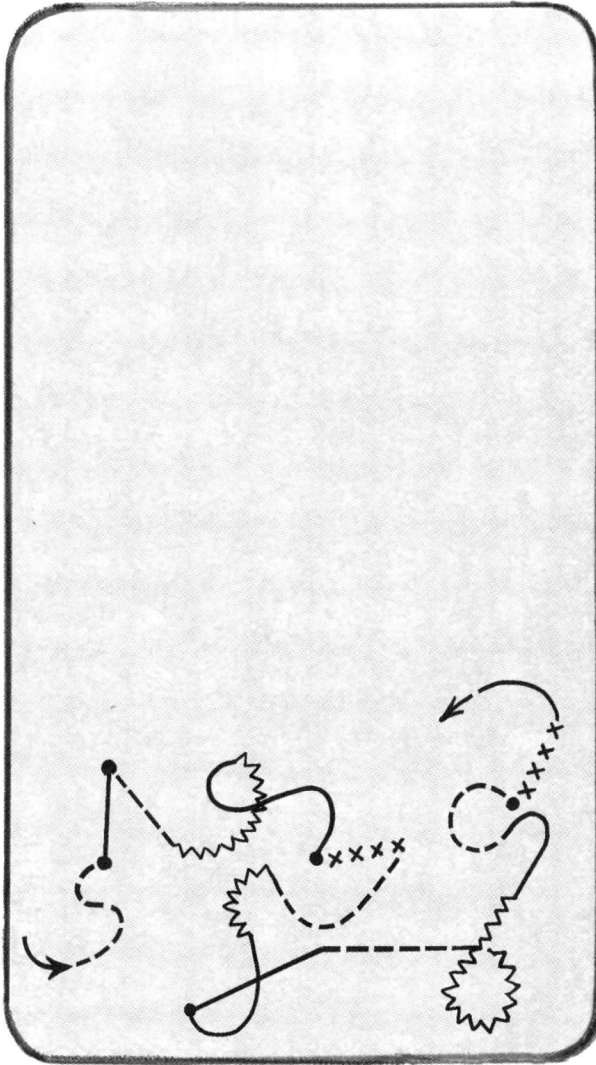

17.2 Embroidery is random, not planned, but this is a sample of what one pattern might look like. This exercise supples the horse's body but also focuses his mind on the rider.

with your body that the object is meaningless and deserves no attention. Don't stop to let the horse stare at a distractor. Rest is a huge reward. If an item is so compelling that your horse can't zero in on you—the grinding maw of a garbage truck with an overhead bin dangling upside down, for example—change the circumstances so he can. Move to a different area temporarily, or revert to groundwork near the novel scene. Change the context, but not the task.

To refine the horse's neural tuning, teach cue sensitivity. Suppose you ask a Daydreamer to canter by sitting tall and straight while pressing with your outside leg. You get nothin'. Zilch. Require the horse to wake up and canter immediately. We don't expect a horse to do something he has not yet learned, but if he knows the cues and you have supplied them clearly, insist that he respond posthaste.

You can sharpen neural tuning further by teaching lighter cues for transitions. Perhaps your horse departs to a canter well with 2 pounds of outside leg pressure and a dollop of inside hand. Begin to expect the depart with 1½ pounds of leg and only a speck of hand. To develop cue sensitivity, you need an independent seat and excellent balance. If you expect your horse to respond to tiny cues, you have to deliver them with precision.

As your horse learns to concentrate, move to busier environments with greater distractions. With all training, proceed bit by bit, showing the horse what is expected without scaring him or dulling his motivation.

Building Equine Concentration

- Assign an uncommon task
- Build concentration time slowly
- Ride unpredictable patterns
- Pass and ignore external distractors
- Teach cue sensitivity
- Practice in increasingly busy environments

An attentive horse will do well to concentrate on you, and on his performance, for several minutes at a time. To expect him to maintain focus for half an hour is cruel. Improve concentration with plenty of brief rests and rewards for good behavior, but ask only for what his brain can give.

Individual Differences

A few horses and a few humans are highly attentive to each other, and others remain Busybodies or Daydreamers unless they get daily training. Some of this variety is genetic. For example, missing genes on chromosome 22 impair focus in humans, especially when patients try to zero in on a particular area of space or moment in time. Brain damage can cause a very rare disorder called Balint's Syndrome, in which patients can attend to only one object at a time. As soon as they divert to a different object, remaining items in the immediate environment seem to disappear.

The amount of attentional chemicals that genes instruct human and horse brains to make every day—dopamine, acetylcholine, norepinephrine, cortisol, and nicotine—changes from one individual to the next. If your horse produces a little more nicotine than most, he will be a little more vigilant—and vice versa.

Hot-blooded breeds are usually more distractible and more sensitive than Warmbloods or Drafts. Like most traits in humans, our best strengths are also our strongest weaknesses. Extreme sensitivity to your aids and intentions go hand in hand with the propensity to leap sideways when a pin drops. The slightest encouragement yields instant response, but the slightest error leads to a tantrum. When selecting performance horses, consider each individual's natural sensitivity and match it to the appropriate discipline. The perfect beginner's horse should be far less alert than the Grand Prix jumper.

Individual differences are also environmental: If you grew up in a home where focused attention was modeled often, you are likely to have a greater capacity for concentration. Likewise, horses who have had a lot of quality training listen for subtle cues from advanced riders; they have learned to pay close attention to people. We have a responsibility to ride well for these horses. They expect to be directed by their human leaders and are confused when that leadership is weak.

Horses offer attention to people who deserve it. We can remind our horses that we are there, and we can reward them for turning their engagement toward us. Beyond that, we must earn their interest through kindness and motivation. Remember the synonyms? Care, courtesy, consideration….

CHAPTER EIGHTEEN
Equine Emotion

Wildflowers carpeted the Arizona desert as five of us rode southeast toward our camp. There, an old ocotillo round pen stood waiting. It was rough but secure and offered a natural source of water—a good place to overnight the horses and sleep on the ground nearby, spend the second day exploring, and ride home the third.

Near the end of the first day's ride, we entered a cholla forest. Teddy-bear *cholla* ("CHOY – uh") is an ill-mannered cactus about 4 feet tall, covered with balls of inch-long spines. These masses of superfine thorns require pliers and a bullet for removal. (You jerk barbed needles out of your skin while biting the bullet to endure pain.) Negotiating a stand of several hundred cholla packed closely together is complicated on foot and even more tricky on horseback. But fences forced us to traverse it, so we moved forward in a slow line. I brought up the rear on Hemi—a tough buckskin Quarter Horse who had been on desert trails for most of his life.

My eyes were on the cacti and my seat in the saddle when suddenly both my feet touched ground. The earth under these cholla looked solid on the surface but had been hollowed out by rodents a couple feet below. Evidently, the undergirding had deteriorated under the weight of four previous horses and had now given way. Hemi's legs dangled loose in an invisible hole. His body was supported by narrow strips of solid ground on each side, and we were girdled in cholla.

Hemi was not struggling; he just continued to dangle, seeking purchase by waving his feet around underground. I stepped off in super-slow motion, like defusing a bomb, silently accepting 50 cholla needles in my left arm and back. Encouraged to move forward, Hemi thrashed a bit, then bull-frogged his way to safety.

An entertaining story—for you, maybe!—but the aftermath was tough on the horse. His legs were fine and he stood in place, but his entire body shook. No amount of soothing would help. It was less distance to proceed than turn back, so I led Hemi as he trembled for about 3 miles. The horse was afraid the ground could swallow him again at any time, in one giant gulp. He quivered while I removed his tack, fed and watered him, and turned him loose in the ocotillo pen. The next morning, we led the horse to the nearest phone, where he was trailered home. A veterinarian determined that physically Hemi was fine, but mentally he was traumatized by fear.

So, Do Horses Have Emotions?

You bet they do! But until a few years ago, and still today in many academic circles, animals were not believed to have the capacity for emotion. Anyone who's been around horses for long knows better. And as researchers begin to explore animal emotions, a growing body of evidence backs us up.

Hang with me for a definition or two, so we're all on the same page. *Emotions* are observable states that drive behavior. We perceive them in a horse's facial expressions, vocalizations, eyes, ears, posture, and physical movements. If human noses were up to snuff, we could smell emotion in an animal's body odor, as many species do. Even people have trouble hiding or faking emotion, and horses have no reason to try.

Emotions drive behavior, but not in the same way that instincts do. An *instinct* is like a reflex—it occurs automatically in the same way each time, and it causes one very specific behavior to occur. Plop a mouse down in front of a cat, and instinct will drive the cat to crouch, stalk, and pounce. An emotion, on the other hand, leaves room for a number of potential behaviors. Sad people might sob in front of a group, tear up silently, turn red and puffy in the face but remain dry-eyed, display complete numbness, laugh in an effort to deflect, or stay home under the covers. We have some choice in the behavior an emotion causes. Likewise, a horse who is afraid might whirl and bolt, freeze in place, tremble all over, leap back on full alert, or look for human guidance.

Emotions are physical and external, but *feelings* are internal mental states that cannot be observed. They're private and subjective. Someone else knows what we feel only if we tell them, or if they have enough experience with us to make an educated guess. Private feelings come from observable emotions—we discover we feel angry when we notice blood rising in our faces and tension tightening our muscles—but they're not the same as emotions.

No one disputes that animals have instinct. Whether they experience emotion remains controversial, but evidence in favor is stacking up. And few people believe that animals have feelings, or at least that they experience feelings as humans do. There's plenty of slop factor in the use of these three terms: Many people use them inaccurately, and often an experience is made up of instinct, emotion, and feelings in varying mixtures.

The science on these issues is in flux and will depend on the results of many experiments yet to be done. We have solid evidence of complex emotions in primates—but primates are omnivorous predators with a prefrontal cortex. Horses, by contrast, are herbivorous prey animals with no prefrontal cortex and a tendency to flee rather than bunch up like other prey animals do when in danger.

Fear

Thanks to the evolutionary need for survival, the equine brain is driven primarily by fear, perhaps the strongest mammalian emotion of all. Is it really an emotion? Well, horses express it outwardly (check), it drives their actions (check), and the actions vary across a range of possibilities (check).

Verifying True Emotion

- Is it observable?
- Does it drive the horse's behavior?
- Does the behavior vary among horses and situations?

Life without fear sounds heavenly, doesn't it? You could ride the hottest bronc, speak about sexual positions to an audience of thousands, and tell teenage strangers to behave. But in fact, fearlessness leaves people at great risk of harm. S.M. is a woman whose rare disease caused calcium deposits to form on her *amygdalas* ("uh-MIG-duh-luhs"), twin areas deep inside the brain that mediate emotions in humans and horses. She cannot feel fear, interpret it on other people's faces, draw a face showing fear, or imagine what it feels like. Without access to such a critical emotion, S.M. has been held at gunpoint twice and at knifepoint twice, largely because her brain cannot warn her to avoid dangerous situations.

In human brains, the amygdalas are connected to prefrontal cortex, so we can evaluate fear and make decisions that reduce risk. S.M. cannot assess danger because her amygdalas are damaged. Horses cannot do it for a different reason: they have brawny amygdalas but no prefrontal cortex to connect to. They can use their knowledge—gained through training, memory, observation, and trust—but they don't have the hard wiring to assess fear in the moment (figs. 18.1 A & B).

Managing Fear and Anxiety

Anxiety is a first cousin to fear. It occurs when we are afraid of something that hasn't happened yet—but it might! Humans and horses who experience high anxiety have larger amygdalas. Anxiety varies a lot across horses—by breed, background, and training. Some dance away from their own shadows or piaffe for an hour instead of walking and trotting. Their ears are alert enough to slice cheese, the whites of their eyes limn the lids, and any rider can feel the meltdown about to occur. Other horses nod along the same path without a care in the world.

The best techniques for reducing fear and anxiety are similar across the horse-and-human team. They center on:

- Relaxation. Relaxing a horse's body calms him enough to heed your guidance. When he realizes you're not afraid, he loses some of his own fear.

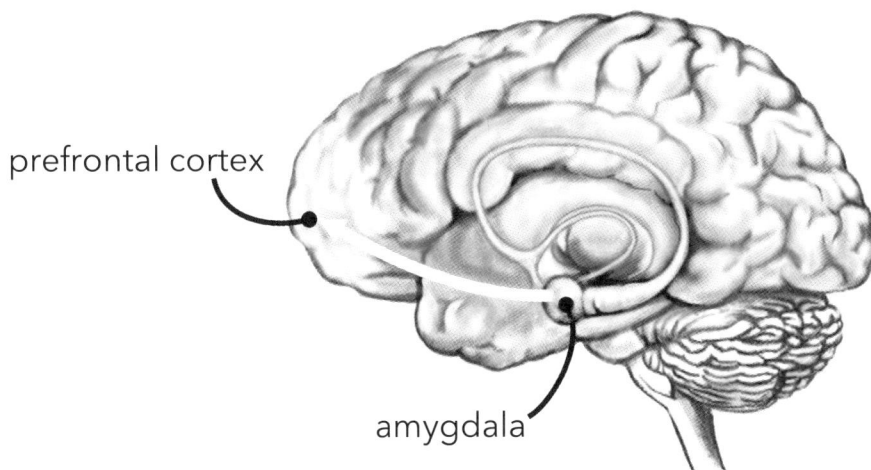

18.1 A Two amygdalas are set off to each side of the human brain and are connected to prefrontal cortex, creating hardwired pathways from emotion to evaluation.

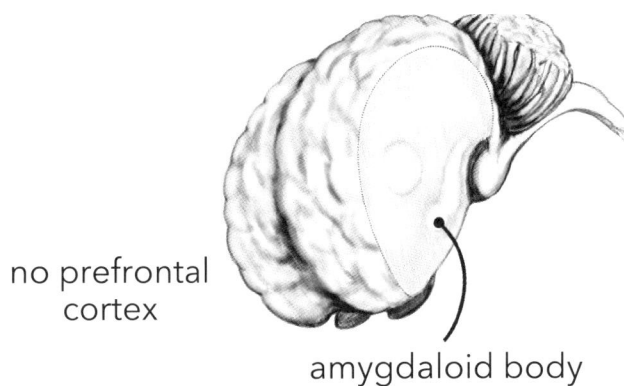

18.1 B The horse has two amygdaloid bodies to process emotion, but no prefrontal cortex for evaluation.

- Consistency. Nibbling your sleeve can't be wrong today but cute tomorrow. Consistency allows the principles of learning to work.
- Predictability. When a horse knows what to expect, he can begin to predict. Prediction yields a sense of control, which reduces fear.

Equine Emotion | 235

Reduce Anxiety through Prediction

Increase predictability by forming routines in a nervous horse's life. Feed, work, rest, turn out, and blanket at roughly the same time every day. Lead to cross-ties or turnout along the same path, preserve the order of feeding or turnout within a group, and build a consistent grooming regimen. In as little as two weeks, the nervous horse will begin to settle in the cross-ties when he can predict that first you will curry, then brush, then pick hooves in the same order and direction every time. The order you choose doesn't matter, just stick with it.

The same is true under saddle—calm a worrywart by creating a habit of sequence—maybe walking three times around the arena each way, then walking serpentines or figure eights, moving into an easy trot, and so on. This degree of consistency doesn't have to last forever, just until equine anxiety calms and the horse begins to trust you.

The Anti-Fear Arsenal

Dusty was a 12-year-old bay Arabian settling into the barn. She had delicate legs and a dished face, with a perky personality but the vigilance of her hot-blooded breed. We were still getting to know each other when I led her into her stall one day from the back (paddock) side. As we walked toward the front of the stall, Dusty's eyes and nostrils opened wide, her head rose in giraffe mode, and every muscle went taut. She came to a sudden halt and bounced all four feet outward in a rapid splay, frightened out of her wits. I glanced across the aisle and saw the new barn mate she was staring at. It was—hold your breath, take cover—a *leopard Appaloosa*. Spots! Everywhere!

How do you manage a sudden fright like this? Through respect and calmness. Whatever scares the horse—spots, plastic bags, bicycles—you must respect as a valid object of equine fear. Your human opinion of its scariness is irrelevant. If you feel fear as well, control it. The best attitude is what I call "patho-calm." Pathological calmness is a useful skill on the ground, in the saddle, and in any emergency. (It's not bad in the boardroom, either.) To learn it, close your eyes for a moment, take a deep breath in and out, and instruct yourself that your horse needs you. Reassure and guide the horse now—go have a nervous breakdown later. Show the horse through your body language that there is nothing to be afraid of.

Sometimes, equine fear mirrors your own—you see someone about to power up a leaf blower and predict that the horse might shy. Your anxiety then transfers to his brain. Equine scientists recently studied this effect. They had people ride or lead horses past a location where only the humans knew an umbrella would be opened. Anxiety about the upcoming reaction increased human heart rates, of course. But it also increased the horses' heart rates—even before the umbrellas appeared. So it's best with fear to accept the team view: If either party is scared, manage that fear together.

Patho-calm includes several activities that relax horses. Breathe slowly and steadily. Most people underestimate the effect of human breathing on the equine mind. Dressage riders use exhalation to halt a horse, hunter riders use rhythmic breathing to steady pace on course, race riders use inhalation to help start a horse, equine massage therapists blow raspberries through their lips to mimic mellow snorts, and any rider or handler can use inhalation and exhalation to quiet a horse. You don't have to pant—horses hear and feel normal human breathing.

Soften your muscles and adopt a relaxed stance—your four-legged fraidy-cat will mirror your body language. Shift your eye contact away from his. Direct eye contact acts as a warning to a horse, scolding or applying pressure—we're predators, remember? Let the horse move around to get a different view, scent, or sound if he wants to. Keep hold of the horse by his lead or reins, but avoid the death grip. We're trying to relax here, not stand at attention for a Marine Corps dress inspection.

A slow low-pitched voice can work miracles, both to encourage relaxation and to serve as a reward. Content doesn't matter much, but tone does. Save higher pitch to motivate or animate a horse. And, of course, remember to reward when the anxious horse begins to settle. Stroking serves as a reward and an aid to reducing the team's heart rate—your horse's and your own.

Relaxing a Horse

- Adopt the "patho-calm" attitude
- Breathe slowly and steadily
- Soften your muscles and stance
- Shift your eyes away from the horse's eyes
- Allow the horse to choose his position
- Lighten the death grip
- Use a low, slow voice
- Stroke the horse's shoulder as he relaxes

How do you know when a horse is relaxed? He lowers his head, extends his necks outward, allows his ears to fall slightly to the sides, loosens his muscles, and unclamps his tail. His eyelids ease to cover the white sclera that appears during fear. A strong sign of relaxation is the long easy snort during exhalation. When you see these changes, reward your prey animal for settling down in the face of his fear!

Other Emotions in Horses

Fear and anxiety are common equine emotions, but they're certainly not the only ones. Horses show sadness, happiness, confidence, frustration, jealousy, and surprise, and they might also experience disgust, betrayal, pride, and more. They probably don't suffer embarrassment, but you might want to leave the holiday reindeer antlers off your bridle just in case.

Sadness is so apparent in horses who are confined to long-term stall rest that it is now used as an animal model for research on human depression. Horses who are suddenly confined mug bypassers for attention at first, but soon retreat to the back of their stalls. Their heads face the wall, necks flat and extended, weight on the forehand, ears still and slanted back, eyes fixed or dull and rarely blinking. This stance differs from normal waking and sleeping positions in undistressed horses.

Depressed animals lose interest in unusual noises, ignore light touches to the skin, pay little attention to their environment, yet become abnormally reactive in scary situations. Some even lose interest in treats. Why bother? Horses might not feel sadness the way humans do, but they display the emotion.

Happiness? Have you seen horses play when it's frisky outside? Even the older four-leggeds bob and weave with their pals, strutting around the pasture and kicking up their heels. Under saddle, happy mounts bounce in their gaits and toss or swing their heads softly. We notice the spring in their step. We can't say whether these cuties *feel* happy, but it sure looks that way.

Even a rookie can see the difference in confidence between green babies and experienced horses. Imagine the two are trotting a big circle under saddle. The youngster's circle is bumpy and uneven, he looks away from it frequently, his pace speeds up and slows down, he is captivated by nearby horses, he wiggles and stares, he startles when a bystander swats a fly. Heaven help you if a baby stroller appears on the horizon! As an emotion, confidence is a building block of horse training. The young horse grows confidence by learning how to handle human environments and expectations. With that confidence, he becomes much more relaxed and secure.

Frustration is often seen in horses. After all, they have to suss out expectations from an inconsistent species, with no common language and lots of mixed messages. To express frustration, horses switch their tails, tighten their backs and muzzles, balk when asked to move forward, grind their teeth rapidly under wrinkled lips, or flip their heads upward. Some even squeal or grunt, and a few pull the all-out, buck-rear-kick maneuver. One of my training horses displayed all these gestures upon returning to his stall after a very difficult trailer-loading lesson. He then flung himself onto his shavings with a huff, every bit the petulant diva.

The most potent display of jealousy I've ever seen—human or otherwise—occurred when two of my horses got a new barnmate. You remember Cory, the big dark bay Thoroughbred, and my palomino school horse

Princess, both introduced earlier. They knew each other for years, but were never turned out or stabled together and didn't seem attached. Cory knew how to attract the ladies, arching his neck and peering sideways at them with huge puppy dog eyes, but he never offered that sort of flirtation to Princess. She wouldn't have stood for it.

When the Shakespearean Jealousy Pageant began, Princess and Cory were located in the same barn five stalls apart from each other, but within viewing distance in their outer paddocks. A new Arabian gelding moved into the stall next to Princess. He was on his best behavior, hanging back to see who's who in the hierarchy. Her Royal Majesty pretty much ignored him. But Cory—oh, Cory wasn't having any of it! He immediately kicked up a fuss, whinnying desperately toward Princess, his eyes shooting daggers at the newbie, breathing hard, sweating buckets, puffing up, and running to and fro along the fenceline. Persistent as a mule, he kept this up for *two weeks*. Every woman in the barn watched with wide eyes as Cory tutored us in the power of male jealousy.

Even a decade ago, these anecdotes would have been viewed by scientists as hopelessly human-centered. The idea was that people are so desperate to see human qualities in their animals that we unconsciously attribute to them emotions that horses cannot have. Equine fear and jealousy would have been seen as instincts; happiness, sadness, and frustration nothing more than human projection. But we now have a growing body of evidence that animals of many kinds—apes, birds, dolphins, whales, pigs, goats—express emotions that drive behavior in non-instinctual ways.

Building Trust

Given the equine capacity for emotion, what's the best way to bond with a horse? The first step is to adopt the right rank. All horses are aware of the hierarchy within their groups and hold complex representations in their minds about social rank. To simplify for human consumption, we can say that some herdmates are equals, others are subordinate, and a few are leaders who must be obeyed. One or two individuals in a group usually act as liaisons.

Horses will transfer their respect for a superior herdmate to any human who offers consistent guidance that yields safe results. Most horses learn to misbehave when humans try to be equals or subordinates. Neither do they respond well to people who lord a bunch of self-important superiority over them. In addition, they distinguish between people with positive as opposed to negative attitudes toward them. A horse needs a reliable guide, similar to a parent—a person whose kind leadership he can trust to provide help in negotiating the human world.

As a guide, you are in a position to allay the fear that drives so much equine behavior. A horse who trusts will hold back his natural reaction to fear until his human guide weighs in. He then considers her suggestions, choosing behavior that leads to reward.

Bonding takes years of tiny successive steps—each one easy enough for the horse to complete successfully without becoming fearful. Eventually, the horse comes to believe that you will not place him in harm's way. Why not? Because you haven't done so yet. We prove our devotion over time, becoming worthy of the horse's trust through 10,000 positive experiences.

Nurturing an ill or injured horse back to health also builds trust. Hand-grazing, taking easy walks, visiting buddies, comfort scratching, grooming for horses who enjoy it, soothing wounds with warm water, bandaging gently, stroking, talking softly, cold-hosing hot sore legs, expecting nothing for a change—all these are ways to show your horse that you are interested in his comfort and welfare. Add some of these luxuries to your weekly equine agenda instead of waiting for an injury to occur.

It takes only a minute to break a horse's trust but months to rebuild it. Don't make the horse do something that scares him. Instead, break the task down into easy pieces, and allow as much time as the horse needs to master each piece. When necessary, revert to a slower gait or an easier version of the task temporarily. Groundwork is an excellent means of reversion. Sometimes even the best riders interfere with equine movement or mindset, so it's helpful to remove the rider and still teach the horse the same basic lesson. Once he's mastered it, reintroduce the rider.

In general, bonding with a horse is like gaining the trust of a skittish child. You must encourage relaxation, offer leadership and nurturing, teach with small steps and gentle guidance, proving that you have the child's best interest at heart. With time and consistency over many experiences, both child and horse learn that you won't hurt them—you're always on their side.

Facial Expression in Cross-Species Communication

To make a good team, horses and humans must be able to read each other's emotions. Horses have one of the most expressive faces of all species, pulling from 17 distinct movements that can be combined in any number of ways. (Any math nerds out there? 17 movements yield over 355 trillion possible combinations. That's a *lot* of facial expression!) Add to that their wide range of body language, and you'll see why horses don't require speech to make their needs known. Even among humans, body language is better than verbal language at conveying subtle meanings through gaze, posture, tempo, gesture, tone, position, and pupil size.

Equids express positive and negative emotions on their faces, just as humans do. These facial expressions are key precursors to body language—it's a lot safer to respond to the look on a horse's face rather than waiting until he has to kick or bite his message across. In one study of facial expressions, a researcher groomed young horses for 10 minutes a day using standard or gentle techniques. The standard technique was similar to typical daily grooming in which we curry and brush from head to tail regardless of equine response. Horses in this group showed their displeasure in wide eyes with white showing, contracted lips, asymmetrical ear positions, and high heads. When these expressions were ignored, the horses moved away, pinned their ears, gestured with a hind leg, or snapped at the groomer.

The gentle technique included scratching and stroking, to find grooming locations that each horse seemed to enjoy. Each horse was still groomed everywhere, but with attention to his personal likes and dislikes. The gently groomed horses displayed tranquil expressions with eyes half-closed, muzzles forward, upper lips extended, ears resting softly outward or backward, and heads at medium height. So, all the horses in this study were exhibiting significant facial differences connected to positive and negative emotions.

One year later, the researchers groomed the same horses again. This time they used a neutral technique intermediate to the standard and gentle protocols. The animals showed no body language, but they displayed the same facial expressions as before. Their emotions were now expressed strictly through facial display. Pay attention to your horse's face, and you'll see a lot more of what he's thinking.

Horses also read emotional expressions on other horses' faces. This practice occurs whether they are familiar with the other horse or not, and it helps to regulate social interactions within an equine group. Have you ever seen a young buck approach an alpha mare's food? She pins one ear, but he's too naive to get the message. When she takes her memo one step further, you'll see a nasty expression with ears pinned flat, teeth bared, nostrils wrinkled back, and an open jaw snapping hard in the direction of the little whippersnapper. No one would mistake it for a kind and loving reminder.

But mild expressions also direct social behavior among equines. Horses who see photographs of positive, attentive, relaxed equine faces approach and spend more time viewing them. Their heart rates slow slightly, suggesting relaxation, but return to normal without delay. In contrast, horses are reluctant to approach photographs of aggressive equine faces, and their heart rates increase and remain heightened for a longer time.

Even more remarkable, equines can read human facial expressions, not only in real life but also in photographs. Horses avoid photographs of angry human faces and display a rapid increase in heart rate upon seeing them. Photographs of relaxed, smiling human faces do not elicit avoidance and do not alter heart rate. So, the next time you're frowning at the barn for some silly human reason, remember you're sending a message to your horse. Try a soft eye and an easy smile instead (fig. 18.2). Human facial expressions are useful in training horses. For example, you can shoot visual lasers at a disobedient horse but adopt a soft indirect gaze when he shapes up.

Equine Therapy

Equine brains are built to experience emotion (the amygdalas) without evaluation (the prefrontal cortex). This architecture creates an emotional

18.2 Horses prefer relaxed pleasant human faces with very soft or slightly diverted eye contact.

but non-judgmental animal who mirrors human attitudes. For that reason, horses excel at teaching people assertiveness, emotional awareness, and social responsibility. Therapy horses help to treat PTSD, mood or anxiety disorders, substance abuse, autism, trauma, and grief. They are also useful in rehabilitating prison inmates and physically disabled individuals.

There are about 900 certified equine therapy centers in the United States today, and they help to heal more than 66,000 children and adults every year. Almost any quiet horse can do this work—it doesn't require special emotional training or years spent scouting for the perfect mount. By nature, equine brains have the capacity to heal human wounds. Maybe the racehorse trainer Federico Tesio said it best, "A horse gallops with his lungs, perseveres with his heart, and wins with his character."

CHAPTER NINETEEN
Pointing Fingers

The barn owner's face was red. "Tiny peed in his feed bucket," she spat in place of, "Hello." I had just arrived for the morning, and she was cleaning stalls. "Little stinker," I giggled, to commiserate with her annoyance. But in fact, it didn't surprise or annoy me.

Measurements alone would dictate that this horse might hit his bucket when urinating. Tiny is 17.2, with skyscraper legs. When this big boy stretches out to pee in his pasture, he covers far more space than the length of his stall. So every now and then, his urine is going to strike a flat bucket that's not fastened into a corner. That's what bleach and soap are for, right?

"No," she intoned in a deeper pitch. "He peed in his feed bucket, *on purpose!*" She was convinced that Tiny had engaged in some careful strategic thought just to ruin her day. And her anger projected to me…as if I had instructed the beast to come up with just such a plan.

Hmm, well. This was a different sort of accusation altogether. No equine plots in advance to retaliate against a human being. Yet similar snippets had reached my ears from several otherwise reasonable adults:

- "I fell off and Smoky didn't wait for me. He ran away and left me lying in the field. He made me limp all the way home, bleeding."
- "Rainbow lifted her hoof up, looked around to see where I was standing, and stepped down on my toes—pinning me to the floor so I wouldn't be able to ride her!"
- "Shandy won't let me catch her. Sh-She doesn't love me."
- "McDreamy's gone nuts, racing around his pen and crashing through fence posts for no reason! He's insane! Help! Hurry!"

It turned out that this last gentle gelding's foot had become entangled in a ground-level loop of electric wire set at a voltage that had knocked down a grown man—the kind of loop that has no business within a mile of a horse farm. That plus a bunch of panicked shrieking is pretty good reason to charge around like a lunatic.

Equine Forethought

Science offers many demonstrations of superb intelligence in horses. But there is no evidence of the purposeful advance planning we see in humans, apes, and some types of birds. This makes perfect sense: Forethought would be an evolutionary disadvantage to any prey animal relying on immediate flight for survival. If the horse's brain was wired to consider each action before it occurred, much time would be wasted in fleeing from danger. In turn, ancient horses would have been killed by predators, and the species would not have survived. That it has survived so well demonstrates the importance of action over thought in the equine mind. To stay alive, some species need to plan—but the horse needs to *not* plan.

Still, many people believe that horses strategize future actions with human-like intent. This misguided assumption is a common problem today, one that's risky for both sides of the horse-and-human team. Its results are not so bad when horses behave well and get credit for positive analysis they have not carried out. But in the event of misbehavior, assuming pre-planned strategies translates all too easily into pointing fingers of blame. And with blame comes punishment.

Pets Rule

Why do we so fervently associate equine misbehavior with planning? Because we humans often misbehave with purpose, so we figure animals do, too. Society has become much more pet-oriented over the last three decades. More and more of us imagine that our animals think and reason just like we do.

Unlike pets of yore, dogs and cats now sleep in our beds, ride in the car, join us at work, and vacation with us in hotels. Some enjoy more play dates than their owners do. In 2019, 67% of Americans said their best friend was a dog or cat, and 78% considered these pets part of their family. More than a third confessed that they prefer their pets to their own children!

But what about horses? Well, more Americans than ever before consider their horses pets. Plenty of equids relax under warm showers every day, cruise around in fancy RVs, get their hooves painted, wear clothing, and enjoy toys, massages, chiropractors, and even psychics. People in the United States spend $67 billion a year pampering their animals. Stacked tight in 100-dollar bills, that much cash would stand 45 miles high. Every year.

Pets have become emotional touchstones. Unlike many human family members, pets offer unconditional love, affection on demand, joyful greetings, and instant forgiveness. They're easy to please—just fork over a treat and all is well. We talk to them like people, confiding our most private thoughts into their velvet ears. New books abound on the moral, emotional, and spiritual lives of animals, while movies and television commercials are rife with animals chatting in human-like conversation.

During the 1990s, the number of Americans who called themselves a pet's "mother" or "father" increased by 28%. Forty years ago it was rare to use a human name for a horse—now it's ubiquitous. By 2017, most owners considered their horses to be their best friends, full members of their human families.

I'm not saying all this is wrong. I talk to four-legged creatures every day and can pamper with the best of horse moms. But it's important to explore the unconscious thought process that often accompanies this kind of conduct. We can love and respect our horses while still appreciating the immense differences between human and equine brains. Equating animal behavior with human behavior causes problems for both parties.

Consider the parents who let their toddlers kiss the sweet horsie's face—loving humans do this, so why not human-animal pairs? They don't realize the horse can sling his huge head around in an eye-blink, shattering the child's face without a morsel of regret. Or the owner who scratches her horse's belly from the ground while he grazes. If spooked, his brain will command instant flight with no regard to her location. The same attitude causes a zoo visitor to climb into a jaguar enclosure for a selfie, getting her arm ripped half off. It allows a father to kick the house cat because it scratched the seven-month-old baby who pulled its tail. Who gets blamed for these mishaps? Well, of course—the horse, the jaguar, and the cat.

A horse's intent is not to make human lives miserable. It's to avoid work, return to the barn, join the homies, or munch clover in the north forty. Equine misbehavior has nothing to do with us personally. Animals are *animals*. Treating them as if they're human sets up impossible expectations and endangers our lives as well as theirs.

"But I Was Only Joking!"

Not everyone who mentions malevolent equine forethought does so with a straight face. Many of us joke about the horse who spends the night "planning his next evasion" or "figuring out a new trick." We spin yarns of late-night equine parties and chuckle at horse antics that resemble human play. We enjoy sayings in which the older horse explains to a youngster, "You can lead humans to knowledge, but you can't make 'em think." I'm guilty of kidding around in these ways, too.

Let's not quash good humor on horse property—we need more of it! But to square this humor with reality, we must be sure our friends know we are laughing about *imaginary* equine capacities.

All joking aside, common language can fuel misunderstandings about equine thought. When horses obey, we say they're "willing to please." When they learn to associate our cues with certain behaviors, we say they "understand" us. Horses who are trained to keep a safe distance from humans "respect" our space. If they step out eagerly on a lead line, they "have a good work ethic." When they perk up at an event mobbed with equine buddies, we say they "love" the show ring. Ponies whose young riders have allowed them to become gate-sour are "taking advantage," and those who bite at the constant treats children offer become "mean."

In theory, we could alter our manner of speech, saying that a horse "has learned to maintain a distance of 2 feet circumference around my body" rather than "respects me." But this is unrealistic and unnecessary. Language is hard to change from the outside. A better way to modify thought is to explain the underpinnings of brain differences to those who have the mental capacity to understand them: humans, in other words. We need to comprehend why horses do not have the powers to plan, moralize, think critically, or evaluate consequences the way we do.

Back to Prefrontal Cortex

Prefrontal cortex is responsible for executive function, right? This includes analysis, strategy, planning, forethought, assessment, judgment—all the capacities we're discussing in relation to whether horses are culpable for misbehavior. The amount of brain tissue devoted to executive function varies dramatically among species.

Proportion of Prefrontal Cortex in the Brain	
Humans	33%
Monkeys	15%
Dogs and Cats	5%
Horses	0%

Aside from hogging so much of our noggins, human prefrontal cortex is also deeply interconnected to distant neural structures that regulate thoughts and feelings. This hard wiring allows us to assess current and future feelings, plan our actions, and strategize about intent on the fly. Prefrontal cortex affects nearly everything humans do; it's a primary component of the human mind, churning through every interaction we have. Most of the time, we are not even aware of its constant activity.

When asked to record every future-oriented thought they have, people report them on average 59 times a day. That's once every 16 minutes of time spent awake. When pinged electronically to record whatever they're thinking at a given moment, people report pondering the future three times more often than they think about the past. But other than the conditioned anticipation of very short-term events, future thinking is not a component of the equine mind at all.

In general, brains grow partly by sending out shoots (called *dendrites*) on neurons, much as a plant grows new stems in the spring (fig. 19.1). Dendrites that do not connect with other neurons through use are killed in a kind of pruning that allows better organization of functional brain tissue. That's what we mean when we say of brain cells, "Use it or lose it!" The greatest number of neurons and dendrites die when children are about two years old. Another big chop occurs around puberty. In much smaller numbers throughout life, unused dendrites are pruned out. Pruning saves oxygen and glucose for active neurons—the ones that read this book and ride your horse.

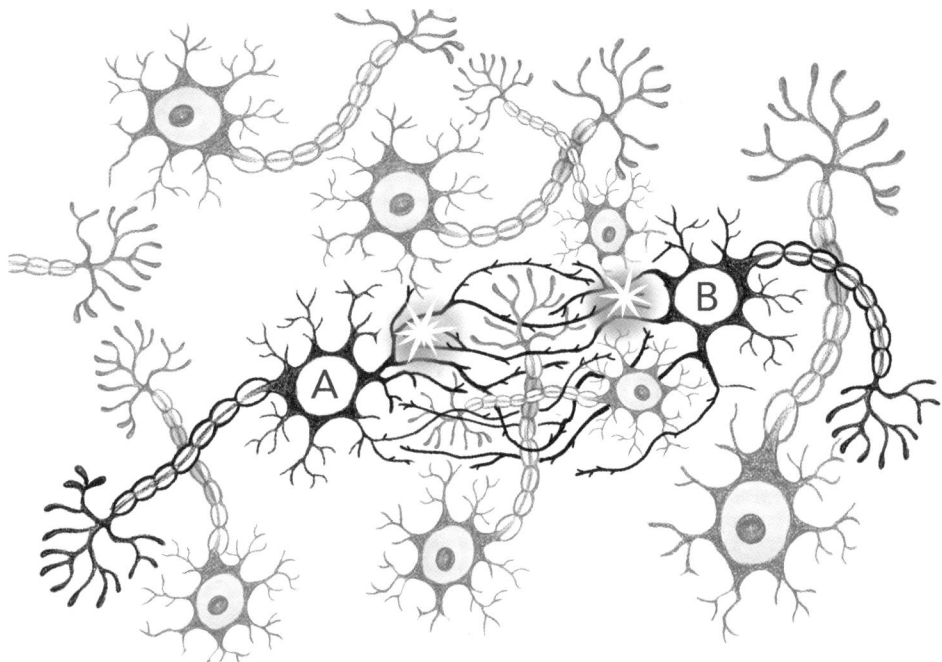

19.1 Dendrites grow outward between neurons A and B to make new connections that will mediate various brain functions.

Across the animal kingdom, human prefrontal cortex is unique in at least three ways:

- It's the last area to be heavily pruned for maximum organization, around 25 years of age. In other words, its complexity requires significantly more time for development than any other part of the brain. Cortex containing massive numbers of unpruned dendrites at age 30 is linked to schizophrenia, mental retardation, and drug- or stress-related psychosis.
- It's unique in size relative to the whole brain. All nonhuman primates (gorillas, chimps, monkeys) have prefrontal cortex. But even they do not have anywhere near the prefrontal equipment that we have. In humans, 21 to 26% of prefrontal tissue is made up of working neurons—tiny analyzers assessing every tidbit of thought and emotion. By comparison, nonhuman primates have only 13 to 17% of neurons hustling about in their prefrontal areas. The volume of connective tissue among prefrontal cells differs too, with humans at about 12% compared with nonhuman primates at 5 to 7%.
- Certain areas of the human prefrontal cortex have no counterpart even in nonhuman primates. An area called the *lateral frontal pole*, for example, does not exist at all in macaque monkeys—or horses. Why do we care? Because that is the area most strongly responsible for human strategizing, planning, and decision-making. Exactly the functions we're questioning in the horse.

In short, the human brain evolved for executive function to a degree that is unprecedented among all other species. To suggest that a horse should have similar executive function is like expecting a newborn to beat a world champion's best game.

A Caveat about Anatomy

The fact that horses do not have prefrontal cortex does not necessarily mean that they have zero capacity for executive function. It just means that such capacity would have to be mediated by another, as-yet-unknown area of the equine brain. But there are some big stumbling blocks here. For one thing, there is no "spare" area of the equine brain that is likely to hold such powers. We can't point at the soft tofu beneath the horse's forehead and say, "Hey, look! There's a lump that's not doing anything—maybe that's prefrontal cortex, sitting in a surprise location!"

More importantly, equine behaviors do not require the function of such an area. A horse's actions—peeing in a bucket, running home after a fall, refusing to be caught, stepping on human feet, freaking out in a paddock—can be explained in much simpler ways. Some are natural, others are learned. In science, the correct explanation is the simplest one that accounts for consistently observable results. If it walks like a horse and neighs like a horse, it's a horse.

Agency

In addition to intent and forethought, brain science explores *agency*–the capacity of an animal to choose to act independently. Horses certainly have free will–they'll buck when *they* feel like it, not when *you* feel like it. And they'll refuse to cross a bridge despite your most contrary persuasions. Horses have the agency to choose actions, but they do not have the mental machinery to analyze consequences like humans do. Riding is that rare sport in which the "equipment" is alive, with a mind of its own.

Assessing Blame

Once we invest horse minds with malevolent intent, it's only a short step to blame them when they misbehave. But "misbehavior" is a human construct. Kicking, biting, striking, bolting, shying, attacking to protect foals, fighting to kill, running away—all these are normal aspects of equine behavior. Only humans see them as misbehavior. So in a human world, the horse must learn to control these natural impulses and behave in a more artificial manner.

Human impulses are controlled partly by learning and partly by reasoning. Using the *hippocampus* ("hip-uh-KAMP-uhs"), basal ganglia, and cerebellum, we learn during early childhood that we can't just haul off and punch the little frenemy who stole our favorite toy (fig. 19.2 A). Horses also have that learning capacity, using the same areas of their brains (fig. 19.2 B). But we *homo sapiens* have an ace up our sleeve—the

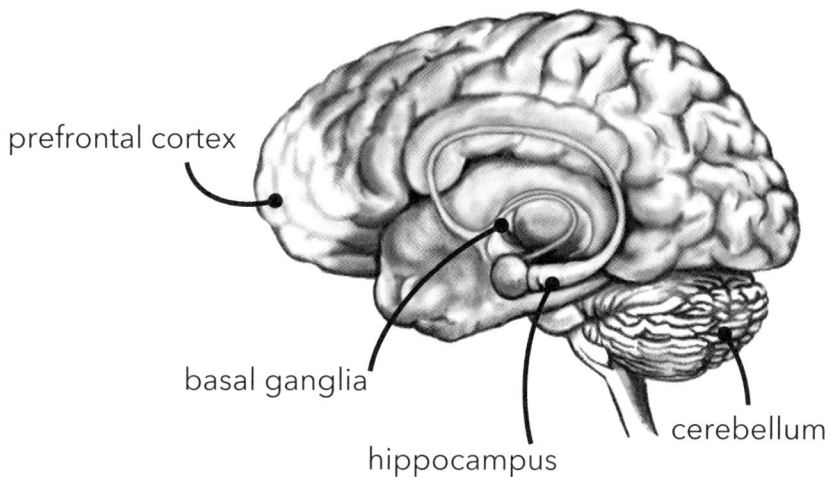

19.2 A Human areas of learning include the basal ganglia, hippocampus, and cerebellum. Areas of reasoning include the prefrontal cortex. Learning and reasoning work together in the human brain.

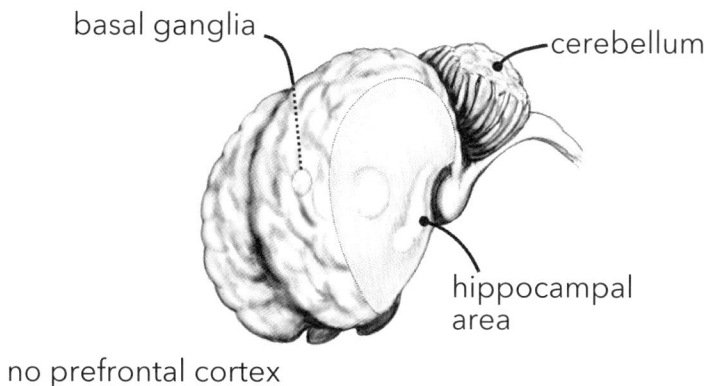

19.2 B The horse also learns using the basal ganglia, hippocampal area, and cerebellum. But there is no prefrontal cortex for reasoning. So the horse learns more directly than humans do, but his brain cannot apply much reasoning to the task.

prefrontal area that supplies risk analysis as a brake: "If I hit that kid, I'm going to get into trouble." Without this futuristic reasoning ability, impulses would have much greater power to derail us—just as they derail the horse.

Prefrontal Dysfunction

Sociopaths are good examples of people whose prefrontal cortex does not inhibit impulses well. They tend to be deceitful and aggressive, with no empathy or remorse and little regard for laws or morals. Their behavior is often criminal. Brain scans show that sociopaths average 11% less brain tissue and significantly less activity in the prefrontal cortex compared to the normal population. That's why their criminal impulses are not inhibited.

Like horses, they still have the neural machinery to learn some impulse control. However, many criminals suffer from poor education and few positive experiences, so their learning is limited. And the impulse toward violence is so immediate that we need both learning and executive function to hold it back. These findings open the door to an important legal question: Are criminals with an impaired prefrontal cortex still culpable for their misbehavior? In turn, we must ask the same of our horses.

When assessing blame in an animal with no prefrontal cortex, there's a lot to consider. As a teenager, I was grooming a grey Quarter Horse filly tied to a large trailer. Asia pressed her left side against the trailer and refused to move over when cued from the front. I should have untied and repositioned her. But I was in a hurry—three words that are so often the prelude to injury—and annoyed at the three-year-old's attitude, so I moved around behind her and pressed my hand against her left hip. She leaned into my pressure and flattened her ears, plastering herself to the trailer even more. Because she didn't yield to my hand, I slapped the left side of her butt. In the blink of an eye, she fired both back legs into my knees.

Who's to blame? Well, who stood behind Asia and slapped her? My prefrontal cortex wasn't fully formed yet, but I had enough horse smarts and brainpower to anticipate the consequences. She did not. She was simply reacting in a horse's natural way. It was the first time she had kicked at anyone. She warned me ahead of time with pinned ears. And she was a green bean—she didn't know yet that refusing to yield was bad manners. I couldn't punish her. For one thing, I was busy driving myself to the hospital with two broken kneecaps. But more importantly, the harm wasn't the horse's fault.

Harm x Intent x Culpability = Punishment

The human prefrontal cortex takes harm and intent into account when assessing blame and determining punishment. An act that causes harm is considered more blameworthy than the same act that does not. If we decide the harm is severe and premeditated, we tend to punish. It's a natural brain equation, one that's very hard to turn off. Through evolution, this unconscious mental processing has allowed us to enforce rules of cooperation and fairness.

Because it's our neural nature, we tend to think in the same terms about animals. But a horse cannot judge harm. A horse who kicks and breaks a couple of knees feels no greater guilt than one who kicks and misses. He just kicks to defend himself, the way humans might raise an involuntary hand to hold off an unwanted touch. Asia is a good example—she intended to kick and she definitely caused harm, but that doesn't mean she should have been punished.

With current equipment, scientists can isolate tiny areas of the human brain and impair them briefly without affecting surrounding tissue. The brain can still think normally except for whatever function that one impaired spot carries out. In one study, researchers temporarily knocked out a little chunk of prefrontal cortex while people read scenarios of misbehavior. In some cases the misbehavior caused severe harm; in others, very little. Each version was accompanied by a different degree of intent.

When the focal spot of prefrontal cortex was out of commission, people assigned blame but did not punish the instigator as severely as when their brains were fully functional. This square-inch of prefrontal tissue is the seat of punishment, the spot that decides whether and how severely to punish for misbehavior. It's exactly the chunk that equestrians must learn to control when working with horses.

"It's Never the Horse's Fault"

Trainers use this tired old slogan when something goes wrong, to everyone's aggravation. Steeped in prefrontal tissue, we humans tend to assume that someone has to be at fault. If an action can't be the horse's fault, then it must be *the human's* fault. And it's really hard to blame yourself when you've just been scraped against a tree or buried face-first in the dirt.

A more accurate phrase would be, "It's not the horse's *intent*." Horse brains can't plan vindictive long-term strategies. Whether good or bad, equine actions rarely carry blame—they simply occur. Do we let misbehavior pass? Not at all! We look at what happened, then plan how to avert or correct it instantly the next time. Asia certainly earned her share of yielding lessons in the weeks after our spat! Let's teach our horses good behavior instead of blaming them for bad behavior. It's more effective and more fun—and the same principle works with people, by the way.

But what about the bear of a horse—that rare thug who attacks whenever you come close? His behavior has nothing to do with plotting. It's caused by poor training, abuse, inappropriate punishment, extreme trauma, illness, pain, or brain dysfunction. Maybe he's just learned that when he assails, you leave—and he gets to eat his hay in peace. Typically, it's a combination of these problems.

Even some humans can't function in a human world. Why would we expect every horse to succeed at it? Bad actors require extensive time with trainers who specialize in misbehavior. Often, that means daily work for many years. Few owners can invest that kind of money in an animal that endangers people and won't perform.

One of the best reasons to hang around horses—even the tough ones—is that they are 100% true. They do not deceive, judge, hoodwink, or manipulate. They're the essence of WYSIWYG: What You See Is What You Get. We humans don't find that kind of authenticity very often in life—maybe that's why it's so hard for us to accept. Let's cherish it, rather than trying to change it. Horses aren't like us, and we shouldn't want them to be.

PART FIVE

Horsemanship Is More Than Knowledge

CHAPTER TWENTY
True Horsemanship

In this book, we've explored the equine brain's evolutionary design and its myriad ways of perceiving the world. We've delved into its superb methods of learning and remembering, of noticing every jot and jiggle yet remaining capable of developing focus. We've seen that the equine brain uses emotion to drive behavior as well as expression, but it does not have the ability to plot against us or judge our actions. This scientific knowledge can be applied to every horse to ease the tensions of equine life in a human world.

It's not just the equine brain that we need to consider. In a horse-and-human team, the inner workings of both brains are equally important. We've investigated some of the differences and similarities between both species' noggins. In recent years, animal researchers have encouraged greater focus on the similarities. But equestrians do best to center on the differences. We already tend toward the mistake that horse minds are similar to our own; it's the differences we are unlikely to see. And for safety, it's the differences that are most critical. Armed with knowledge of equine and human brains, you can begin to understand equine behavior at a deep level. From there, you can build your horse's brain—and your own—to better suit your purpose.

Much more is known about equine brains than this one book can relate, but much also remains to be explored. We need equine scientists to drill down on the horse's sense of smell, ability to seek cause, categorical perception, and potential for observational learning. There's room to delve more deeply into equine concept categorization and positive equine emotions. Hundreds of experimental paradigms wait for application to the horse, each with the potential to demonstrate equine surprises we might never imagine.

Whatever we learn about that soft tofu between our four-legged creatures' ears, we must apply to its human counterpart, so that team function advances in equal measure. During all forms of mounted performance, and some forms of ground handling, horse and human brains can work not just simultaneously, but quite literally together. In effect, the quality team has one very large brain that can do far more than its human and equine halves.

Cross-Species Communication at Its Peak

Brain scientists and comparative psychologists have overlooked horses long enough. Although equids are difficult to house and test, the results are likely to pay off in basic science, veterinary medicine, equine studies, and animal communication. Researchers who want to understand how two widely differing species communicate with each other—such as the dog and human, or the chimp and crow—should focus first on the best example we have. That example is found in the nonverbal communication between horses and riders. From such study, scientists will learn much that can be applied to communication between humans and all other animal species. New knowledge will also yield lessons in ethics, philosophy, anatomy, physiology, language, medicine, and communication systems.

As a cognitive scientist, I am well aware that my opinion on the need for greater equine study will shock most academics. Horses? You've gotta be kidding! But I'm confident enough in my knowledge of horses and brains to step out on a limb and invite brain scientists of all flavors: Come learn about horses and the ways they interact with people, then develop rebuttals if you still don't believe me. There's a level of communication here that simply does not exist in even the closest human relationships with dogs and cats.

We've seen that cross-species communication is not just theoretical or abstract—it's physical. A horse's neurons fire in direct response to human neurons, and vice versa, as if the synaptic gap crosses skin. Riders in this communication loop have the unprecedented privilege of experiencing a prey animal's brain from within. We become part of the horse's brain when working together, and he becomes part of our human brain as well. Humans can learn so much from this perspective about how animals experience the world. Of course, excellence in this ability takes years of training and hundreds of horses to develop. You don't just plop your bottom on your first pony and wait for divine intervention to occur!

Thinking through other minds is not the worst skill to awaken, regardless of whether you use it in the saddle. As the world grows smaller and more diverse, we all benefit from learning to walk in someone else's shoes. Meld your mind with a horse, and you'll find it easier to understand your human neighbors, dogs and cats, even your kids and parents!

Solid knowledge of equine and human brain science takes time and effort to grasp. So why bother? I hope this book has already answered that question: to boost performance, to improve safety, to tailor training to a specific horse, to clarify your horse's understanding of your requests and yours of his. But here in these final paragraphs, I'd like to offer one more reason for all that extra work. It has to do with an old-fashioned but much needed definition of horsemanship.

The Gift of True Horsemanship

A teen and her trainer stand near the gate at a show, watching a lovely Thoroughbred exit his hunter stake flat class. The rider of the horse is delighted—smiling, stroking his neck, and cooing praise into his handsome ears. The teen knows that the horse placed dead last and did not perform well in an absolute sense: He was visibly nervous, brought a little too much hand-gallop to the game, and shied once in the back corner of the indoor arena. He also failed to remain at a four-poster halt for 30 seconds while all the Warmbloods grew roots in the sand. So the teen asks her trainer why the rider is patting the horse. "That's horsemanship," the trainer answers. "The horse did the best he could, and the rider is comparing today's performance to previous performances, not to the other horses in the ring. It doesn't matter that he wasn't perfect." The teen listens carefully, but her face furrows in puzzlement.

The word "horsemanship" gets thrown around a lot nowadays. It has acquired definitions that dilute its true meaning and sometimes contradict its basic spirit. We have horsemanship clinics in which participants learn about equine nutrition, evolution, welfare, first aid, and barn management—all key topics. We have natural horsemanship in which people train horses according to one school of thought. We have horsemanship lessons in every discipline: cutting, roping, jumping, dressage, driving, reining, trail, and so on. I've used it in the phrase "brain-based horsemanship." Magazines on horsemanship include topics like tack care, hoof trimming, and barn dogs. So many topics can be included under the umbrella of the term that it has come to mean almost anything about horses.

The kind of true horsemanship I'm talking about can be summed up in four simple words: *"The horse comes first."* Good horsemen—and there is no greater compliment to a woman or man who works with these magnificent animals—don't even have to think about equine priority. As children, their breakfasts and dinners arrived only after the horses were fed. That way, they'd never forget to feed. Neglecting to water a horse would have been akin to murdering a friend. The shame of it was so severe that no further punishment was needed.

Because we hold them captive in barns or pastures, horses must have our protection. They have no choice but to rely on us for nutritious food, fresh water, and solid shelter. They must depend on us for safety: low-risk fencing, clean housing, veterinary care, farrier visits, regular exercise, and prudent socialization with equine pals. We have an obligation to expand our horse knowledge fully so that we can take the best possible care of our captive steeds. Developing the necessary knowledge requires devotion to education and daily experience with many different mounts—over long periods of time. Maintaining a horse is a highly specialized task, nothing like owning a dog or cat.

True horsemen remain lifelong learners who are always willing to ask for help without fear of embarrassment. Every horse teaches something new. When problems crop up—from training turmoil to human drama—their key question is, "What's best for the horse?" True horsemen never risk a horse's health or welfare with performance-enhancing drugs, inhumane practices, or human temper tantrums. They step in at any cost when a horse is mistreated or endangered. Trash talking their animals is like telling new parents their infant is ugly—seek refuge, because you're in for an earful. No true horseman is too proud to muck out a stall, pick a hoof, or clean a sheath. These women and men hold the highest respect for the honor and dignity of horses.

Most horsemen, of course, are women—not because women take better care of horses, but because horse sports have become populated primarily by female riders and handlers. The term hangs on because we have not yet developed a genderless word that conveys the spirit of true horsemanship. Anyone can learn to ride, drive, handle, or maintain horses. But to be a true horseman is to stand a step above the most highly qualified of these individuals because of that spirit in which the horse comes first.

What the Horse Gives Back

Horses are generous, but those who are bonded deeply to a true horseman will try their hearts out. Ask that horse to run, and he will run his fastest until the very stride in which he collapses and dies. That's why we have to keep our expectations in check.

In return for our best care and kindest attention, equids give us so much. Modern horses can run 44 miles an hour while carrying a saddle and rider—faster than any other land mammal on earth. They can travel 500 miles in mountainous endurance races, leap obstacles more than 8 feet high, fly around the world in airplanes, and dance in place to the rhythm of music. A pair can pull the weight of two 2019 Ford F-350 Super Duty pickup trucks. Try that sometime! Horses can walk 33 feet on their hind legs. And why do they do all this? Simply because we ask them to.

Horses perform these amazing athletic feats, and yet they still rest the weight of their heads gently on our shoulders and breathe softly into our ears. They stand quietly next to us while we cry. They connect with all manner of troubled people—abused children, battered wives, and traumatized combat veterans; at-risk teens, rape victims, parents grieving tragic losses—offering their hearts to let people heal. "Here I am," they imply in peace. "Let's just be."

Few endeavors teach the same degrees of confidence and humility as the daily work of learning to control an enormous but agile animal with mental training, physical conditioning, and emotional kindness. Horses show us how to set clear boundaries, master nonverbal communication, break goals into ordered steps, and practice the best principles of learning and motivation. They teach us to conquer our fears, offer compassion, build trust, let go of anxiety, and behave with transparency. Honed on animals, these skills transfer to human interactions to everyone's benefit. If we all treated people the way true horsemen treat horses, the world would be a better place.

Source Notes

P. ix | "The Brain—is wider..."—There are several versions of this poem, but I have chosen to reprint the original exactly as Dickinson wrote it. THE POEMS OF EMILY DICKINSON, edited by Thomas H. Johnson, Cambridge, Mass.: The Belknap Press of Harvard University Press, Copyright © 1951, 1955 by the President and Fellows of Harvard College. Copyright © renewed 1979, 1983 by the President and Fellows of Harvard College. Copyright © 1914, 1918, 1919, 1924, 1929, 1930, 1932, 1935, 1937, 1942, by Martha Dickinson Bianchi. Copyright © 1952, 1957, 1958, 1963, 1965, by Mary L. Hampson.

CHAPTER 1

P. 3 | Earliest evidence of horses being ridden and milked— https://www.sciencedaily.com /releases/2009/03/090305141627.htm

P. 3 | American Horse Council Foundation statistics, 2017—They report 7.2 million horses in the United States, not counting ponies or minis. https://www.horsecouncil.org/about-us /ahc-programs/ahc-foundation/

P. 3 | 27 million Americans ride— https://www.sportsbusinessdaily.com /Journal/Issues/2017/01/09/Marketing -and-Sponsorship/Equestrian.aspx

P. 4 | 833 breeds—Estimates of living horse breeds in the world vary from 200 to 1600 because they are so difficult to establish. After extensive discussion with the United Nations Food and Agriculture Organization, the most accurate number they can provide at this time is about 833 non-extinct and transboundary horse breeds around the world. This number comes from the Commission on Genetic Resources for Food and Agriculture, "Status and Trends of Animal Genetic Resources – 2022," (January 18-20, 2023, Rome). https://openknowledge.fao.org/ server/api/core/bitstreams/c8121641- 5385-404f-bf98-6a584bec2e7b/content.

P. 9 | Highest puissance wall jumped is 8' 1"—https://en.wikipedia.org/wiki /Puissance

P. 11 | Xenophon—Xenophon, *The Art of Horsemanship* (New York: Dover Publications, 350 BC/2006 AD).

P. 12 | Scottsdale population—10,026 in 1960 census, 3.8 square miles. https://scottsdalehistory.org/page-18189

P. 15 | "Simplicity is…"—usually attributed to Leonardo da Vinci, but the exact source is uncertain. https://quoteinvestigator.com/2015/04/02 /simple/

P. 15 | "Where in this wide world…"— is the first stanza of a poem by Ronald Duncan, *The Horse* (London: Souvenir Press Ltd, 1990). © (Copyright of) the Ronald Duncan Estate.

CHAPTER 2

P. 18 | Human brain maturation to age 25—J. N. Giedd, "Structural Magnetic Resonance Imaging of the Adolescent Brain," *Annals of the New York Academy of Sciences,* 1021 (2004): 77–85.

P. 18 | Equine physical maturity takes five to seven years—Isabella Edwards, "When are Horses Mature?," *Equine Wellness,* April 17, 2014.

P. 18 | New neurons born throughout adulthood—Aurèlie Ernst and Jonas Frisèn, "Adult Neurogenesis in Humans—Common and Unique Traits in Mammals," PLOS Biology, 13 (2015): doi 10.1371/journal.pbio.1002045

P. 18 | Effects of the Ice Age 35 million years ago—https://www.science20.com/news_releases/why_did_ice_antarctica_suddenly_appear_35_million_years_ago_co2_says_study

P. 19 | Splint bones were outer toes—https://www.inverse.com/article/40590-horse-toe-feet evolution-metacarpal-equus-mesohippus; and https://ker.com/equinews/horse-splints/

P. 19 | Natural history of the horse—Wendy Williams, *The Horse* (New York: Scientific American/Farrar, Straus and Giroux, 2015). This bestselling book describes the horse's natural history in entertaining detail. It contains photographs of equine fossils and explains how archeologists date them.

P. 20 | Equine axon length—The longest equine axon is the recurrent laryngeal nerve which runs from the brainstem to the larynx, a few inches away. For interesting evolutionary reasons, it takes an indirect route from the brainstem all the way to the horse's heart, then loops back up to the larynx. Michel-Antoine Leblanc, *The Mind of the Horse,* trans. Giselle Weiss (Cambridge, MA: Harvard University Press, 2013), 73; and Janet L. Jones, "Cory's Second Wind," *EQUUS* 470, (November 2016): 32-42.

P. 20 | Equine axon speed—Zoe Davies, *Equine Science* (Hoboken, NJ: John Wiley & Sons, 2018).

P. 20 | Glucose consumption—Human brain comprises 2% of body weight https://faculty.washington.edu/chudler/ffacts.html. Horse brain weighs 1 ½ to 2 pounds http://www.ebhrc.com/article2.

html. Calculating the horse's average weight at 1000 pounds, the ratio of brain to body weight is .002. Horse uses 25% of body's glucose - American Association of Equine Practitioners, *Equine Veterinary Education,* (October 2017). Available online: https://aaep.org/site-search?search=glucose+brain.

P. 21 | Human pathway from vision to action—A second pathway in human brains reduces prefrontal analysis under certain circumstances, but it is still not as fast as the equine route. Joseph LeDoux, *The Emotional Brain* (New York: Simon and Schuster, 1996).

P. 22 | Brain link between human navigation and smell—Louisa Dahmani, Raihaan M. Patel, Yiling Yang, M. Mallar Chakravarty, Lesley K. Fellows, and Veronique D. Bohbot, "An Intrinsic Association Between Olfactory Identification and Spatial Memory in Humans," *Nature Communications* 9, (October 16, 2018): 4162.

P. 24 | Hard-wired social interaction—Lauren Wingfield, "Glimpses Into Brain Uncover Neurological Basis for Processing Social Information," *Neuroscience News* (November 5, 2018).

P. 26 | 6000 years of domestication—Wendy Williams, *The Horse* (New York: Scientific American/Farrar, Straus and Giroux, 2015).

P. 26 | Przewalski horse—Wendy Williams, *The Horse* (New York: Scientific American/Farrar, Straus and Giroux, 2015).

P. 26 | Przewalski horse descended from domesticated horses—Elizabeth Pennisi, "Ancient DNA upends the horse family tree," *Science* (February 22, 2018). Available online: https://www.sciencemag.org/news/2018/02/ancient-dna-upends-horse-family-tree

P. 27 | Brain texture like soft tofu— Katrina Firlik, *Another Day in the Frontal Lobe* (New York: Random House, 2006).

P. 27, 28 | Weight and dimensions of the equine brain—Bruno Cozzi, Michele Povinelli, Cristina Ballarin, and Alberto Granato, "The Brain of the Horse: Weight and Cephalization Quotients," *Brain Behavior and Evolution* 83, no. 1 (December 2013): 9-16.

P. 27 | Volume of the equine brain— Bruno Cozzi, DMV, PhD, 2019, e-mail messages to author, September 17-18.

P. 28 | Number of neurons in human brain—Suzana Herculano-Houzel, *The Human Advantage: A New Understanding of How Our Brain Became Remarkable* (Cambridge, MA: The MIT Press, 2017).

P. 28 | Number of neurons in equine brain—Michel-Antoine Leblanc, *The Mind of the Horse,* trans. Giselle Weiss (Cambridge, MA: Harvard University Press, 2013).

P. 28 | Each pyramidal neuron allows up to 10,000 connections—John Morrison, Professor of Neurology at University of California, Davis. https:// www.brainfacts.org/thinking-sensing -and-behaving/learning-and-memory /2019/the-short-answer-what-is-a -synapse-072519

CHAPTER 3

P. 32 | Blindsight in animals—Jason Holt, *Blindsight and the Nature of Consciousness* (Peterborough, Ontario: Broadview Press, 2003).

P. 32 | Edelman quote—"If our view of memory is correct, in higher organisms every act of perception is, to some degree, an act of creation, and every act of memory is, to some degree, an act of imagination." Gerald M. Edelman and Guilio Tononi, *A Universe of Consciousness:* *How Matter Becomes Imagination* (New York: Basic Books, 2000), 101.

P. 33 | Equine eye size—Michel-Antoine Leblanc, *The Mind of the Horse,* trans. Giselle Weiss (Cambridge, MA: Harvard University Press, 2013).

P. 33 | Normal equine acuity—Zoe Davies, *Equine Science* (Hoboken, NJ: John Wiley & Sons, 2018).

P. 33 | Near- and far-sighted horses— Michel-Antoine Leblanc, *The Mind of the Horse,* trans. Giselle Weiss (Cambridge, MA: Harvard University Press, 2013).

P. 34 | Horse vs. human view of a jump—See photograph credited to Alison Harman in Paul McGreevy, *Equine Behavior 2e* (Sydney: Saunders Elsevier, 2012), 41.

P. 34 | Variations in acuity with age and breed—Michel-Antoine Leblanc, *The Mind of the Horse,* trans. Giselle Weiss (Cambridge, MA: Harvard University Press, 2013).

P. 36 | Equine eyes can move independently—www.horsewyse.com.au /howhorsessee.html

P. 36 | 340-degree range of view—*Merck Veterinary Manual.* Available online: https://www.merckvetmanual.com /horse-owners/eye-disorders-of-horses /eye-structure-and-function-in-horses

P. 42 ‖ 55 types of retinal cells—Richard H. Masland, "The Fundamental Plan of the Retina," *Nature Neuroscience* 4 (2001): 877-886.

P. 42 | 210 million rods and cones— Margaret W. Matlin and Hugh J. Foley, *Sensation and Perception 4e* (Needham Heights, MA: Allyn and Bacon, 1997).

P. 42 | Half second to perceive a sight— David Eagleman, *The Brain: The Story of You* (New York: Pantheon Books, 2015).

P. 45 | "Decapitating" with the blind spot—Vilayanur S. Ramachandran,

Phantoms in the Brain (New York: William Morrow and Company, Inc., 1998), 91.

CHAPTER 4

P. 49 | Pupillary adaptation time and sensitivity—Zoe Davies, *Equine Science* (Hoboken, NJ: Wiley Blackwell, 2018).

P. 50 | Humans see 66% less light at age 60—Atul Gawande, *Being Mortal* (New York: Metropolitan Books, 2014).

P. 51 | Depth perception—This section focuses on binocular disparity, but human and equine vision systems use monocular cues for depth perception as well. For example, motion parallax is important to both species.

P. 51 | Human depth perception of ⅛ inch at 16½ feet—O.J. Braddick, Binocular Vision. In H.B. Barlow and J.D. Mollon (Eds.), *The Senses* (Cambridge: Cambridge University Press, 1982).

P. 51 | Equine depth perception of 9 inches at 16 ½ feet—calculated from information provided in B. Timney and K. Keil, "Local and Global Stereopsis in the Horse," *Vision Research* 39, (1999): 1861-1867.

P. 53 | Half the area visible to two human eyes is visible to two horse eyes—Francis Burton, *Ultimate Horse Care* (Lydney, UK: Ringpress Books, 1999). Leblanc specifies that the equine binocular field is about 60 degrees compared to a human binocular field of 120 degrees. Michel-Antoine Leblanc, *The Mind of the Horse,* trans. Giselle Weiss (Cambridge, MA: Harvard University Press, 2013).

P. 54 | Human visual system uses almost ⅓ of brain—David Eagleman, *The Brain: The Story of You* (New York: Pantheon Books, 2015).

P. 56 | Red jacket against green grass—Wendy Williams, *The Horse* (New York: Scientific American/Farrar, Straus and Giroux, 2015).

P. 56 | Steeplechase colors—Bianca Britton, "New Research on Horse Eyesight Could Improve Racecourse Safety," *CNN News* (October 23, 2018). Available online: https://edition.cnn.com/2018/10/23/sport/racecourse-safety-horse-vision-spt-intl/index.html

P. 56 | 201 racehorses died in 2018—Marcus Armytage, "Horse Deaths at Racecourses Reach Highest Level for Six Years," *The Telegraph* (January 28, 2019). Available online: https://www.telegraph.co.uk/racing/2019/01/28/horse-deaths-racecourses-reach-highest-level-six-years/

P. 57 | Video contrasting horse and human views—I have been unable to verify the origin of this video but believe it was created and posted by the French Riding School, Le Haras de la Cense, 2016. Available online: https://www.agdaily.com/video/simulation-shows-horse-eye-view/.

CHAPTER 5

P. 60 | Loudness and pitch thresholds for horses and cattle—Rickye S. Heffner and Henry E. Heffner, "Hearing in Large Mammals: Horses (*Equus caballus*) and Cattle (*Bos taurus*)," *Behavioral Neuroscience* 97 (1983): 299-309. The landmark study of equine auditory thresholds, this research is well designed. However, it only includes results from three very young horses. To generalize from a small number of immature individuals to the 60 million horses worldwide is a matter of concern.

P. 60 | Pitch thresholds for dogs—Henry E. Heffner, "Hearing in Large and Small Dogs: Absolute Thresholds and Size of the Tympanic Membrane," *Behavioral Neuroscience* 97 (1983): 310-318.

P. 60 | Pitch thresholds for cats—Rickye S. Heffner and Henry E. Heffner, "Hearing Range of the Domestic Cat," *Hearing Research* 19, no. 1 (1985): 85-88.

P. 60 | Pitch range on piano—
http://hyperphysics.phy-astr.gsu.edu/hbase/Music/pianof.html

P. 61 | Male horses pay more attention to sound—Rickye S. Heffner, "Your Horse's Hearing," *Practical Horseman* (August 2000). Available online: https://practicalhorsemanmag.com/health-archive/eqhearing933-11344

P. 61 | Hearing loss by age 17-22 in horses—Elaine Pascoe, "All Ears: Horse Hearing Problems," *Practical Horseman* (November 2014). https://practicalhorsemanmag.com/health-archive/ears-horse-hearing-problems-25832

P. 63 | "High" and "canter"—Susan McBane, *Horse Senses* (London: Manson Publishing Ltd, 2012), 84-5, 90.

P. 64 | Quotes from victims of amusia—Oliver Sacks, *Musicophilia: Tales of Music and the Brain* (NY: Knopf, 2007) 105, 113.

P. 64 | Brainwaves synchronize over music—Jens Madsen, Elizabeth Hellmuth Margulis, Rhimmon Simchy-Gross, and Lucas C. Parra, "Music Synchronizes Brainwaves Across Listeners with Strong Effects of Repetition, Familiarity, and Training," *Nature: Scientific Reports* 9 (March 5, 2019), Article 3576.

P. 65 | Music calms horses and improves performance—Anna Stachurska, Iwona Janczarek, Isabela Wilk, and Witold Kedzierski, "Does Music Influence Emotional State in Race Horses?" *Journal of Equine Veterinary Science* 35, no. 8 (August 2015): 650-656.

P. 65 | 16 muscles per ear—Several freelance writers state that horses have 10 muscles per ear. Burton and Leblanc, both respected experts in equine sensory perception, state there are 16 muscles per ear. Francis Burton, *Ultimate Horse Care* (Lydney, UK: Ringpress Books, 1999); and Michel-Antoine Leblanc, *The Mind of the*

Horse, trans. Giselle Weiss (Cambridge, MA: Harvard University Press, 2013).

P. 66 | Sound localization in horses—Rickye S. Heffner and Henry E. Heffner, "Localization of Tones by Horses: Use of Binaural Cues and the Role of the Superior Olivary Complex," *Behavioral Neuroscience* 100 (1986): 93-103. Also Brian Timney and Todd Macuda, "Vision and Hearing in Horses," *Journal of the American Veterinary Medical Association* 218, no. 10 (May 15, 2001): 1567-1574.

P. 69, 70 | Whinny analysis—Several related studies are described in Michel-Antoine Leblanc, *The Mind of the Horse,* trans. Giselle Weiss (Cambridge, MA: Harvard University Press, 2013), 308-319.

P. 70 | Equine identification of human voices—L. Proops and K. McComb, "Cross-modal Individual Recognition in Domestic Horses (*Equus caballus*)," *Proceedings of the National Academy of Sciences of the USA* 106 (2012): 947-51.

CHAPTER 6

P. 73 | Bending light in 1666—Isaac Newton, "Optics," (1704), in *Great Books of the Western World*, ed. R.M. Hutchins (Chicago: Encyclopedia Britannica, Inc., 1952).

P. 73 | Predicting the scent of a molecule's structure—Andreas Keller, et al., "Predicting Human Olfactory Perception from Chemical Features of Odor Molecules," *Science* 355, no. 6327 (February 24, 2017): 820-826.

P. 73, 74 | Information gleaned from sniffing—Susan McBane, *Horse Senses* (London: Manson Publishing, 2012) and Michel-Antoine Leblanc, *The Mind of the Horse*, trans. Giselle Weiss (Cambridge, MA: Harvard University Press, 2013).

P. 74 | Casting for scent—Stephen Budiansky, *The Nature of Horses* (New York: Free Press, 1997), 170.

P. 75 | Masking scents to change behavior—Karen Briggs, "Equine Sense of Smell," *The Horse* (December 11, 2013). Available online: https://thehorse.com /13971/equine-sense-of-smell/

P. 76 | Sniffing humans and clothing—Susan McBane, *Horse Senses* (London: Manson Publishing, 2012).

P. 77 | Effects of smelling predators—Michel-Antoine Leblanc, *The Mind of the Horse*, trans. Giselle Weiss (Cambridge, MA: Harvard University Press, 2013).

P. 77 | Vomeronasal organ for pheromones—Peter A. Brennan, "Pheromones and Mammalian Behavior," in *The Neurobiology of Olfaction*, ed. A. Menini. Boca Raton, FL: CRC Press/Taylor & Francis, 2010. Available online: https:// www.ncbi.nlm.nih.gov/books/NBK55973/

P. 78 | Diseases dogs can sniff out—Maureen Maurer, Michael McCulloch, Angel M. Willey, Wendi Hirsch, and Danielle Dewey, "Detection of Bacteriuria by Canine Olfaction," *Open Forum Infectious Diseases* 3, no. 2 (March 9, 2016) Available online: https://doi.org/10.1093 /ofid/ofw051. Also, https://massivesci.com /articles/dogs-smell-diseases-diagnose -cancer-diabetes/ and https://www.mnn. com/family/pets/stories/6-medical -conditions-that-dogs-can-sniff

P. 78 | Comparison of canine to equine olfaction—Michel-Antoine Leblanc, *The Mind of the Horse,* trans. Giselle Weiss (Cambridge, MA: Harvard University Press, 2013), 337-341.

P. 78 | Humans' 6 million olfactory receptor cells—Estimates vary. Leblanc estimates there are 10 million olfactory receptors in the human system, based on a 1982 study. But a newer and more reliable source estimates 6 million – Michael W. Levine, *Fundamentals of Sensation and Perception 3e* (Oxford: Oxford University Press, 2006), 465.

P. 78 | Bloodhounds have 300 million olfactory receptor cells—Stanley Coren, *How Dogs Think* (New York: Free Press, 2004), 55.

P. 80 | 80% of taste is from smell; dimensions of equine tongue—Michel-Antoine Leblanc, *The Mind of the Horse,* trans. Giselle Weiss (Cambridge, MA: Harvard University Press, 2013), 354.

P. 81 | Variety in pasture grass—Susan McBane, *Horse Senses* (London: Manson Publishing, 2012).

CHAPTER 7

P. 83 | Patch—Eliza McGraw, "A One-eyed Horse named Patch has a Chance of Winning the Kentucky Derby," *The Washington Post Animalia*, May 3, 2017. Available online: https://www.washingtonpost.com/news /animalia/wp/2017/05/03/a-one-eyed -horse-named-patch-has-a-chance-of -winning-the-kentucky-derby/?noredirect =on&utm_term=.177417e41d34

P. 83 | Gunner—Colonel's Smoking Gun https://www.usef.org/media/press-releases /2570_the-reining-horse-gunner-becomes -million-dollar-sire

P. 83 | Addy—Adventure de Kannan was "the only horse to win the Speed Derby, the Eventing Grand Prix, the All England Grand Prix, the Queen Elizabeth II Cup and the British Jumping Derby." These events are among the most difficult show jumping challenges in the world. http://www.hickstead.co.uk/news/2017 /the-one-eyed-wonder-horse-adventure -de-kannan-to-be-retired-at-this-year-s -al-shira-aa-hickstead-derby-meeting/ https://www.independent.ie/irish-news /news/wonder-horse-astonishing-success -of-showjumping-champ-with-just-one -eye-30495783.html

P. 84 | Splashed-white deafness—Ed Kane, "Hearing Loss in Veterinary Equine

Patients," *Veterinary News DVM360*, March 19, 2015.

P. 84 | Tough Sunday—earnings as of March 2020. https://www.google.com /search?q=Tough+Sunday+earnings&rlz =1C1AVFC_enUS886US886&oq=Tough +Sunday+earnings&aqs=chrome..69i57 .11598j0j7&sourceid=chrome&ie=UTF-8-

P. 84 | Karen Law—http://www. ejbevents.co.uk/press/karen-law -britains-first-blind-show-jumper/

P. 85 | Kristen Knouse—https://apnews. com/1b308a6abc7ff2667fc8d25eec1ccf68

P. 85 | Blind people have better hearing—Elizabeth Huber, Kelly Chang, Ivan Alvarex, Aaron Hundle, Holly Bridge, and Ione Fine, "Early Blindness Shapes Cortical Representations of Auditory Frequency within Auditory Cortex," *The Journal of Neuroscience* (April 22, 2019): 2896-2918.

P. 87 | Hidden stress during trailering—Hajime Ohmura, Seiji Hobo, Atsushi Hiraga, and James H. Jones, "Changes in Heart Rate and Heart Rate Variability during Transportation of Horses by Road and Air," *American Journal of Veterinary Research* 73, no. 4 (April 2012): 515-521.

P. 87 | Hidden stress during clipping—Kelly Yarnell, Carol Hall, and E. Billett, "An Assessment of the Aversive Nature of an Animal Management Procedure (Clipping) using Behavioral and Physiological Measures," *Physiology and Behavior* 118 (June, 2013): 32-39.

P. 89 | Stabilized retinal images disappear—Margaret W. Matlin and Hugh J. Foley, *Sensation and Perception 4e* (Boston: Allyn and Bacon, 1997), 96-97.

CHAPTER 8

P. 98 | "The horse moved like a dancer…"—Quote from Mark Helprin, *Winter's Tale* (New York: Mariner Books, 1983).

P. 99 | Ian Waterman lost proprioception—Jonathan Cole, *Pride and a Daily Marathon* (London: MIT Press, 1991). Video clips of Mr. Waterman are available on youtube.

P. 99 | Spindles detect differences in muscle length of .002%—Richard C. Fitzpatrick, Douglas K. Rogers, and Dierdre I. McCloskey, "Stable Human Standing with Lower-Limb Muscle Afferents Providing the Only Sensory Input," *Journal of Physiology* 480 (October 15, 1994): 395-403.

P. 100 | Proprioception corrects errors in less than half the time vision does—Jennifer A. Stone, Nina B. Partin, Joseph S. Lueken, Kent E. Timm, and Edward J. Ryan, "Upper Extremity Proprioceptive Training," *Journal of Athletic Training* 29 (1994): 15.

P. 100 | Muscle spindle illusions—Guy M. Goodwin, Dierdre I. McCloskey, and P. B. Matthews, "Proprioceptive Illusions Induced by Muscle Vibration: Contribution by Muscle Spindles to Perception?" *Science* 175, no. 4028 (March 24, 1972): 1382-1384.

P. 101 | Joint angle receptor sensitivity in hip and toe—Grigore C. Burdea and Philippe Coiffet, *Virtual Reality Technology, Volume 1* (Hoboken, NJ: Wiley, 2003), 95.

P. 101 | Dorsal columns of the spine carry proprioceptive data—Dale Purves, George J. Augustine, and David Fitzpatrick et al., "The Major Afferent Pathway for Mechanosensory Information: The Dorsal Column-Medial Lemniscus System," *Neuroscience 2e* (Sunderland, MA: Sinauer Associates, 2001).

P. 102 | Stork toe raise—*Women's Health*, November 2014, p. 64.

P. 107 | The man who lost his leg—Oliver Sacks, *A Leg To Stand On* (New York: Touchstone, 1984), 54-60.

P. 107 | Human sensorimotor cortex— E. Bruce Goldstein, *Sensation & Perception 7e* (Belmont, CA: Thomson Wadsworth, 2007).

P. 107 | Mapping of equine motor cortex—Jonathan M. Levine, Gwendolyn J. Levine, Anton G. Hoffman, and Gerald Bratton, "Comparative Anatomy of the Horse, Ox, and Dog: The Brain and Associated Vessels," *Compendium Equine* (April 2008): 153-164. Magnetic Resonance Imaging (MRI), Computer Tomography (CT) scans, and transcranial magnetic stimulation can now be used on the equine brain. Although such images are rarely precise enough to map networks representing specific body parts, they do help us explore general areas.

P. 109 | Sheep and horse brains are similar—Yvette Nout-Lomas, DVM, PhD, 2020, e-mail messages to author, January 16.

P. 109 | Locating somatosensory cortex in sheep— Mortimer Gierthmuehlen, et al., "Mapping of Sheep Sensory Cortex with a Novel Microelectrocorticography Grid," *The Journal of Comparative Neurology* 522 (2014): 3590-3608.

P. 109 | Equine Parkinsonism from toxic weeds— Thomas Gore, Paula Gore, and James M. Giffin, *Horse Owner's Veterinary Handbook 3e* (Hoboken, NJ: Wiley, 2008), 432-433.

CHAPTER 9

P. 112 | Weight of a housefly—https://animaldiversity.org/accounts/Musca_domestica/

P. 112 | Weight of dandelion seeds— http://www.agroatlas.ru/en/content/weeds/Taraxacum_officinale/

P. 112 | Horse's ability to sense a fly—Statistics are calculated from information in Michel-Antoine Leblanc, *The Mind of the Horse*, trans. Giselle Weiss (Cambridge, MA: Harvard University Press, 2013); Carol A. Saslow, "Understanding the Perceptual World of Horses," *Applied Animal Behaviour Science* 78 (2002): 209-224; the online source www.agroatlas.ru; www.biokids.umich.edu; "How Sensitive is Human Touch?" Available online: www.isciencetimes.com; Michael S. Fleming and Wenqin Luo, "The Anatomy, Function, and Development of Mammalian A-beta Low-Threshold Mechanoreceptors," *Frontiers in Biology* 8, no. 4 (2013): 408-420; and Stanley Coren, Lawrence M. Ward, and James T. Enns, *Sensation and Perception 6e* (New York: Wiley, 2004).

P. 112 | Sensitivity in noticing the nod of a head— Statistics are calculated from information in Michel-Antoine Leblanc, *The Mind of the Horse,* trans. Giselle Weiss (Cambridge, MA: Harvard University Press, 2013), 31; and Joseph S. Lappin, Duje Tadin, Jeffrey B. Nyquist, and Anne L. Corn, "Spatial and Temporal Limits of Motion Perception Across Variations in Speed, Eccentricity, and Low Vision," *Journal of Vision* 9, no. 1 (2009): 1-14.

P. 112 | Equine discrimination for head movement—Clever Hans was able to detect a head movement of .20 millimeters – Michel-Antoine Leblanc *The Mind of the Horse,* trans. Giselle Weiss (Cambridge, MA: Harvard University Press, 2013), 31.

P. 112 | Human discrimination for head movement—Joseph S. Lappin, Duje Tadin, Jeffrey B. Nyquist, and Anne L. Corn, "Spatial and Temporal Limits of Motion Perception Across Variations in Speed, Eccentricity, and Low Vision." *Journal of Vision* 9, No. 1 (2009): 1-14.

P. 112 | Equine pressure detection—Lea Lansade, Gaelle Pichard, and Mathilde Leconte, "Sensory Sensitivities: Components of a horse's temperament dimension," *Applied Animal Behavior Science* 114, No. 3-4 (2008): 534-553.

P. 112 | Weight of an "average" grain of sand—https://www.quora.com/How-many-atoms-are-there-in-a-grain-of-sand

P. 112 | Human pressure detection—Jack Loomis, "An Investigation of Tactile Hyperacuity," *Sensory Processes* 3 (1979): 289-302; and M. Hollins and S. R. Risner, "Evidence for the Duplex Theory of Tactile Texture Perception," *Perception & Psychophysics* 62 (2000): 695-705.

P. 113 | Blind people comprehend speech almost three times faster—Susanne Dietrich, Ingo Hertrich, and Hermann Ackermann, "Ultra-Fast Speech Comprehension in Blind Subjects Engages Primary Visual Cortex, Fusiform Gyrus, and Pulvinar - A Functional Magnetic Resonance Imaging (fMRI) Study," *BMC Neuroscience* 14 (July 23, 2013): 74.

P. 113 | More cortex for fingertip control in guitar players—Thomas Elbert, Christo Pantev, Christian Wienbruch, Brigitte Rockstroh, and Edward Taub, "Increased Cortical Representation of the Fingers of the Left Hand in String Players," *Science* 270, No. 5234 (October 13, 1995): 305-307.

P. 113 | More cortex for spatial memory in taxi drivers—Eleanor Maguire, Katherine Woollett, and H. J. Spiers, "London Taxi Drivers and Bus Drivers: A Structural MRI and Neuropsychological Analysis," *Hippocampus* 16, No. 12 (2006): 1091-1101.

P. 113 | Cortex is built by training—Katherine Woollett and Eleanor Maguire, "Acquiring 'the Knowledge' of London's Layout Drives Structural Brain Changes," *Current Biology* 21, (December 20, 2011): 2109-2114.

P. 123 | "What goes around comes around"—often attributed to Paul Crump, *Burn, Killer, Burn!* (Chicago: Johnson Publishing, 1962).

P. 123 | Proprioception declines with age—Fernando Ribeiro and Jose Oliveira, "Aging Effects of Joint Proprioception: The Role of Physical Activity in Proprioception Preservation," *European Review of Aging and Physical Activity* 4, (2007): 71-76.

CHAPTER 10

P. 135 | "What fires together, wires together"—These words are from page 64 of Carla Shatz, "The Developing Brain," *Scientific American* 267 (1992): 60-67. But the theory behind them is from Donald O. Hebb, *The Organization of Behavior: A Neuropsychological Theory* (New York: Wiley and Sons, 1949).

P. 136 | Learning by association—Also known as classical conditioning, its scholarly roots date back at least to Aristotle, but Pavlov worked out the details. Ivan P. Pavlov, "Conditioned Reflexes: An Investigation of the Physiological Activity of the Cerebral Cortex," trans. G. V. Anrep, *Nature* 121 (1927): 662-664.

P. 136 | Instrumental or operant conditioning—Burrhus Frederick Skinner, *About Behaviorism* (New York: Vintage, 1976).

P. 137 | Bobo doll studies—Albert Bandura, Dorothea Ross, and Sheila A. Ross, "Transmission of Aggression through Imitation of Aggressive Models," *Journal of Abnormal and Social Psychology* 63 (1961): 575-582.

P. 137 | Dogs learn by imitation—Stanley Coren, "Dogs Learn by Modeling the Behavior of Other Dogs," *Psychology Today*, January 23, 2013. Available online: https://www.psychologytoday.com/us/blog/canine-corner/201301/dogs-learn-modeling-the-behavior-other-dogs

P. 137 | Wild dolphins tail-walking—WDC (Whale and Dolphin Conservation)

"Wild Dolphins Learn From Each Other to 'Walk on Water'… but It's Just a Fad," August 29, 2018. Available online: https://us.whales.org/news/2018/08/wild -dolphins-learn-from-each-other-to-walk -on-waterbut-its-just-fad

P. 137 | Horses learn by observing dominant horses—Konstanze Krueger and Jurgen Heinze, "Horse Sense: Social Status of Horses (Equus Caballus) Affects their Likelihood of Copying Other Horses' Behavior," *Animal Cognition* 11 (July 1, 2008): 431-439.

P. 137 | Foals learn to be groomed by watching—Christa Leste-Lasserre, "Study: Dams Shape Foals' Relationships with Humans," *The Horse*. Available online: https://thehorse.com/112179 /study-dams-shape-foals-relationships -with-humans/

P. 138 | Foals accept scary objects by watching—J. W. Christensen, "Early-Life Object Exposure with a Habituated Mother Reduces Fear Reactions in Foals," *Animal Cognition* 19 (January 2016): 171-179.

P. 138 | Horses learn to open gates by watching—Temple Grandin, *Animals in Translation* (New York: Simon and Schuster, 2005), 247.

P. 138 | Horses learn join-up by watching—"Join-up" refers to a horse following a human. Often assumed to be purely natural, equine scientists have now shown that the effect is at least partly learned by observation. Konstanze Krueger and Jurgen Heinze, "Horse Sense: Social Status of Horses (Equus Caballus) Affects their Likelihood of Copying Other Horses' Behavior," *Animal Cognition* 11 (July 1, 2008): 431-439.

P. 139 | Horses learn by observing humans—Aurelia Schuetz, Kate Farmer, and Konstanze Krueger, "Social Learning Across Species: Horses (Equus Caballus) Learn from Humans by Observation," *Animal Cognition* 20 (May 1, 2017): 567-573.

P. 140 | Mirror neurons—Marco Iacoboni, *Mirroring People* (New York: Farrar, Straus and Giroux, 2008).

P. 141 | Brain chemicals that consolidate memories of emotional events—Paul E. Gold, "Modulation of Emotional and Nonemotional Memories: Same Pharmacological Systems, Different Neuroanatomical Systems," in *Brain and Memory: Modulation and Mediation of Neuropasticity*, ed. James L McGaugh, N.M. Weinberger, and Gary Lynch (New York: Oxford University Press, 1995), 41-74.

P. 142 | Trespass livestock—"Mesa Verde Horses," *The Durango Herald*, March 25, 2014, 10A. Also Jim Mimiaga, "Mesa Verde National Park prefers removal of 'trespass horses'," *The Durango Herald*, April 22, 2018.

P. 142 | Horse waters himself—Wendy Williams, *The Horse* (New York: Scientific American/Farrar, Straus and Giroux, 2015).

P. 143 | Interval testing for human memory—Alan Baddeley, *Human Memory: Theory and Practice* (Needham Heights, MA: Allyn & Bacon, 1998), 112-114.

CHAPTER 11

P. 146 | Horses use displacement by nature—Andrew McLean and Janne Christensen, "The Application of Learning Theory in Horse Training," *Applied Animal Behaviour Science* 190 (2017): 18-27.

P. 148 | Seat pressure sensor pads—Hilary Clayton, "Measurement and Interpretation of Saddle Pressure Data," *Comparative Exercise Physiology* 9 (January 2013): 3-12.

P. 151 | Timing of the swing phase at a trot—Calculated from data in Stig Drevemo, Goran Dalin, I. Fredricson, and G. Hjerten, "Equine Locomotion: 1. The

Analysis of Linear and Temporal Stride Characteristics of Trotting Standardbreds," *Equine Veterinary Journal* 12 (April 1980): 60-65; W. Back et al., "How the Horse Moves: 2. Significance of Graphical Representations of Equine Hind Limb Kinematics," *Equine Veterinary Journal* 27 (January 1995): 39-45; and W. Back, A. Barneveld, H. C. Schamhardt, and G. Bruin, "Longitudinal Development of the Kinematics of 4-,10-, 18-, and 26-month-old Dutch Warmblood Horses," *Equine Veterinary Journal Supplement* 17 (1994): 3-6.

P. 154 | Negative effects of equine punishment—Andrew McLean and Janne Christensen, "The Application of Learning Theory in Horse Training," *Applied Animal Behaviour Science* 190 (2017): 18-27.

CHAPTER 12

P. 157 | 100-pound head—A horse's head comprises about 10% of his total weight. http://www.answers.com/Q /How_much_does_a_horse%27s _head_weigh

P. 159 | Dopamine is released when needs are satisfied—Many brain chemicals release when drives are sated, but dopamine is the most important for signifying pleasure.

P. 159 | Rats use dopamine to death—James Olds and Peter Milner, "Positive Reinforcement Produced by Electrical Stimulation of Septal Area and Other Regions of Rat Brain," *Journal of Comparative Physiological Psychology* 47 (December 1954): 419-427.

P. 160 | Too many extrinsic rewards damage human motivation—Edward L. Deci, Richard Koestner, and Richard M. Ryan, "A Meta-Analytic Review of Experiments Examining the Effects of Extrinsic Rewards on Intrinsic

Motivation," *Psychological Bulletin* 125 (November 1999): 627-668.

P. 160 | The first reward is the strongest—Sebastian D. McBride, Matthew O. Parker, Kirsty Roberts, and Andrew Hemmings, "Applied Neurophysiology of the Horse: Implications for Training, Husbandry and Welfare," *Applied Animal Behaviour Science* 190 (2017): 90-101.

P. 160 | Surprising rewards increase dopamine release—Markus Ullsperger, "Minding Mistakes: How the Brain Monitors Errors and Learns from Goofs," *Scientific American Mind* 19 (August/ September 2008): 52-59.

P. 162 | Stroking reduces heart rate—Haruyo Hama, Masao Yogo, and Yoshinori Matsuyama, "Effects of Stroking Horses on Both Humans' and Horses' Heart Rate Responses*," Japanese Psychological Research* 38 (August 2009): 66-73.

CHAPTER 13

P. 170 | Pop-out occurs across demographic differences—Anne Treisman and Garry Gelade, "A Feature-Integration Theory of Attention," *Cognitive Psychology* 12 (1980): 97-136.

CHAPTER 14

P. 179 | Human brains mature at age 25—J. N. Giedd, "Structural Magnetic Resonance Imaging of the Adolescent Brain," *Annals of the New York Academy of Sciences,* 1021 (2004): 77–85.

P. 183 | 41% of the human cortex is frontal—University of California San Francisco's Weill Institute for Neurosciences Memory and Aging Center, 2019. https://memory.ucsf.edu/executive -functions

P. 183 | Pathways for prefrontal evaluation of fear—Joseph LeDoux, *The Emotional Brain* (New York: Simon and Schuster, 1996).

P. 185 | Fronto-temporal dementia—
University of California San Francisco's
Weill Institute for Neurosciences Memory
and Aging Center, 2019. https://memory
.ucsf.edu/frontotemporal-dementia

**P. 185 | Horse brains focus on one thing
at a time**—Clive Wynne and Monique
Udell, *Animal Cognition 2e* (New York:
Palgrave MacMillan, 2013), 134.

P. 189 | Definition of insanity—
Although this quote is usually attributed
to Albert Einstein, no one has identified
its origin. https://quoteinvestigator.com
/2017/03/23/same/

P. 190 | "Success in Circuit lies"—This
line is from poem 1129, written around
1868, "Tell all the Truth but tell it slant."
Emily Dickinson, *The Complete Poems of
Emily Dickinson,* ed. Thomas H. Johnson
(Boston: Little, Brown and Company,
1960), 506.

CHAPTER 15

P. 193 | Lobes—The definition of a lobe
has changed over the years, but current
sources use it to refer to cortical (surface)
areas of the brain. Michael S. Gazzaniga,
Richard B. Ivry, and George R. Mangun,
Cognitive Neuroscience 5e (New York: W. W.
Norton & Company, 2019).

**P. 194 | Percentage of human cortex
used for various activities—**Eric H.
Chudler, University of Washington
Center for Neurotechnology, "Brain Facts
and Figures." www.faculty.washington
.edu/chudler/facts.html

**P. 194 | Weight and volume of average
equine and human brains—**Eric H.
Chudler, University of Washington
Center for Neurotechnology, "Brain Facts
and Figures." www.faculty.washington.
edu/chudler/facts.html. Also, Michel-
Antoine Leblanc, *The Mind of the Horse*,
trans. Giselle Weiss (Cambridge, MA:
Harvard University Press, 2013).

**P. 194 | Goal-driven vs. stimulus-driven
attention associated with separate brain
areas in humans—**Maurizio Corbetta and
Gordon L. Shulman, "Control of Goal-
Directed and Stimulus-Driven Attention in
the Brain," *Nature Reviews Neuroscience* 3
(March 2002): 201-215.

**P. 195 | Humans produce more dopa-
mine than nonhuman primates do—**
Andre M. M. Sousa, et al., "Molecular and
Cellular Reorganization of Neural
Circuits in the Human Lineage," *Science*
358 (November 2017): 1027-1032.

P. 195 | Dopamine drives higher-order
functions—Andre Nieoullon, "Dopamine
and the Regulation of Cognition and
Attention," *Progress in Neurobiology* 67,
No. 1 (May 2002): 53-83.

**P. 195 | Dopamine limits sensory
awareness—**Christian Beste, Nico
Adelhofer, Krutika Gohil, Susanne
Passow, Veit Roessner, and Shu-Chen Li,
"Dopamine Modulates the Efficiency of
Sensory Evidence Accumulation During
Perceptual Decision Making," *Interna-
tional Journal of Neuropsychopharmacology*
21, no. 7 (July 2018): 649-655.

**P. 195 | Anxiety and docility with
dopamine—**Kirsty Roberts, Andrew J.
Hemmings, Meriel Moor-Colyer, Matthew
O. Parker, and Sebastian D. McBride,
"Neural Modulators of Temperament:
A Multivariate Approach to Personality
Trait Identification in the Horse," *Physiol-
ogy & Behavior* 167 (December 1, 2016):
125-131.

**P. 195 | Dopamine highs and lows
beyond normal—**Kentucky Equine
Research, "Equine Behavior and Dopamine Levels," *EquiNews* (November 16,
2016). Available online: https://ket.com
/equinews/equine-behavior-dopamine
-levels/.

**P. 196 | "There is no such thing as
over-handling"**—I surfed the Web for

less than three minutes and turned up four sites that used those exact words: www.horsegroomingsupplies.com, www.horsehomeschool.homestead.com, www.stockyard.net, and www.vichorse.com. A longer search would probably locate many more.

P. 196 | Grandin's recommendation that horses be habituated slowly—Temple Grandin, "Safe Handling of Large Animals (Cattle and Horses)," *Occupational Medicine: State of the Art Reviews* 14 (April-June 1999). Available online: http://www.grandin.com/references/safe.html

P. 196 | Myers' recommendation that horses not work for long periods—Jane Myers, *Horse Safe: A Complete Guide to Equine Safety* (Clayton VIC, Australia: CSIRO Publishing, 2005), 124.

P. 196 | Hausberger's statement that excessive handling is detrimental—Martine Hausberger, Helene Roche, Severine Henry, and E. Kathalijne Visser, "A Review of the Human-Horse Relationship," *Applied Animal Behaviour Science* 109 (2008): 1-24.

P. 197 | Amounts of handling in 170 horses—Martine Hausberger, Helene Roche, Severine Henry, and E. Kathalijne Visser, "A Review of the Human-Horse Relationship," *Applied Animal Behaviour Science* 109 (2008): 1-24.

P. 197 | Weaving increases with work—Julie L. Christie, Caroline J. Hewson, Christopher B. Riley, Mary A. McNiven, Ian R. Dohoo, and Luis A. Bate, "Management Factors Affecting Stereotypies and Body Condition Score in Nonracing Horses in Prince Edward Island," *The Canadian Veterinary Journal* 47 (February 2006): 136-143.

P. 197 | Equine stress can cause hives—Nancy S. Loving, "Hives in Horses," *The Horse* (January 16, 2019). Available online:

https://thehorse.com/122959/hives-in-horses/

P. 197, 198 | Dimensions of temperament and use of negative reinforcement for aversion-sensitive horses—Lea Lansade and Faustine Simon, "Horses' Learning Performances are Under the Influence of Several Temperamental Dimensions," *Applied Animal Behaviour Science* 125 (June 2010): 30-37.

P. 197, 198 | Positive and negative reinforcement for docile and anxious horses, respectively—Kirsty Roberts, Andrew J. Hemmings, Meriel Moore-Colyer, Matthew O. Parker, and Sebastian D. McBride, "Neural Modulators of Temperament: A Multivariate Approach to Personality Trait Identification in the Horse," *Physiology and Behavior* 167 (2016): 125-131.

P. 198 | Negative reinforcement for horses sensitive to aversion—Orla Doherty, Paul D. McGreevy, and Gemma Pearson, "The Importance of Learning Theory and Equitation Science to the Veterinarian," *Applied Animal Behaviour Science* 190 (2017): 111-122.

P. 199 | A normal horse eats 70% of the time—Sebastian McBride and Daniel Mills, "Psychological Factors Affecting Equine Performance," *Bio Med Central Veterinary Research* 8 (September 2012). Available online: https://www.ncbi.nlm.nih.gov/pmc/articles/PMC3514365/

P. 200 | Body-clipping produces covert anxiety—Kelly Yarnell, Carol Hall, and E. Billett, "An Assessment of the Aversive Nature of an Animal Management Procedure (Clipping) using Behavioral and Physiological Measures," *Physiology and Behavior* 118 (June 2013): 32-39.

CHAPTER 16

P. 207 | Attention in honeybees—Johannes Spaethe, Jurgen Tautz, and Lars

Chittka, "Do Honeybees Detect Colour Targets Using Serial or Parallel Visual Search?," *Journal of Experimental Biology* 209 (2006): 987-993.

P. 208 | Missing the gorilla—Daniel Simons and Christopher Chabris, "Gorillas in Our Midst: Sustained Inattentional Blindness for Dynamic Events," *Perception* 28 (1999): 1059-1074. Video is available online at https://www.youtube.com/watch?v=vJG698U2Mvo

P. 208 | Missing mealtime changes—Daniel Simons and Daniel Levin, "Failure to Detect Changes to People During a Real-World Interaction," *Psychonomic Bulletin & Review* 5 (December 1998): 644-649.

P. 210 | Neurochemicals in attentional tuning—Steven E. Petersen and Michael I. Posner, "The Attention System of the Human Brain: 20 Years After," *Annual Review of Neuroscience* 35 (July 21, 2012): 73-89. The link to horses is from the equine endocrine table in Francis Burton, *Ultimate Horse Care* (Lydney, UK: Ringpress Books, 1999). Available online: www.gla.ac.uk/external/EBF/EndocrineTable.html.

P. 210 | Nicotine in equine attention—Gene ID report, CHRNA1 Cholinergic Receptor Nicotinic Alpha 1 Subunit [Equus Caballus (Horse)], (January 14, 2019). Available online: https://www.ncbi.nlm.nih.gov/gene/100065034. Also see Matthew S. Hestand, Theodore S. Kalbfleisch, S. J. Coleman, Zhenling Zeng, Jian Hua Liu, L. Orlando, and James N. MacLeod, "Annotation of the Protein Coding Regions of the Equine Genome," *PLOS One* 10 (June 24, 2015).

P. 210 | Acetylcholine in equine attention—Peter H. Kay, Roger L. Dawkins, Ann T. Bowling, and Domenico Bernoco, "Polymorphism of the Acetylcholine

Receptor in the Horse," *The Veterinary Record* 120 (April 11, 1987): 363-365.

P. 210 | Supplementary motor area—William H. Calvin, *The River that Flows Uphill: A Journey from the Big Bang to the Big Brain* (San Francisco: Sierra Club Books, 1986).

P. 211 | Neural cell tuning—Tirin Moore and Marc Zirnsak, "Neural Mechanisms of Selective Visual Attention," *Annual Review of Psychology* 68 (2017): 47-72.

CHAPTER 17

P. 219 | Attention is the basis of training—Celine Rochais, Severine Henry, Carol Sankey, Fouad Nassur, A. Goracka-Bruzda, and Martine Hausberger, "Visual Attention, An Indicator of Human-Animal Relationships? A Study of Domestic Horses (*Equus Caballus*)," *Frontiers in Psychology* 5 (2014): 108-117.

P. 219 | Fruit fly learns faster when engaged—Bruno van Swinderen and Ralph J. Greenspan, "Salience Modulates 20-30 Hz Brain Activity in Drosophila," *Nature Neuroscience* 6 (2003): 579-586.

P. 221 | Multi-tasking increases time and mistakes by 50%—John Medina, *Brain Rules* (Seattle, WA: Pear Press, 2008), 87.

P. 221 | Multi-tasking decreases productivity by 40%—Joshua S. Rubinstein, David E. Meyer, and Jeffrey E. Evans, "Executive Control of Cognitive Processes in Task Switching," *Journal of Experimental Psychology: Human Perception and Performance* 27 (2001): 763-797.

P. 221 | Horses and cattle kill the most Americans annually—Jared A. Forrester, Thomas G. Weiser, and Joseph D. Forrester, "An Update on Fatalities due to Venomous and Nonvenomous Animals in the United States (2008-2015)," *Wilderness and Environmental Medicine* 29 (March 2018): 36-44.

P. 222 | Love and fear activate most of the brain—Saarimaki, Heini. "Decoding Emotions from Brain Activity and Connectivity Patterns." PhD dissertation, Aalto University, 2018. Available online: https://medicalxpress.com/news/2018-02 -visible-brain-restricted-region.html.

P. 222 | Reticular activating system is not in attention textbooks—Michael Posner (Editor), *The Cognitive Neuroscience of Attention 2e* (New York: Guilford Press, 2011); and George Mangun, *The Neuroscience of Attention: Attentional Control and Selection* (Oxford: Oxford University Press, 2012).

P. 223 | Size of VENs—Susan Casey, *Voices in the Ocean* (New York: Penguin Random House, 2015).

P. 224 | VENs limited by species—Sandra Blakeslee and Matthew Blakeslee, *The Body has a Mind of Its Own* (New York: Random House, 2007).

P. 224 | VENs in the horse—Mary Ann Raghanti, Linda B. Spurlock, F. Robert Treichler, Sara E. Weigel, Raphaela Stimmelmayr, Camilla Butti, J. G. M. Hans Thewissen, and Patrick R. Hof, "An Analysis of Von Economo Neurons in the Cerebral Cortex of Cetaceans, Artiodactyls, and Perissodactyls," *Brain Structure & Function* 220, No. 4 (July 2015): 2303-2314.

P. 225 | Horses distinguish humans by familiarity, sense human focus, learn which humans require attention—Celine Rochais, Severine Henry, Carol Sankey, Fouad Nassur, A. Goracka-Bruzda, and Martine Hausberger, "Visual Attention, An Indicator of Human-Animal Relationships? A Study of Domestic Horses (*Equus Caballus*)," *Frontiers in Psychology* 5 (2014): 108-117.

P. 229 | Missing genes on chromosome 22 impair focus—Tony Simon and Steven J. Luck, "Attentional Impairments in Children with 22q11.2DS Chromosome Deletion Syndrome" in Michael Posner (Ed.) *The Cognitive Neuroscience of Attention 2e* (New York: Guilford Press, 2011): 441-453.

P. 229 | Balint's Syndrome—E. Bruce Goldstein, *Sensation and Perception 7e* (Belmont, CA: Thomson Wadsworth, 2007), 133. Also see Jeremy Wolfe, Keith Kluender, Dennis Levi, Linda Bartoshuk, Rachel Herz, Roberta Klatzky, and Susan Lederman, *Sensation & Perception* (Sunderland, MA: Sinauer Associates, 2006), 193.

CHAPTER 18

P. 232, 233 | Definitions of instinct, emotion, feeling—Frans de Waal, *Mama's Last Hug* (New York: W. W. Norton & Company, 2019).

P. 233 | Bunching vs. fleeing prey animals—Temple Grandin, *Animals in Translation* (New York: Simon and Schuster, 2005).

P. 234 | S.M. feels no fear—Rachel Feltman, "Meet the Woman Who Can't Feel Fear," *Washington Post* (January 20, 2015). Available online: https://www. washingtonpost.com/news/speaking -of-science/wp/2015/01/20/meet-the -woman-who-cant-feel-fear/

P. 234 | High anxiety linked to large amygdalas—Shaozheng Qin, Christina B. Young, Xujun Duan, Tianwen Chen, Kaustubh Supekar, and Vinod Menon, "Amygdala Subregional Structure and Intrinsic Functional Connectivity Predicts Individual Differences in Anxiety During Early Childhood," *Biological Psychiatry* 75, No. 11 (June 1, 2014): 892-900.

P. 237 | Human anxiety increases equine heart rate—Linda J. Keeling, Liv Jonare, and Lovisa Lanneborn, "Investigating Horse-Human Interactions: The

Effect of a Nervous Human," *Veterinary Journal* 181 (July 2009): 70-71.

P. 237 | Low pitch soothes horses— Across all mammals, high pitch is associated with calls of distress. Temple Grandin, *Animals in Translation* (New York: Simon and Schuster, 2005), 35.

P. 238 | Stroking reduces heart rate in horse and human—Haruyo Hama, Masao Yogo, and Yoshinori Matsuyama, "Effects of Stroking Horses on Both Humans' and Horses' Heart Rate Responses,"*Japanese Psychological Research* 38, No. 2 (1996): 66-73.

P. 238 | Stroking below and behind withers reduces heart rates—Susan McBane, *Horse Senses* (London: Manson Publishing Ltd, 2012).

P. 238 | Horses as research models for human depression—Carole Fureix, Patrick Jego, Severine Henry, Lea Lansade, and Martine Hausberger, "Towards an Ethological Animal Model of Depression? A Study on Horses," *PLOS One* 7 (June 28, 2012). Available online: https://journals.plos.org/plosone/article?id=10.1371/journal.pone.0039280

P. 239 | Depression in horses—Celine Rochais, Severine Henry, Carole Fureix, and Martine Hausberger, "Investigating Attentional Processes in Depressive-Like Domestic Horses (*Equus caballus*)," *Behavioural Processes* 124 (March 2016): 93-96.

P. 240 | Apes, birds, dolphins, whales, pigs express emotion—Frans de Waal, *Mama's Last Hug* (New York: W. W. Norton & Company, 2019).

P. 240 | Goats distinguish emotions— Luigi Baciadonna, Elodie F. Briefer, Livio Favaro, and Alan G. McElligott, "Goats Distinguish between Positive and Negative Emotion-Linked Vocalisations," *Frontiers in Zoology* 16 (2019): 25.

P. 241 | Horses distinguish between people with positive or negative attitudes toward them—Haruyo Hama, Masao Yogo, and Yoshinori Matsuyama, "Effects of Stroking Horses on Both Humans' and Horses' Heart Rate Responses," *Japanese Psychological Research* 38, No. 2 (1996): 66-73.

P. 242 | Equine face is highly expressive—Frans de Waal, *Mama's Last Hug* (New York: W. W. Norton & Company, 2019).

P. 242 | 17 movements can be combined in over 355 trillion ways— https://www.calculatorsoup.com/calculators/discretemathematics/permutations.php

P. 242 | Facial expressions during grooming—Lea Lansade, Raymond Noak, Anne-Lyse Laine, Christine Leterrier, Coralie Bonneau, Celine Parias, and Aline Bertin, "Facial Expression and Oxytocin as Possible Markers of Positive Emotions in Horses," *Scientific Reports* 8 (October 2, 2018): article 14680.

P. 243 | Horses viewing equine facial photographs—Jennifer V. Wathan, Leanne Proops, Kate Grounds, and Karen McComb, "Horses Discriminate between Facial Expressions of Conspecifics," *Scientific Reports* 6 (December 20, 2016): article 38322.

P. 243 | Horses reading human facial expressions—Amy Victoria Smith, Leanne Proops, Kate Grounds, Jennifer Wathan, and Karen McComb, "Functionally Relevant Responses to Human Facial Expressions of Emotion in the Domestic Horse (*Equus caballus*)," *Biology Letters* 12 (2016): doi 10.1098/rsbl.2015.0907.

P. 244 | 900 certified equine therapy centers and over 66,000 patients— Robin Roenker, "Horses of Hope and Joy," *U.S. Equestrian* (Fall, 2018): 127-135.

P. 244 | "A horse gallops…"—Quote by Federico Tesio, https://www.azquotes.com/quote/609305

CHAPTER 19

P. 247 | Percentages of Americans who consider pets to be best friends, members of the family, and preferable to their own children—Survey conducted by OnePoll for www.iandloveandyou.com, July 11-25, 2019. Available online: https://www.studyfinds.org/survey-a-third-of-parents-say-their-favorite-child-is-their-pet/

P. 247 | In 2016 the US pet industry brought in $66.75 billion, up every year since 1994—http://www.americanpetproducts.org/press_industrytrends.asp

P. 247 | Height of $67 billion—https://www.ehd.org/science_technology_largenumbers.php

P. 247 | Pet parents—Rebecca Gardyn, "Animal Magnetism," *American Demographics* 24 (2002): 30-37.

P. 247 | Horses as family members—Market Research Report, *U.S. Equine Market Third Edition* (Rockville, MD: Packaged Facts Press, 2017). https://www.packagedfacts.com/Equine-Edition-10706833/

P. 248 | Jaguar—Lindsey Bever, "A Woman Was Trying to Take a Selfie With a Jaguar When It Attacked Her, Authorities Say," *The Washington Post* (March 10, 2019). Available online: https://www.washingtonpost.com/science/2019/03/10/woman-was-trying-take-selfie-with-jaguar-when-it-attacked-her-authorities-say/

P. 248 | House cat—Rene Lynch, "22-Pound Pet Cat Holds Family Hostage until Police Arrive," *Los Angeles Times* (March 11, 2014). Available online: https://www.latimes.com/nation/la-sh-22-pound-house-cat-traps-family-20140311-story.html

P. 248 | "You can lead a human to knowledge…"—Jerre Kelsh, 2014.

P. 248 | Horses who "understand" and "respect"—Paul McGreevy, *Equine Behavior 2e* (Sydney: Saunders Elsevier, 2012).

P. 249 | Prefrontal cortex across species—Earl Miller, Professor of Neuroscience at Massachusetts Institute of Technology, as quoted in Alina Tugend, "Multitasking Can Make You Lose… Um… Focus," *New York Times* (October 24, 2008). Available online: https://www.nytimes.com/2008/10/25/business/yourmoney/25shortcuts.html

P. 249 | Future thoughts 59 times a day—Arnaud D'Argembeau, Olivier Renaud, and Martial Van der Linden, "Frequency, Characteristics, and Functions of Future-Oriented Thoughts in Daily Life," *Applied Cognitive Psychology* 25, No. 1 (2011): 96-103.

P. 249 | Three times more future thinking—Martin E. P. Seligman and John Tierney, "We Aren't Built to Live in the Moment," *New York Times Sunday Review* (May 20, 2017): SR 1.

P. 250 | Neuronal death in childhood—R. W. Oppenheim, "Cell Death During Development of the Nervous System," *Annual Review of Neuroscience* 14 (1991): 453-501.

P. 251 | Prefrontal pruning at age 25; schizophrenia, retardation, psychosis—Zdravko Petanjek, Milos Judas, Goran Simic, Mladen Roko Rasin, Harry Uylings, Pasko Rakic, and Ivica Kostovic, "Extraordinary Neoteny of Synaptic Spines in the Human Prefrontal Cortex," *Proceedings of the National Academy of Sciences of the United States of America* 108 (August 9, 2011): 13281-13286.

P. 251 | Humans have greater percentage of prefrontal neurons and connections—Chad Donahue, Matthew Glasser, Todd Preuss, James Rilling, and David Van Essen, "Quantitative Assessment of Prefrontal Cortex in Humans relative to Nonhuman Primates," *Proceedings of the National Academy of Sciences of the United States of America* 115 (May 29, 2018): E5183-E5192.

P. 251 | No lateral frontal pole in macaques—Franz-Xaver Neubert, Rogier B. Mars, Adam Thomas, Jerome Sallet, and Matthew F. S. Rushworth, "Comparison of Human Ventral Frontal Cortex Areas for Cognitive Control and Language with Areas in Monkey Frontal Cortex," *Neuron* 81, no. 3 (February 5, 2014): 700-713.

P. 251 | No lateral frontal pole in horses—Martin J. Schmidt, Carola Knemeyer, and Helmut Heinsen, "Neuroanatomy of the Equine Brain as Revealed by High-Field (3Tesla) Magnetic-Resonance-Imaging," *PLOS One* (April 1, 2019): doi 10.1371/pone.0213814.

P. 252 | Horses are not malevolent or culpable—Andrew McLean and Janne Christensen, "The Application of Learning Theory in Horse Training," *Applied Animal Behaviour Science* 190 (2017): 18-27.

P. 254 | Less prefrontal tissue in sociopaths—Adrian Raine, Todd Lencz, Susan Bihrle, Lori LaCasse, and Patrick Colletti, "Reduced Prefrontal Gray Matter Volume and Reduced Autonomic Activity in Antisocial Personality Disorder," *Archives of General Psychiatry* 57 (2000): 119-127; and Erin D. Bigler, Adrian Raine, Lori LaCasse, and Patrick Colletti, "Frontal Lobe Pathology and Antisocial Personality Disorder," *Archives of General Psychiatry* 58 (2001): 609-611.

P. 254 | Culpability of criminals with impaired prefrontal cortex—Dean Mobbs, Hakwan C. Lau, Owen D. Jones, and Christopher D. Frith, "Law, Responsibility, and the Brain," *PLoS Biology* 5, no. 4 (April 17, 2007): doi 10.1371/pbio.0050103.

P. 256 | Biological seat of punishment—Joshua W. Buckholtz, Justin W. Martin, Michael T. Treadway, Katherine Jan, David H. Zald, Owen Jones, and Rene Marois, "From Blame to Punishment: Disrupting Prefrontal Cortex Activity Reveals Norm Enforcement Mechanisms," *Neuron* 87 (September 23, 2015): 1369-1380. The area of temporary impairment was in the dorso-lateral prefrontal cortex.

CHAPTER 20

P. 261 | Greater focus on similarities—Frans de Waal, *Mama's Last Hug* (New York: W. W. Norton & Company, 2019).

P. 265 | Run 44 mph, jump 8' 1", walk 10 m on hind legs—http://www.guinnessworldrecords.com/search?term=horse

P. 265 | 500-mile race—In the early 1920s, the Arabian stallion Shahzada completed a 500-mile race successfully over difficult terrain. The longest endurance race for a single horse-and-rider team today is named after him: the annual 249-mile Shahzada Race in Australia, which is spaced over a period of five days. https://www.horsetalk.co.nz/features/cj-2001shahzada-prev.shtml

P. 265 | Heavyweight pull—Two horses broke the heavyweight pull record in 2012 by dragging 13,400 pounds a distance of 14 feet. https://www.horsetalk.co.nz/2012/07/17/heavyweights-show-their-stuff-stampede/ That's equivalent to the weight of two F-350 trucks. https://www.ford.com/trucks/super-duty/models/f350-xl/

Glossary

Accommodation Bending of the eye's lens to focus on near objects.

Acetylcholine Abundant brain chemical in the horse, important for muscle activation and memory.

Activation Electrical and chemical process that ignites a neuron to send a message.

Acuity Ability to see fine detail.

Adductors Human inner thigh muscles.

Adrenaline A natural chemical that increases blood flow in the fight or flight response, also called epinephrine.

Agency Origin of a cause.

Agnosia Inability to perceive related sights or sounds wholistically.

Aids Cues to the horse delivered by the rider's body, especially hands, seat, legs, back, and weight distribution.

Amusia Inability to perceive related tones as music.

Amygdala Area of brain that processes emotion.

Angle receptors Cells that tell the brain how much and in which direction a joint is bent.

Anterior cingulate Area near the center of the brain that regulates heart rate and blood pressure along with some emotional and cognitive processes.

Artificial selection Selection of male and female individuals to enhance traits in a species.

Auditory cortex Area of the brain's surface where hearing is processed.

Axon The part of a brain cell that transmits an electrical impulse from one neuron to another.

Balint's syndrome Rare disorder in which people can focus on only one object at a time.

Banamine A bitter-tasting equine pain medicine.

Barrel (of a horse) The round body of the horse between shoulders and hips.

Basal ganglia A set of neural structures deep in the brain important for motor control and learning.

Blindsight Knowledge of an object's location despite inability to see it.

Capriole Dressage maneuver in which a horse leaps upward, kicking both hind legs to the rear.

Categorical perception Human brain bias in which items with individual variation are grouped together automatically.

Cerebellum Portion of the brain that is important for coordinated movement and learning.

Cerebrospinal fluid Nutrient liquid contained in the spine and certain passages of the brain.

Chestnuts Hard scaly deposits on a horse's inner legs.

Ciliary muscle Muscle that pulls the eye's lens into shape when focusing.

Classical conditioning Associating a new stimulus, like a bell, with an established behavior.

Cognitive psychology Study of the normal human mind.

Cognitive science Interdisciplinary study of the human mind and brain.

Comparative psychology Study of the human mind and brain in comparison to animal minds and brains.

Cones Cells in the eye that encode color.

Cortex Surface of the human and equine brains, containing cells that mediate perception, memory, language, and thought.

Cortical blindness Blindness at the level of the brain; the eyes still function normally.

Corticosterone Stress hormone in rodents, birds, and reptiles.

Cortisol Stress hormone in horses and humans.

Counter-canter An exercise in which horses canter on the outside lead with an outside bend.

Counter-condition To substitute a related behavior for an undesired behavior.

Crest The top of a horse's neck, where the mane grows.

Cribbing A vice in which horses hold the edge of an object and inhale sharply.

Cross-modal perception Perceiving through multiple organs, like seeing and hearing simultaneously.

Cue sensitivity A horse's heightened response to aids.

Dark adaptation Process of pupil contraction in which the eye adapts from bright to dark surroundings.

Decibels (dB) Measurement of loudness.

Dendrites Small branches on neurons that receive information from other neurons.

Displacement The horse's natural habit of yielding away from pressure.

Domestication Breeding for traits that allow easier training, like calmness.

Dopamine Reward chemical made by the brain.

Downward transition A change from a faster gait to a slower gait.

Draft Breeds built for strength and power, such as Clydesdales and Percherons.

Emotion An observable state of mind that drives optional behaviors.

Epinephrine A natural chemical that increases blood flow in the fight or flight response, also called adrenaline.

Equus caballus The species name for modern horses.

Ergots Hard callouses under the fetlocks.

Ethology Study of animal behavior.

Executive function The human brain's ability to plan, reason, and strategize.

Extinction Process of undoing a learned association.

Fast-twitch muscles Muscle fibers that produce speed and sudden power.

Feeling An internal subjective mental state that cannot be observed.

FEI Fèdèration Equestre Internationale, which governs international horse shows.

Fetlock The primary equine joint between knee (carpus) and hoof, sometimes called the ankle.

Flehmen The lifting of the equine upper lip to trap air inside the vomeronasal organ.

Frontal cortex Portion of the surface of the human brain, located behind the forehead and back to the crown.

Frontal lobe Portion of the human brain behind the forehead and back to the crown, responsible for speech, movement, personality, executive function, and more.

Fronto-temporal dementia A form of dementia in which the frontal and temporal lobes shrink, impairing reason while memory and language remain intact until late stages.

Generalization Applying learned behaviors across different contexts.

Glial cells Brain cells that clean up after neurons.

Glucose Sugar used for brain fuel.

Golgi organs Cells that tell the brain how much tension is applied to a muscle.

Groundwork Unmounted horse training.

Gustation The sense of taste.

Half-halt Rider's maneuver that slows a horse or changes to a slower gait.

Half-seat A position used by hunter riders, in which the seat is lifted slightly off the saddle.

Half-pass Diagonal movement with the horse's head flexed slightly to the inside and his body straight.

Hard wiring Permanent pathways of the brain.

Hertz (Hz) Measurement of frequency in sound waves.

Hippocampus Area of the brain reponsible for consolidating new memories.

Horsemanship Philosophical spirit of placing the horse's needs first, based on detailed equine knowledge.

Hotblood A nervous excitable breed, like a Thoroughbred or Arabian.

Inattentional blindness Human failure to notice obvious stimuli when attention is focused elsewhere.

Incentive A lure offered prior to desired behavior.

Indiscriminate rewards Rewards given in association with no particular behavior.

Instinct A specific inborn behavior.

Instrumental conditioning Teaching by consequence of reward, negative reinforcement, or punishment; also called operant conditioning.

Iris Colored portion of the eye.

Jig A prancing trot that occurs when nervous horses won't walk.

Join-up A horse's movement toward and following of a handler.

Leg-yield Horse moves away from the rider's leg, on a diagonal line, with his head straight or slightly flexed to the outside.

Lens Portion of the eye that bends light to focus an image.

Levade Dressage maneuver in which a horse stands on bent hind legs.

Light adaptation Process of pupil dilation in which the eye adapts from dark to bright surroundings.

Lobes Sections of human cortex including frontal, parietal, temporal, and occipital areas.

Longe line A 25- to 30-foot line on which a horse circles a handler at various gaits.

Long-term potentiation Heightened potential for activation in neurons.

Loudness Perceived differences in volume.

Mammalian Related to all mammals.

Mirror neurons Brain cells that prepare motor neurons for action; they activate even when we only watch someone else take an action.

Motion detector cells Visual cells that pick up movement and send the information to the brain.

Motor cortex A strip of brain tissue that contains neurons designed to initiate the movement of specific body parts.

Multipolar neuron A standard brain cell that transmits and receives impulses.

Multi-tasking The illusory effort to increase productivity by doing several tasks at once.

Muscle spindles Muscle cells that tell the brain how fast and how much a muscle is extending its length.

Natural selection Survival and reproduction of individuals who are best adapted to the environment.

Negative reinforcement Teaching by release of pressure.

Neural fatigue The natural time limit of a neuron's ability to remain activated.

Neural network A group of neurons connected to each other, representing a particular ability or concept.

Neural tuning Process of limiting the specific stimulation to which a neuron responds.

Neuron The basic brain cell of mental function; there are also other types of brain cells.

Nicotine A chemical made by the brain that increases vigilance.

Norepinephrine A natural chemical that prepares the body for action, increasing the fight or flight response; also called noradrenaline.

Occipital lobe Area of the human brain responsible for vision.

Olfaction Sense of smell.

Olfactory bulbs Area of the brain that collects information from receptor cells about scents.

Operant conditioning Teaching by consequence of reward, negative reinforcement, or punishment; also called instrumental conditioning.

Optic disk Eye area where rods and cones cannot transmit information.

Optic nerve Nerve that carries information from eye to brain.

Oxer A jump in which at least two poles are spread apart in width.

Pacing A vice in which horses move rapidly back and forth in a line.

Parietal lobe An area of the brain located between the crown and back of the head.

Patho-calm My term for a human attitude of near-pathological calmness that frantic or nervous horses sometimes require.

Pheromones Natural chemicals that trigger animal behaviors.

Piaffe A dressage maneuver in which the horse trots in place.

Pitch Perceived differences in auditory frequency, for example between bass and soprano notes.

Poll Location between a horse's ears.

Pop-out Automatic processing of certain stimulus attributes like color and tilt.

Power moment My term for common activities during which reward is especially effective.

Predator An animal designed to kill, having front-facing eyes for depth perception during a chase.

Prefrontal cortex The portion of the brain's surface that is located behind the forehead and above the eyes.

Prey An animal designed to escape predators, with side-facing eyes for range of view and motion detection.

Proprioception The ability to sense one's own body position and movement.

Pruning The killing of unused brain cells.

Punishment An unpleasant consequence following undesired behavior, to be distinguished from abuse.

Pupil Portion of the eye that dilates and contracts to adjust the amount of light.

Receptor cells Cells in sensory organs that are designed to receive incoming stimulation, like rods and cones.

Reflex An automatic response at the level of the spinal cord that is not controlled by the brain.

Reticular activating system An area of the brain responsible for wakefulness.

Reward A pleasant experience given after performance of a desired behavior.

Rods Cells in the eye that encode motion.

Sclera The white portion of the eye.

Search asymmetry A human brain bias in which we notice presence more easily than absence.

Self-carriage The horse's ability to maintain position, speed, balance, or gait without a rider's aids.

Somatosensory cortex Area of the brain that receives information from the body about skin touch, pressure, movement, and temperature.

Sound localization The ability to determine where a sound is coming from.

Splashed-white A hereditary form of equine deafness.

Splint bones Small vestigial bones in the horse's lower legs.

Sprezzatura The ability to make the difficult seem simple.

Stereoacuity The brain's ability to compute depth with views from two eyes.

Stimulus An external item or event that stimulates the brain.

Supplementary motor area An area of the human cortex that processes obscene language.

Swing phase Brief moment between lifting a hoof and setting it down again.

Tapetum Shiny fibers of the horse's eye that reflect light in dim surroundings.

Taste buds Receptor cells in the tongue that pick up information about taste.

Tempi changes A dressage move in which the horse completes flying changes every one or two strides on a straight line.

Temporal lobe An area of the brain just above each ear, helpful in processing sound, music, and memory.

Testing A natural means of equine learning, to be encouraged.

Thalamus A neural structure that coordinates incoming data from all the senses.

Transduce To transform an external sensory stimulus (like light) into electrical impulses the brain can understand.

Two-point position A riding exercise for balance and strength, in which body weight is balanced on the balls of the feet.

USEF The United States Equestrian Federation, which governs American horse shows.

Vasopressin A hormone that controls blood pressure and kidney function, often elevated during stress.

Vertical jump A jump with height but no width.

Visual capture The human brain's bias toward prioritizing vision.

Visual cortex Area of the brain's surface where visual data are processed.

Vomeronasal organ The horse's second "nose," capturing odors for extra processing.

Von Economo neuron A large type of neuron that is specialized for promoting attention.

Warmblood Breeds initiated by crossing drafts and hotbloods.

Weaving A vice in which horses shift their weight side to side repetitively.

Withers The bony area at the base of the top of the horse's neck.

About the Author

Janet Jones is a cognitive scientist who applies brain research to the training of horses and riders. She began riding at age 7 and qualified for the United States Olympic jumping program at 17. She has schooled hundreds of young horses, competing in hunter, jumper, halter, reining, and Western Pleasure events. A strong advocate of true horsemanship, Jones believes every rider should know horses from the ground up. Using basic principles of dressage and groundwork as a foundation for each horse, she encourages cross-training among equestrian disciplines.

Jones earned her Ph.D. in cognitive science at UCLA with original research on the human brain's ability to resolve ambiguity in language. That project won UCLA's Gengerelli Distinguished Dissertation Award in 1989. She taught the neuroscience of perception, language, memory, and thought to college students for 23 years. She is a member of Phi Beta

Kappa, the Association for Psychological Science, the United States Equestrian Federation, the United States Hunter/Jumper Association, and the Society for Neuroscience.

Horse Brain, Human Brain is Jones' fourth book. Previous titles include texts on scientific research and human memory. She has also written for *EQUUS*, the *Journal on Excellence in College Teaching, Innovative Higher Education, Current Psychology: Research and Reviews, Liberal Education*, the *Quarter Horse Journal*, the *Association for Psychological Science*, and the *Journal of Psycholinguistic Research*.

Jones lives in the Rocky Mountains with a three-year-old Dutch Warmblood who sharpens her skills every day. In her spare time, she enjoys music, literature, and nature. Learn more at www.janet-jones.com.

Acknowledgments

Horse Brain, Human Brain has been a labor of love supported by a remarkable cast of encouraging characters. My editor at *EQUUS* magazine, Laurie Prinz, gave breath to my earliest articles on the neuro-science of horsemanship. She kindled the spark with care and edited my manuscripts with an incisive eye but a gentle hand. *EQUUS* readers wrote to me often with questions, opinions, and the positive feedback that every writer needs.

Wendy Williams, science journalist and author of the bestselling book *The Horse*, served as a sounding board during the incubation of this project, long before the book proposal was ready for outside eyes. She remains happy to share her knowledge of the publishing industry with a fellow scribbler, and that interaction makes my work easier and more fun.

Rebecca Didier, my editor at Trafalgar Square Books, responded to the idea of this book with instant enthusiasm and has remained a supportive companion every step of the way. Trafalgar's publisher Caroline Robbins edited the manuscript with tender loving care, saving me from some misguided word choices and an irreverent sense of humor. Martha Cook, managing director and marketing guru, led me through the landscape of of social media and book promotion. All of these smart women have been excellent guides.

While maintaining an easy camaraderie, equine artist Susan Harris created beautiful illustrations of difficult concepts. Many of them are first-ever drawings of the interior of the equine brain, based on cutting-edge veterinary research. Others required seeing like a horse—a feat harder than it sounds for even the best artists. Tim Holtz designed each page with pleasing visual variety, and Andrea Jones produced a comprehensive index. Rebecca Didier performed her magic as a graphic artist to finalize all the illustrations and create a beautiful cover.

Several people read the manuscript and offered generous advice. Thanks to Rebecca Didier, Denny Emerson, Jonathan Field, Gerry Jones, Tik Maynard, Caroline Robbins, Eric Smiley, Karen Spear, PhD, Jeffrey Warren, DVM, and Wendy Williams for their attention to detail, constructive ideas, and identification of mistakes. Remaining errors are mine alone.

I am indebted to two veterinary neurologists who answered questions about the horse brain with good cheer: Bruno Cozzi, DMV, PhD, Professor of Veterinary Anatomy at the University of Padova, Italy; and Yvette Nout-Lomas, DVM, PhD, Associate Professor of Equine Internal Medicine at Colorado State University, USA. In addition, I appreciate the hard work of all the veterinary researchers and equine scientists whose publications have contributed knowledge to this book.

To the owners of all the horses brought to me for training and to my riding students who have posted without irons or slowed the lope longer than they wished, thank you. I am lucky to have had such a close-knit group of highly motivated clients who appreciated my passion even when it made their muscles sore.

My friends have shared my excitement in writing this book and in offering to the public my way of understanding horses. We raise one another up and take true joy in each other's achievements. I thank all of them for their integrity and good will. Those who took an especially deep interest in the project, offering motivation whenever my energy flagged, include Ro Babcock, Jennifer Beck, Carolyn Bidinger, Debbie Bishop, Tavvy Bowers, Zinnia Cantrell, Sandra Eisemann, Shirley Fleming, Kathy Greene, Gail Koser, Cindy Lawrence, Francie Olson, Meredith Page, Suzanne Reilly, Karen Rider, Pat Stelter, Carol Teall, and Kelly Ziegler. My sister in friendship, Karen Spear, offered a sympathetic ear and abundant guidance through every chapter of this book, as she does through every chapter of my life.

Writing demands months of solitary confinement, and those family members who slip symbolic food under the door are cherished. My father Gerry Jones understands solitude through his own art and architectural work, still keeping him busy well into his nineties. In addition, thanks to Beth and Joe Hendel, Leslie Jones, Lois and Kevin McDermott,

Diane Moles, Lynne Norris, Joan and Frank Pavlica, Cindy Prevost, Sandy Roman, Ray Torres, and my cousin-sister Diana Torres.

Credit also goes to the many hundreds of horses in my past. Each one taught me something new about the equine brain, though a few could have been less dramatic in their lessons. They showed me the range of unique personalities among equines and reminded me always to be prepared for anything. Every day, horses teach me more.

Finally, I offer deepest thanks to my friend Jeffrey Warren, who has encouraged my work on the neuroscience of horsemanship for ten years. Jeff is that rare individual who brings warmth, laughter, humility, and intelligence to every interaction. In many ways, he set the tone for this book and I only aspired to achieve it.

Index

Page numbers in *italics* indicate illustrations.

Cortisol, 75, 87, 210–12, 229
Counter-conditioning, 177
Cribbing, 195, 199
Criminal behavior, 254
Crops, 92, 217
Cues. *See* Aids
Cushing's disease, 195
Cutting, 52

da Vinci, Leonardo, 15
Dancing analogy, 98
Daydreamer horses, 215–17, 227
Deafness, 84
Death-by-animal statistics, 221
Decision-making, neural basis for, 251
Dementia, fronto-temporal, 185
Dendrites, *20, 135,* 250–51, *250*
Depression, 195, 238–39
Depth perception, 36, 51–54, *52*
Desensitization, 68, 198, 217
Dickinson, Emily, 190
Digestion, motion and, 199
Direct training, 180–81, 187–190
Disabilities, 83, 84, 85
Displacement, 146. *See also* Movement
Dissonance, 64
Distance assessment, 51, 104–5
Distractibility. *See also* Attention
   in horses, 220, 226, 229
   in humans, 214
   neurology of, 207–12
   training considerations, 212–17, 225–28, 227

Do or Don't thinking, 173–74
Docility, dopamine role, 195
Dogs
   communication with, 9, 124, 262
   neurology of, 249
   observational learning in, 137
   sense of smell, 78–79
Dolphins, 137, 224
Domestication, 3, 18, 26–27
Dopamine, 159, 160, 194, 195, 209–12, 229
Dressage, 89
Drilling, of movements, 226
Dull horses, 215
Duncan, Ronald, 15

Ears, 65–66, 224–25. *See also* Hearing
Edelman, Gerald, 32
Einstein, Albert, 189
Embroidery pattern riding exercise, 225–26, 227
Emotions
   defined, 232–33
   vs. feelings, 233
   in horses, 69, 238–39, 242 (*see also* Fear)
   horse's sensitivity to, 63, 75
   learning by, 141
   music and, 64–65
   in observational learn-ing, 138, 140
   rider/handler control of, 6, 237–38
Empathy, 57, 96, 189
Engagement (physical), 98, 104, 120–21. *See also* Attention
Environmental conditions
   in equine learning, 132, 226, 229

in natural selection, 17, 18–19
Epinephrine, 141
Equine brain. *See also* Case histories; Human brain
   attention in, 207–12
   compared to human brain, 5–7, 179, 192–96, 251–52, 261
   evolution of, 17–19, 183, 209
   physical characteristics, 27–28
   somatosensory areas in, 107, *108,* 109
   as stimulus-driven, 194–96, 200
   visual processing in, 21–22, *21*
   working with, 5, 190
Equine therapy, 243–44
Errors, learning from, 132
Eventing, 90
Evolution. *See* Natural selection
Executive function, 179–180, 183–87, *184,* 249–252
Expectations, managing, 173–78, 197–200, 251–52, 265–66
Experience, 4–5, 28, 136, 234
Extinction, of associative learning, 167–68
Eye contact, 237
Eyes. *See also* Vision
   damage to, 32
   dark/light adaptation, 48–51
   position of, 36
   size of, 33
   structure of, 35, *35,* 42, 43, *45,* 47–48
Eye-shine, 48

Optic nerves, 43–44, *45*
Outdoor riding areas, 88
Over-handling, 191–92, 196–200
Overreactive horses, 198

Pain, perception of, 101
Parietal lobes, 193, *193*
Parkinson's disease, 109, 195
"Patho-calm," 237–38
Pawing, 167, 197
Perception. *See also specific organs and senses*
  as act of creation, 32
  case histories, 23, 31, 37–41, 55, 59, 71–72, 81
  categorical, 84, 92–96, *93, 96*, 133, 212
  cross-modal, 70
  evolution of, 20
  interpretation of, 32
  neural fatigue and, 84, 89–92
  of presence vs. absence, 169–174
  sensory compensation in, 32–33, 50, 54, 76, 84–88
  study of, 72–73
Peripheral vision, 36, 42–43, 51–52, 67
Pets, interpretation of behavior of, 246–48
Pheromones, 77
Physical fitness, 114, 199
Physical therapy, 103
Pitch, 60–62, *60*, 68–70
Planning, capacity for, 245–46, 251, 252–57
Pleasure riding, 177–78, 191–92, 196–200
Pop-outs, 170–73, *172*
Postural balance assessment, 105

Potentiation, long-term, 147
"Power moments," 163–64
Praise
  benefits of, 176, 187
  context in, 263
  timing of, 189
  verbal, 162, *163*
Predators
  emotions in, 233
  neurology of, 51–52, 77, 78, 246
  prey animals and, 25–26, 124, 262–63
Predictability, in managing fear, 199, 235, 236
Preferences, 75, 81
Prefrontal cortex
  dysfunction in, 254
  fear and, 234, *235*
  features of, 179–180, 250–51
  intention and, 249–252, 255–56
  lacking, in horses, 22, 23, 183, *184*
  learning role, 183, *184*, 253–54
  visual processing role, 21–22, *21*
Presence, perception of, 169–174, *172*
Pressure (sensation), 122, 146–47
Pressure and release training, 91–92, 145–153
Prey animals
  characteristics of, 19, 25
  emotions in, 233
  neurology of, 51–52, 77, 78, 246
  predators and, 25–26, 124, 262–63
Primates, nonhuman, 224, 233, 249, 251
Priming, of neurons, 147, 158, 224

Problem-solving, 133, 141–42, 222–24
Productivity, 221
Projection, 246–48, 261
Proprioception
  brain damage/dysfunction and, 106–9
  in horse/human interactions, 97–98, 111, 122–28, *125–27*
  loss of, 109–10
  physiology of, 99–101
  rider assessments, 102–6
  rider training in, 112, 113–19
  vision and, 103, 112
Protection, horse's need for, 264
Pruning, of neurons, 20, *250*
Przewalski horse, 26
Psychosis, 251
Punishment
  vs. corrections, 91, 154
  downsides of, 154–55
  harm and intent in, 255
  vs. negative reinforcement, 145
Pupils, contraction of, 49
Pushy horses, 161

Quadratus lumborum muscles, *121*

Racing and racehorses, 56, 65, 83, 84, 90, 237
Radios, in barns, 63–65, 87
Ranking, among horses, 70, 240
Rearing, 181, 239
Redirection
  for addressing vices, 165
  for distracted horses, 213–14, *215*, 216
  in indirect training, 182, 186–87, 189

Reflex actions, 22. *See also* Instinct
Rein aids, 81, 89, 92, 119
Reinforcement
    in conditioned learning, 136–37
    unintended, 151–52, 157, 161, 164, 167
Reining, 83
Relaxation
    in horses, 65, 234, 237–38
    in humans, 6, 64, 237–38, *244*
Release
    defined, 91
    neural fatigue and, 153
    in pressure and release training, 91–92, 145–153
    rest as, 148, 227
Repetition, of movements, 226
Research studies
    animal emotions, 232–33, 240, 243
    handling/over-handling, 197
    harm and intent, 255–56
    on horses, lacking, 6–7, 66–67, 261–62
    inattentional blindness, 208–9
    music in barns, 65
    observational learning, 139
Resistance, 98, 186–87
Respect
    of horse's fear, 237
    for rider's leg, 92, 100–101, 146
Rest
    from attentional demands, 192, 196–200
    as release/reward, 148, 227

Reticular activating system, 222
Reversion, 241
Rewards
    accidental/unintentional, 164
    breaking tasks down for, 174–75
    dopamine release in, 159, 160
    edible, 81, 157, 161, 162
    self-delivered, 166
    sensitivity to, 197
    timing of, 162–64, 189
    training by, 157–167
    types of, 161–62, *163*
Riders/handlers
    attentiveness to horses, 86, 141, 192, 200, 217, 266
    distractibility of, 214
    horse's observational learning from, 139
    over-handling by, 191–92, 196–200
    responsibilities of, 14, 178, 264–65
    as source of problems, 133, 151–52
Riding
    brain-to-brain communication in, 124–28, *125–27*
    demands of, 11
    vs. groundwork, 41
    learning by reward in, 165
    proprioception in, 97–98
Rods, in eyes, 42, 56
Romantic attraction, 23
Round pens, 214
Routines, 199, 235, 236
Rubber bit material, 81

Sacks, Oliver, 107

Saddles, in rider training exercises, 116–19, *117*
Sadness, 238–39
Safety considerations, 12, 50, 56, 88
Salt, 80
Scary objects, approach to, 37–41, *37, 39,* 180–83, *184,* 187–190
Scent, information potential of, 74. *See also* Smell, sense of
Schizophrenia, 195, 251
Science, attitudes toward, 11. *See also* Research studies
Seat, of rider, 102–6, 113–19, 126, *127,* 148
Seat bones, 121
Seeing. *See* Vision
Selection. *See* Natural selection
Self-carriage, 91–92
Self-regulation, in human learning, 160
Sensation. *See also* Perception; Proprioception; *specific organs and senses*
    attentiveness to, 207–9
    of emotions, 232
Sensitive horse case histories, 83, 85–86, 175–76
Sensitivity. *See also* Nervous horses
    to aids, 83–84
    to body language, 133
    breed considerations, 229
    as equine adaptation, 9, 68, 112
    overreaction as, 198
Sensory compensation, 32–33, 50, 54, 76, 84–88. *See also* Neural recruitment